MILTON'S STYLE

Milton's Style:

The Shorter Poems, Paradise Regained, and 'Samson Agonistes'

Archie Burnett

Ex Libris

MHM

Mitchell M. Harris

Longman
London and New York

Longman Group Limited
Longman House
Burnt Mill, Harlow, Essex, UK

Published in the United States of America
by Longman Inc., New York

© Longman Group Limited 1981

First published 1981

British Library Cataloguing in Publication Data

Burnett, Archie
　Milton's style.
　1. Milton, John – Criticism and interpretation
　I. Title
　821′ .4　　PR3588　　80–49807

　ISBN 0–582–49128–2
　ISBN 0–582–49129–0 Pbk

Printed in Singapore by Chong Moh Offset Printing Pte Ltd

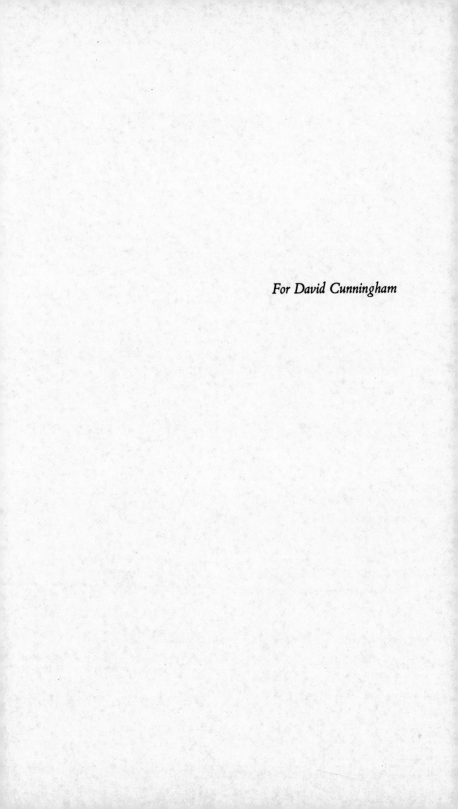

For David Cunningham

Contents

Preface

Milton's style has been both a celebrated and highly controversial subject. Discussion has concentrated hitherto on *Paradise Lost* – understandably. But though the rest, or other half, of the poetry has hardly been neglected (nothing goes neglected in Milton studies), there has to date been no detailed and wide-ranging study of Milton's stylistic achievement from 'L'Allegro' and 'Il Penseroso' to *Paradise Regained* and 'Samson Agonistes'. (This is perhaps strange, for the twentieth-century debate about Milton has shown a marked concern with allegations that his style lacks delicacy and flexibility.)

This book has various aims: to give close readings of Milton's poems other than *Paradise Lost*; to take into account the criticism on these poems, focusing on major issues; and to investigate the variety and consistency of their style. Detailed analyses of the styles of 'L'Allegro' and 'Il Penseroso', the 'Nativity Ode', 'Comus', 'Lycidas', *Paradise Regained,* and 'Samson Agonistes', as well as of some psalms and sonnets and other minor poems, are included; and the review of the criticism is undertaken on the basis of these analyses. The result is a kind of compact critical variorum.

The decision not to write on *Paradise Lost* – in this book, anyway – is a purely practical one. The main consideration is the almost unmanageable bulk and complexity of Milton scholarship. In the real world it would be highly improbable that anyone could locate, read, digest, and evaluate all of it, and write on all of the poetry as well. The proliferation of scholarship, much of it superb, and to the serious reader indispensable, is one of the problems of our age. In 1969 John Gross said of the scholarship on Alexander Pope:

A generation or so ago very little of real note had been added to what the eighteenth-century critics had to say. Today there are, I suppose, at least half-a-dozen full-length critical studies which are worth reading, while a leading American scholar has edited an anthology entitled *44 Essential Articles on Pope*. None of this represents wasted labour. But what are we all going to do when there are forty-four essential *books*?

(*The Rise and Fall of the Man of Letters* (1969; rpt., 1973), p. 319)

The state of affairs envisaged in that last sentence is fast becoming a reality in Milton scholarship (and, no doubt, such as Milton is will Pope be). In fact, the volume of publication on Milton has even increased dramatically in the 1960s and 1970s. And if specialists find it difficult to keep up to date, their problem is slight in comparison with that of students and teachers in general, whose time available for any one author is necessarily limited. Accordingly, it seemed best to do what could reasonably be done (and done reasonably) in one book.

Each of Milton's poems discussed is taken on its own terms. The significance of any feature of a poet's style is by no means constant in every poem, and strict adherence to any single principle of analysis can resemble eating soup with a fork. It is important that attention should be given to whatever is emphasized in the individual poem, irrespective of the means whereby it is emphasized. However, it has often proved useful, both for discovering some of the significant patterns in the language of each poem, and for outlining Milton's stylistic development, to consider his adjective usage. Figures are given for this, and should be referred to the complete table at the end of the book. The more technical and theoretical problems of analytical procedure are discussed in an appendix. However, no particular technical knowledge should be necessary for understanding the readings of the poems.

At Milton's style in *Paradise Lost* Marvell exclaimed:

Where couldst thou Words of such a compass find?
Whence furnish such a vast expense of Mind?
('On Mr. Milton's Paradise lost', *ll.* 41–2)

His phrase 'Words of such a compass' could be applied aptly to the rest of the poetry, and even to the style within the structure of individual poems. It is this book's concern to find the measure of that stylistic compass.

Acknowledgements

Many people have given help in the course of this study. I thank all of them most heartily, and take full responsibility for any errors that may remain. As this is a first book, I should like to acknowledge my first university tutor of English, Ruth Mateer, whom it was my good fortune to meet at Edinburgh, and who has remained a constant source of encouragement ever since. So, too, has my student contemporary, John McGavin, now at Southampton University. In an earlier phase this work took the form of an Oxford D.Phil. thesis. It was supervised in a manner that I consider ideal by Professor John Carey, and without his vigilance, liveliness, and kindness it would never have come to much. The examiners of the thesis, Dennis Burden and Colin Williamson, made useful suggestions about content and format. The President and Fellows of St John's College elected me to a Junior Research Fellowship, and generously extended it for a fourth year – and all without insurance regarding a refund! Without this award this work would not have been possible. The staffs of St John's College Library, the English Faculty Library, the Taylorian Institute, and the Bodleian provided cheerful and efficient service at all times. I should also like to place on record the exemplary cooperation received from Longman. My last acknowledgement is of my greatest debt of all, to my wife Lesley. It was Burns who exclaimed, 'Ah, gentle dames, it gars me greet, / To think how monie counsels sweet, / How monie lengthen'd sage advices / The husband frae the wife despises!' He could have spoken with less irony and shed fewer tears on my score; but, then, I have had the constant advice of an expert lexicographer as well as tolerance when I have been intolerable.

Archie Burnett,
Oxford,
May, 1980.

Abbreviations

'Another'	– 'Another on the Same' (the second poem on the University Carrier)
Carey and Fowler	– *The Poems of John Milton*, ed. John Carey and Alastair Fowler (1968)
CE	– *College English*
'Circumcision'	– 'Upon the Circumcision'
CL	– *Comparative Literature*
CQ	– *Critical Quarterly*
'Cromwell'	– 'To the Lord General Cromwell'
'Cyriack Skinner'	– 'To Mr Cyriack Skinner upon his Blindness'
EC	– *Essays in Criticism*
ELH	– *A Journal of English Literary History*
ES	– *English Studies*
ESEA	– *Essays and Studies by Members of the English Association*
'Fairfax'	– 'On the Lord General Fairfax at the siege of Colchester'
'Fair Infant'	– 'On the Death of a Fair Infant Dying of a Cough'
FQ	– *The Faerie Queene*
HLQ	– *Huntington Library Quarterly*
JEGP	– *Journal of English and Germanic Philology*
JHI	– *Journal of the History of Ideas*
'May Morning'	– 'Song. On May Morning'
MLN	– *Modern Language Notes*
MLQ	– *Modern Language Quarterly*
MLR	– *Modern Language Review*
MP	– *Modern Philology*
MQ	– *Milton Quarterly (Milton Newsletter* till 1970)
MS	– *Milton Studies*

N & Q	– *Notes and Queries*
'Nativity Ode'	– 'On the Morning of Christ's Nativity'
'New Forcers'	– 'On the New Forcers of Conscience under the Long Parliament'
NM	– *Neuphilologische Mitteilungen*
OED	– *The Oxford English Dictionary*
PL	– *Paradise Lost*
PMLA	– *Publications of the Modern Language Association of America*
PQ	– *Philological Quarterly*
PR	– *Paradise Regained*
RES	– *Review of English Studies*
SAMLA	– *South Atlantic Modern Language Association*
'Samson'	– 'Samson Agonistes'
SEL	– *Studies in English Literature*
'Solemn Music'	– 'At a Solemn Music'
SP	– *Studies in Philology*
SQ	– *Shakespeare Quarterly*
TLS	– *The Times Literary Supplement*
TSLL	– *Texas Studies in Literature and Language*
'Univ. Carrier'	– 'On the University Carrier'
UTQ	– *University of Toronto Quarterly*
'Vac. Ex.'	– 'At a Vacation Exercise in the College'
'Vane'	– 'To Sir Henry Vane the Younger'
Variorum Commentary	– *A Variorum Commentary on the Poems of John Milton,* ed. Merritt Y. Hughes *et al.* (1970–)
'Winchester'	– 'An Epitaph on the Marchioness of Winchester'

NOTES

1. All quotations from Milton's poetry, apart from those used by other writers, are from the text of *The Poems of John Milton,* ed. John Carey and Alastair Fowler (1968).
2. Archaic spellings with 'u' and 'v' have been normalized to accord with modern convention.
3. Some standard linguistic abbreviations have been used: 'adj.' for adjective, 'advb.' for adverb, 'N.' for noun, 'Vb.' for verb, 'sg.' for singular, 'part.' for participle, and 'pl.' for plural. Two oblique markers enclosing a letter denote a phoneme: thus, the line 'Swinging slow with sullen roar' alliterates on the sound '/s/'.

CHAPTER ONE
'L'Allegro' and 'Il Penseroso'

Anyone who has carried out a survey of the scholarly and critical writing on 'L'Allegro' and 'Il Penseroso' is likely to be impressed by the sheer bulk of what has been done on, or in some cases to, the poems, the wide variety of approaches taken, and, happily, the way that these two early works of Milton emerge, rather like fresh grass from an overlay of solid concrete, persistently appealing. It has generally been the case, as Rosemond Tuve says, that 'no willing student of these poems has been able to resist them';[1] but as commentary, of varying quality, proliferates, it is hard not to feel one's delight that the poems have proved so attractive change to dismay that so many students have been so willing. As controversy develops, or even as opinions multiply and tend to diverge, it becomes increasingly important to reread the poems themselves with care, so that the merits both of poems and commentary can be assessed. The poems have certainly been found charming, but it is hardly sufficient to say, as Christopher Ricks (astonishingly) does, that 'there is little to be said about charm':[2] to do this is, in effect, to disdain to analyse poetic effects and to overlook just how much has been said already. With the conviction that charm is worthy of examination, I propose in this chapter to offer a close reading of 'L'Allegro' and 'Il Penseroso'. I shall also use the information acquired through analysing the style of the poems in an appraisal of the existing criticism.

The poems have not pleased everyone. Rosemond Tuve's statement about the irresistibility of the poems may be taken to represent the prevailing consensus of critical opinion, but for a few readers the poems have held only a very limited appeal. Not unpredictably, perhaps, these readers have been T. S. Eliot, Robert Graves, William Empson, and F. R. Leavis. Eliot's criticism is concerned with one short passage in 'L'Allegro' that he was willing to resist, and will be discussed fully below. Graves regards the whole of 'L'Allegro' as 'a dreadful muddle' that sacrifices 'commonsense'

1

to 'cunning verbal music'.[3] But the dreadful muddle is very much the result of Graves's own theories (which are not supported by any reliable biographical or textual evidence) about the composition of the poem. He substantiates his speculations only with displays of what might be called close misreading; and as he is concerned, therefore, with the details of specific passages, his criticisms will also be considered below. What must be questioned at once is Graves's critical manner:

In *Il Penseroso* [Milton] had sown Classical allusions with the sack; but apart from Hebe's cheek and a reference at the end to Orpheus and Eurydice, *L'Allegro* might have been written by any poetic bumpkin (Shakespeare, poor fellow, for example – 'father lost his money in the meat trade and couldn't send young Will to college') . . . Here's a Miltonic discovery for the scholars to toss about – if they want something to toss about . . . [4]

This banter soon stales as imitation of Milton's allegedly hack-like ways, to become sterile and irresponsible. It also reduces the credibility of Graves's more precise criticisms of the poems. By comparison, the seriousness of Leavis's manner is welcome. Leavis does not resist the poems, but he does resist disclosing why he thinks they possess little merit: 'I do not myself rank *L'Allegro* (or *Il Penseroso*) very high among Milton's works',[5] he declares, apparently confident that his opinion is self-validating. Of course, it hardly bends the mind to infer from Leavis's other pronouncements on Milton that he must truly despise 'L'Allegro' and 'Il Penseroso'. But his judgement must remain unchallengeable only because his criteria are so obscure. Empson's criticism of the poems resembles Leavis's in that it is short and unsupported by evidence. Unlike Leavis's, however, it is flippant: ' "L'Allegro" and "Il Penseroso" seem to me ponderous trifles with a few good lines in them, so that they are a bad place to look for profound symbols.'[6] Does Empson's oxymoronic phrase 'ponderous trifles' commend a 'gravity and ease' in the style of the poems, or dismiss alleged pedantry? And is the meaning of 'profound symbols' clear enough for the alleged absence of such symbols to be so automatically a fault?

Clearly, if a stalemate of contradictory critical opinions is to be avoided, Graves, Empson, and Leavis cannot be answered in their own kind of critical language: their curt dismissal of the poems needs to be countered by something more substantial than curt approval. Ironically, the critical procedure which seems to promise the best answer to their criticisms is the one that they themselves have followed frequently, though by no means uniformly: inspecting the details of the poetic language. By doing this it will be possible to test the more precise criticisms made by Eliot and Graves, and to show that Milton's stylistic achievement is generally of a higher order than they, or Leavis and Empson, would have us believe.

An impression shared by many readers provides a useful starting point. It has often been remarked that 'L'Allegro' seems to be more extrovert and less exclusively cerebral in disposition than 'Il Penseroso', and that 'Il Penseroso' celebrates a comparatively personalized, even private, experience.[7] Evidence for this difference between the poems can be found in the distribution of first-person pronouns in each:

	I	me	my	mine	us	our	Total
'L'Allegro'	2	2	1	1	1		7
'Il Penseroso'	6	4	4	2		1	17

'Il Penseroso' reminds the reader of its *persona* at least once in every 10 lines; 'L'Allegro', once in every 22 lines.[8] This difference may be highlighted by considering the single occurrence of the plural form of the first-person pronoun in each poem. In 'Il Penseroso' 'our' is found in the first address to Melancholy:

> But hail thou goddess, sage and holy,
> Hail divinest Melancholy,
> Whose saintly visage is too bright
> To hit the sense of human sight;
> And therefore to our weaker view,
> O'erlaid with black staid wisdom's hue.   (*ll*. 11–16)

'Our weaker view', equated with 'the sense of human sight', generalizes impersonally. By contrast, 'us' occurs in a typical social context in 'L'Allegro', where the speaker even assumes that the reader shares his predilections:

> Towered cities please us then,
> And the busy hum of men.   (*ll*. 117–18)

The change from the single to the plural form of the first-person pronoun is made almost imperceptibly in 'L'Allegro'. One has to look back to line 69 before finding the singular form that is nearest to the plural in line 117:

> Straight mine eye hath caught new pleasures
> Whilst the landscape round it measures.

The eye, not strictly the speaker, catches the pleasures, and 'it' in the couplet's second line further depersonalizes the perception. It would seem, on the evidence of the pronouns throughout 'L'Allegro', that the happy man

3

is effaced by the experiences into which he so heartily throws himself. His disposition is to move out of himself and into social experiences that he can share with the reader. As David Miller has noted, the pensive man turns 'inward for meditation', whereas the happy man turns 'outward for observation'.[9] 'L'Allegro' stresses what is perceived rather than who perceives; 'Il Penseroso' follows a process of perceiving in the mind of its *persona*.

The different relationship between the speaker and the reader subtly established in the poems may be explored further through verbs. After the imperatives that banish Melancholy and welcome Mirth, the speaker in 'L'Allegro' moves quietly behind the infinitives 'to live', 'to hear', and 'to come' (*ll*. 39, 41, 45). He thus makes his experiences public by not emphasizing them as his own. Thereafter in the poem his activities are represented by present participles ('list'ning', 'walking', *ll*. 53, 57), which, John Carey notes, are 'only hazily connected with any specific agent'.[10] The reader is not told to whom the happy man bids good morrow, or whom the upland hamlets will invite (*ll*. 46, 92). The words 'loathèd', 'yclept', 'unreprovèd', 'not unseen', 'told', 'pinched', 'pulled', 'set', and 'well-trod' (*ll*. 1, 12, 40, 57, 101, 103, 103, 106, 131) appear without expressed agents. Highly generalized subjects abound: 'men' (*ll*. 13, 118), 'some sager' (*l*. 17), 'young and old' (*l*. 97), 'they' (*l*. 115), 'throngs of knights and barons bold' (*l*. 119), and 'store of ladies' (*l*. 121). Subject and verb together are omitted twice, in the lines 'Then to the spicy nut-brown ale' and 'Then to the well-trod stage anon' (*ll*. 100, 131). Only with the returning imperative in 'Lap me in soft Lydian airs' (*l*. 136) does the speaker reappear, and his previous self-withdrawal is such that his request has the force of 'as for me, lap me in soft Lydian airs'. Throughout 'L'Allegro', then, grammar operates in a way that makes the speaker's experiences the common property of the reader. Hospitable sharing is singled out stylistically as one of the speaker's chief delights.

Already, the language of 'L'Allegro' and 'Il Penseroso' manifests a degree of precision and subtlety that has too readily been overlooked or ignored by critics. And yet the arrangement of the first-person pronouns and verbs in 'L'Allegro' is of central importance to one of the cruces in the poem: in the lines 'Then to come in spite of sorrow, / And at my window bid good morrow' (*ll*. 45–6), is the subject of the verb 'come' the happy man or the lark?[11] It is necessary to place the lines in context when considering the question:

> Come, and trip it as you go
> On the light fantastic toe,
> And in thy right hand lead with thee,
> The mountain nymph, sweet Liberty;
> And if I give thee honour due,

35

> Mirth, admit me of thy crew
> To live with her, and live with thee,
> In unreprovèd pleasures free; 40
> To hear the lark begin his flight,
> And singing startle the dull night,
> From his watch-tower in the skies,
> Till the dappled dawn doth rise;
> Then to come in spite of sorrow, 45
> And at my window bid good morrow,
> Through the sweet-briar, or the vine,
> Or the twisted eglantine.

In this passage, as elsewhere, the grammar of 'L'Allegro' allows the reader to substitute for the happy man by keeping the *persona* obscured. But an obscured *persona* is not a nonexistent one, and the syntax of the request 'Mirth, admit me . . . to live . . . to hear . . . then to come' signifies that he, the happy man, is the subject of the verb 'come'.

This solution of the problem seems straightforward enough. But to the most recent contributor to the debate over the subject of 'come', Stanley E. Fish, it will seem crudely straightforward. He supports his general contention that 'L'Allegro is easier to read than Il Penseroso' [12] by arguing that, in the passage about the lark:

> the ambiguity is *so* complete that unless someone asks us to, we do not worry about it, and we do not worry about it (or even notice it) because while no subject is specified for 'come', any number of subjects – lark, poet, Mirth, Dawn, Night – are available. What is *not* available is the connecting word or sustained syntactical unit which would pressure us to decide between them, and in the absence of that pressure, we are not obliged to decide. [13]

In saying that 'we do not worry about it (or even notice it)' Fish blithely overlooks the very existence of the debate. But the truth remains that the subject of 'come' must be the happy man because any alternative can be chosen only at the expense of the sustained syntactic unit comprising the imperative 'admit me' and its three complementary infinitives. The subject cannot be the lark, for no clear indication is given that the lark is at some point to be substituted for the speaker who says 'Mirth, admit me . . . to live . . . to hear . . . then to come'. And no amount of learned commentary about the habits of larks, or citation of passages in other poems where birds come to windows, can argue this away. For the subject to be the lark or the dawn 'then to come' would have to be replaced by '[and then] come'; but Milton writes 'then to come'. The subject cannot be Mirth: the speaker's request is addressed *to* Mirth, and part of his request is that he should be able to come to his window in spite of sorrow. And the subject can hardly be 'the dull night', for the dawn has risen. Clearly, any number of subjects is *not* available, and four of those proposed by Stanley Fish – lark, Mirth, Dawn, Night – possess little syntactic credibility.

To reason, as some have done, that the speaker would say 'go' rather than 'come' if he were speaking about himself (on the assumption that he does not approach his own window from the outside, but 'goes' to it from the inside) is to miss the significance of Milton's choice of verb. 'Come' suggests that someone is waiting outside the window for the happy man to 'come' and greet him. That is to say, the verb is orientated in place and time towards another person. Thus it endorses, and is endorsed by, the social implications of the consistently omitted agents and objects throughout the poem. It is a detail that reveals the happy man's self-effacing sociability.

Robert Graves is alone in finding a different difficulty in the lines about the lark and those that follow them, but his difficulty also concerns syntax. Of the speaker Graves says:

While distractedly bidding good-morrow, at the window, to Mirth . . . he sometimes . . . goes *'walking, not unseen, by hedgerow elms, on hillocks green.'* Either Milton had forgotten that he is still supposedly standing naked at the open window – the Jacobeans always slept raw – or else the subject of 'walking' is the cock who escapes from the barn-yard, deserts his dames, ceases to strut and, anxiously aware of the distant hunt, trudges far afield among ploughmen and shepherds in the dale. But why should Milton give twenty lines to the adventures of the neighbour's wandering cock? And why *'walking, not unseen'*? Not unseen by whom?[14]

Stanley Fish argues that Graves's last question might well be supplemented by others, such as 'What sees?' (*l.* 77) or 'Hard by what?' (*l.* 81), since 'it is Milton's wish to liberate us from care, and the nonsequiturs that bother Graves are meant to prevent us from searching after the kind of sense he wants to make'.[15] Unfortunately, the fact that Fish's questions are easily answered must damage his case: it is the 'eye' in line 69, twice referred to as 'it' (*ll.* 70, 77), that 'sees'; and the cottage chimney smokes 'hard by' the 'towers, and battlements . . . bosomed high in tufted trees' (*ll.* 77–82). 'L'Allegro' may liberate the reader from care, but surely not by making a careless reader of him? Nevertheless, Fish is right in implicitly criticizing Graves's improvisations on Milton's text. Why is Graves so sure that the happy man bids good morrow to Mirth? And where in the poem is there a figure standing 'naked' at the window? Indeed, though the issue is irrelevant to what Milton has written, where is the evidence for stating, with such easy familiarity, that 'the Jacobeans always slept raw'? (If our own knowledge of our contemporaries in this matter is anything to judge by, collecting the evidence would require at least a certain furtive dexterity.) In Graves's version of the poem the happy man bids good morrow 'distractedly', and the 'neighbour's' cock, 'anxiously aware' of the hunt as it 'escapes' from the barn-yard, 'trudges' far across the countryside. Graves seems to wish to turn Milton's poem into a novel.

Though Graves proves unpromisingly inaccurate in these particulars, some of his confusions over Milton's syntax can be instructive. His muddling of the time distinctions in 'L'Allegro' is especially so. Graves argues that Milton has created confusion by having the happy man bid good morrow at the window at the same time as he is supposedly walking about the countryside. The muddle, once more, is Graves's, for these activities do not take place simultaneously in the poem. The speaker pictures himself '*oft* list'ning' to the sounds of the hunt and '*sometime* walking' across the land; the adverbs signal that he listens frequently and walks at an unspecified time, and not that he does these things while also bidding good morrow at his window. Graves's attempt to impose time restrictions on 'L'Allegro' only reveals how unrestricted the poem is. It is partly by not observing the treatment of time in the poem that Graves also thinks that the subject of 'list'ning' and 'walking' is the cock rather than the speaker in the poem. Only at first sight does this seem plausible:

> While the cock with lively din,
> Scatters the rear of darkness thin,
> And to the stack, or the barn door
> Stoutly struts his dames before,
> Oft list'ning ...
>
> (*ll*. 49–53)

The syntax, in the immediate context, is potentially ambiguous, and the cock appears to be 'list'ning'. But, in the wider context, through which this passage is approached, it is the *speaker* who has asked Mirth to let him come to the window while the cock routs the darkness and struts before his dames who is 'oft list'ning'. And notice that Milton writes 'Oft list'ning *how* the hounds and horn / Cheerly rouse the slumb'ring morn'; not 'list'ning *to*'. Is the implied power of mind not more likely to be attributed to the speaker than to a cock? Indeed, is it not ridiculous for the cock to be taken from its barn-yard and dames, to set off 'walking' far across the countryside, and for twenty or so lines to function as the perceiver in the poem? In lines 69–70 the speaker says, 'Straight mine eye hath caught *new* pleasures / Whilst the landscape round it measures', implying that in the immediately preceding context his eye has already caught some pleasures. It is very likely, therefore, that in that same context the speaker, not the cock, has been walking across the land. Graves's confusions only draw attention to the syntactic devices by which the speaker in 'L'Allegro' is obscured; and although, to function in this way, the syntax cannot be too inflexible, it is not so uncontrolled that it should invite bizarre interpretations. Graves, not the cock in the poem, has trudged far afield. His purely speculative theory about muddled manuscript sheets of 'L'Allegro' resulting in a muddled poem solves a problem of his own invention. (In the *New Republic* of 1957 his remarks were headed 'John Milton Muddles Through'; a year later, in *5 Pens in Hand*, they became, perhaps more sensationally, 'Legitimate Criticism of Poetry'.)

If 'L'Allegro' takes risks with some readers by typically obscuring its speaker, 'Il Penseroso' keeps its speaker well to the fore and channels its experiences through him. The ten imperatives in lines 1–51 parallel those at the beginning of 'L'Allegro', but, as Bridget Gellert Lyons has noted,[16] the verbs which follow them are firmly connected to first-person pronouns: 'I woo to hear' (*l.* 64), 'I walk unseen . . . to behold' (*ll.* 65–7). The speaker twice highlights his isolation by asking that his lamp or he should be seen: 'Or let my lamp at midnight hour, / Be seen in some high lonely tower' (*ll.* 85–6), 'Thus Night oft see me in thy pale career' (*l.* 121). The placing of the pronoun in 'me goddess bring' (*l.* 132) seems to suggest the exclusion of anyone but the speaker. The melancholy man requests 'retired Leisure' (*l.* 49), walks 'unseen' (*l.* 65), withdraws to a 'still removed place' (*l.* 78) or 'close covert by some brook, / Where no profaner eye may look' (*ll.* 139–40), and hears a 'far-off' curfew in a place 'far from all resort of mirth' (*ll.* 74, 81). He is, then, identifiably the spiritual descendant of 'solitary Saturn' and Vesta who met in 'secret shades / Of woody Ida's inmost grove' (*ll.* 28–9). And it is consistent with his temperament that the religious experience described at the end of the poem should be personalized:

> But let my due feet never fail,
> To walk the studious cloister's pale,
> And love the high embowèd roof,
> With antique pillars' massy proof,
> And storied windows richly dight,
> Casting a dim religious light.
> There let the pealing organ blow,
> To the full-voiced choir below,
> In service high, and anthems clear,
> As may with sweetness, through mine ear,
> Dissolve me into ecstasies,
> And bring all heaven before mine eyes.
>
> (*ll.* 155–66)

Emphasis is on 'my due feet', 'mine ear', 'dissolve me into ecstasies', and 'mine eyes'. In a communal religious service, with a 'full-voiced choir' present (but present 'below'), the speaker seems self-engrossed, aware of the setting only inasmuch as it stimulates his spiritual elation.

The emphasis on the speaker in 'Il Penseroso' is such that, when an explicit object is omitted in the poem's language, it seems natural to assume that the speaker is still referring to himself: his wishes would appear to be that the 'still removèd place' will 'fit' him, and that 'gorgeous Tragedy' will 'come sweeping by' him, presenting 'Thebes, or Pelops' line' to him (ll. 78, 97–9). Of course, the reader may identify with the speaker's wish for solitude and personal enrichment; but the sense of being readily welcomed to identify with the speaker is more restricted than it is in 'L'Allegro'. The pensive man typically makes himself inaccessible to others. When, for instance, he says 'Or let my lamp at midnight hour, / Be seen in some high lonely tower' (ll. 85–6), he specifies a time and place that severely limit the number of potential observers. If, as John Carey says, the pensive man 'does not even see a living creature',[17] neither is any living creature meant to see him: only his lamp will be visible, and that from a distance.

The happy man walks 'not unseen'; the pensive man, 'unseen'. The one assumes that someone will see him; the other, that no-one will. When Robert Graves asks, 'Not unseen by whom?' he is failing to perceive the social contrasts achieved by the presence or absence of pronouns and objects in the two poems.

Similarly, Graves's inattention to time markers in 'L'Allegro' can serve only to draw attention to the poem's treatment of time. 'L'Allegro' is written predominantly in the present tense, to lend immediacy and freshness to the experiences it describes. But the poem is not very specific about time. Subordinate temporal clauses such as 'till the dappled dawn doth rise' and 'while the cock with lively din, / Scatters the rear of darkness thin' lose precision through the counterbalancing present tenses in the main clauses to which they are linked. Everything is regulated to a continuous or habitual present. Stanley Fish has commented that time markers like 'while' in 'L'Allegro' provide 'a fulcrum around which . . . events swirl',[18] and though he seems inattentive or unrigorous in not feeling compelled to arrange the components of language 'into an intelligible sequence',[19] it remains true that the time clauses do little more than arrange the progression of events. In a line like 'While the ploughman near at hand', 'while' could be replaced by 'and' without much being lost. When Bridget Gellert Lyons notes that the adverbs 'oft' (ll. 53, 125), 'often' (l. 74), 'sometime' (l. 57), and 'sometimes' (l. 91) recur to 'convey the idea of custom and habit',[20] it should be noted also that these adverbs assign no specific time of occurrence for the repeatable experiences. The happy man's chief wish seems to be that his pleasures will be continually present, permanent: just as he commands Melancholy, 'In dark Cimmerian desert *ever* dwell', so he asks Mirth, '*ever* against eating cares, / Lap me in soft Lydian airs' (*ll.* 10, 135–6).

The sequence of tenses is unusual on two occasions in 'L'Allegro'. The first is at lines 69–70, where 'straight mine eye *hath caught* new pleasures' clashes with the surrounding continuous present tenses in 'whets', 'tells', and 'measures' (*ll.* 66, 67, 70):

> While the ploughman near at hand,
> Whistles o'er the furrowed land,
> And the milkmaid singeth blithe,   65
> And the mower whets his scythe,
> And every shepherd tells his tale
> Under the hawthorn in the dale.
> Straight mine eye hath caught new pleasures
> Whilst the landscape round it measures.   70

The transition made in line 69 is abrupt. In standard grammar 'catches' rather than 'hath caught' would be compatible with 'measures'. 'Hath caught', supported by 'straight', presupposes a specific present moment, but 'measures', in this context, does not. By the combination of the two the speaker is dramatically made to relive an exhilarating moment. It is as though a slide slotted into a projector is taking him back to the exact moment when the original picture was taken. Notice that it is the eye that catches the pleasures, not the pleasures that catch the eye.[21] The eye is eager, scanning the countryside for delights, and the syntax dramatizes the moment – almost of surprise – when the delights are 'caught'. A particular present is singled out from a habitual present, excitedly.

The other passage in 'L'Allegro' which contains unusual tenses is that between lines 100 and 114:

> Then to the spicy nut-brown ale,
> With stories told of many a feat,
> How Faëry Mab the junkets eat,
> She was pinched, and pulled she said,
> And by the friar's lantern led
> Tells how the drudging goblin sweat,   105
> To earn his cream-bowl duly set,
> When in one night, ere glimpse of morn,
> His shadowy flail hath threshed the corn,
> That ten day-labourers could not end;
> Then lies him down the lubber fiend.   110
> And stretched out all the chimney's length,

Basks at the fire his hairy strength;
And crop-full out of doors he flings,
Ere the first cock his matin rings.

Several marked shifts occur here: from 'stories told' to the reported speech of line 103, and then to the stressed present, 'tells'; from the past tense of 'sweat' to 'hath threshed' (where 'threshed' or 'had threshed' would have been normal); and from 'hath threshed' to the historic or habitual tenses of 'lies', 'basks', 'flings', and 'rings'. The whole sequence moves from past to present. In referring to Faëry Mab's words the speaker becomes engrossed in one of the 'stories told', and then he continues with the story in the present. The relation of 'hath threshed' to 'sweat' is similarly dramatic: the leap from the past to a particular present recreates the astonishment that the goblin's work has been magically completed ahead of schedule, and at the same time traces the speaker's deepening involvement in his experiences. The present tenses throughout the passage may be interpreted as being historic or habitual, reporting events as they happen or as they are thought typically to happen: like the tenses in lines 69–70, they combine the specific and the universal. But in reflecting processes in the speaker's mind the present tenses also manifest something of the 'ruminative kind of beauty'[22] detected by Tillyard in the poems (while allaying, in poetic terms, his fear that the 'unconscious element' may be 'dangerously strong').[23] At least Tillyard comes close to recognizing some poetic purpose behind the syntax: it is surprising that D. C. Allen should speak of 'occasional syntactical confusions',[24] and William Riley Parker of 'a few minor problems of syntax',[25] without investigating possible poetic functions of unusual tense sequences.

Although 'L'Allegro' and 'Il Penseroso' naturally have past tenses in their genealogies of Mirth and Melancholy, the poems in general differ markedly in the ways that they treat time. Bridget Gellert Lyons has commented that 'the speaker of "Il Penseroso" has a sense of time that his counterpart in "L'Allegro" lacks, or against which he protects himself.'[26] As evidence she cites the use of time-markers in the poems: 'oft' and 'sometimes' stress 'custom and habit' in 'L'Allegro', she feels, but 'oft' in 'Il Penseroso' 'fixes the experience of the thinking man clearly in time', so that a line like 'There let Hymen oft appear' (from 'L'Allegro') would be 'more explicitly temporal' if it occurred in 'Il Penseroso'. The pensive man sees events 'not merely in succession, but in a variety of temporal relationships', and possesses 'a sense of duration that causes him to see the twenty-four hours he traverses as constituting an analogy to the passage of his life'.[27]

It is always good to have evidence, but the evidence must be good. If the same word – 'oft', for instance – is to be interpreted differently in each poem, then additional contextual evidence is needed to show how this is justified. Imagining a line from one poem occurring in the other only makes the subsequent interpretation of the line imaginary. And if words like 'oft' do occur in 'Il Penseroso' its time scheme is not necessarily confined to twenty-four hours.[28] 'L'Allegro', in outline, progresses from morning till night, and 'Il Penseroso' from night till morning,[29] but the progression is far from rigid. One may, with Gary Stringer, see this daily cycle (in the two poems taken as one) as symbolic of the birth-to-death cycle[30] – indeed, Mrs Lyons also wishes to see this parallel. But, though her general conclusions about 'L'Allegro' and 'Il Penseroso' are very often valid, even illuminating, her handling of the evidence, and sometimes the evidence itself, could be better. The evidence she collects is considerable, but incomplete, and she seems occasionally to draw conclusions, correct in themselves, from areas of the poetic language that do not support those particular conclusions. But before drawing any conclusions it is necessary to extend Mrs Lyons's evidence of the treatment of time in the poems:

	'L'Allegro'	Total	'Il Penseroso'	Total
Temporal adverbs				
oft(en)	*ll.* 53, 74, 125	3	*ll.* 27, 46, 63, 71, 73, 87, 121	7
sometime(s)	*ll.* 57, 91	2	*l.* 97	1
(n)ever	*ll.* 10, 135	2	*ll.* 137, 155	2
straight	*l.* 69	1		
anon	*l.* 131	1		
soon	*l.* 116	1		
long	*l.* 140	1		
ay			*l.* 48	1
first			*l.* 51	1
slow			*l.* 76	1
yet			*l.* 30	1
then	*ll.* 45, 100, 110, 117, 131	5		
once	*l.* 20	1		
Temporal phrases				
on a sunshine holiday (*l.* 98)			long of yore (*l.* 23)	
in one night (*l.* 107)			in Saturn's reign (*l.* 25)	
ere glimpse of morn (*l.* 107)			at midnight hour (*l.* 85)	
thus done the tales (*l.* 115)			of later age (*l.* 101)	
on summer eves (*l.* 130)		5	at last (*l.* 167)	5

Temporal clauses

while / whilst...	ll. 49, 63, 70, 123	4	ll. 30, 59, 126, 142	4
when...	l. 107	1	ll. 128, 131	2
till...	ll. 44, 99	2	ll. 42, 122, 173	3
as...	ll. 20, 33	2	l. 151	1
ere...	l. 114	1		

Temporal Adjectives and Nouns

night-raven (l. 7), spring (l. 18), fresh-blown roses (l. 22), youthful Jollity (l. 26), the dull night (l. 42), the dappled dawn (l. 44), good morrow (l. 46), the rear of darkness (l. 50), the slumb'ring morn (l. 54), the earlier season (l. 89), young and old (l. 97), the live-long daylight (l. 99), day-labourers (l. 109), the first cock (l. 114), matin (l. 114), antique pageantry (l. 128), youthful poets (l. 129), immortal verse (l. 137).	wonted state (l. 37), night (l. 58), accustomed oak (l. 60), even-song (l. 64), highest noon (l. 68), curfew (l. 74), the bellman's drowsy charm (l. 83), nightly harm (l. 84), the immortal mind (l. 91), rare (l. 101), wont (l. 123), minute drops (l. 130), twilight groves (l. 133), day's garish eye (l. 141), old experience (l. 173).	
	18	15

Total	50	44

On average, 'L'Allegro' refers in some way to time once in every three lines; 'Il Penseroso', once in every four. Therefore, to do as Mrs Lyons does, and cite temporal adverbs, phrases, and clauses as evidence of a distinctive concern with time in 'Il Penseroso' is, by itself, inadequate: such time-references are, in fact, more frequent in 'L'Allegro'. Both poems are concerned with time. If they differ, something in the nature of their concern, some other feature of their language, must be responsible for altering the neutral stance revealed by the tabulated evidence.

What the difference appears to be is that 'L'Allegro' is concerned with time, but 'Il Penseroso' is concerned *about* time. Time passing and past time matter more to the pensive man than to his carefree counterpart. This is revealed in their respective artistic tastes. L'Allegro is chiefly interested in the art of contemporary social performances: folklore stories told over drinks of ale (ll. 100–14), 'pomp, and feast, and revelry, / With mask, and antique pageantry' (ll. 127–8), and the plays of Jonson and Shakespeare at the theatre (*ll.* 131–4). The pensive man prefers art from remoter periods (*ll.* 19–21, 88–92, 97–120), and regards good post-classical tragedies as 'rare' (*l.* 101). His interests extend beyond the performing arts: since he avoids crowds it is presumably in reading or in fleeting reminiscence that 'gorgeous Tragedy' will 'come sweeping by' (*ll.* 97–8).[31] He is more precise than the happy man is about the details of the past, mentioning Cassiopea as 'that starred Ethiop queen that strove / To set her beauty's praise above / The sea-nymphs' (*ll.* 19–21), and inserting a footnote on the circumstances of Melancholy's birth – 'His daughter she (in Saturn's reign, / Such mixture was not held a stain)' (*ll.* 25–6). Art from the past is for him a spiritual resource to be drawn on in the present, hence his commands to 'bid' and 'call up' (*ll.* 105, 109). It is perhaps significant that he should wish to revive, not quite Plato and Orpheus, but 'the spirit of Plato' and 'the soul of Orpheus' (*ll.* 89, 105): the resources are to be in mentally assimilable form! In his description of his walk in the moonlight his mind's habitual inclination towards the past is revealed even by a tense-sequence:

> . . . I walk unseen
> On the dry smooth-shaven green,
> To behold the wandering moon,
> Riding near her highest noon,
> Like one that had been led astray
> Through the heaven's wide pathless way; (*ll.* 65–70)

In standard grammar, 'walk' would be compatible with '*hath* been led astray', or a past tense ('walked') with 'had been led astray'; but Milton matches 'walk' with 'had been led astray'. Whereas 'L'Allegro' moves typically from past to present, 'Il Penseroso' here moves in fluent thought from present to past. The syntax strays significantly. The high moon, 'riding' in the night sky, is the pensive man's equivalent of the noonday sun. It both correlates with, and induces, his meditative drift into the past.

Bridget Gellert Lyons really pinpoints the difference in the sense of time in 'L'Allegro' and 'Il Penseroso' when she speaks in her discussion of 'Il Penseroso' of 'the continuous rather than discrete nature of experience filtered through a consciousness of which we therefore become more aware'.[32] The speaker in 'Il Penseroso' is more in evidence than the speaker in 'L'Allegro', and this, rather than any number of time-markers, is the chief means by which the passage of time is suggested. Time does not merely pass by; it passes by the speaker. He has an aim to be realized in time – to attain spiritual maturity and elation in his anticipated 'weary age' (*ll.* 167–74); whereas, as Dr Johnson notes, 'for the old age of Chearfulness [Milton] makes no provision'.[33] Experience in 'Il Penseroso' seems to be reviewed from the standpoint of 'old experience', but in 'L'Allegro' it seems perennially young. In 'L'Allegro' much emphasis is given to 'youthful Jollity', 'many a youth, and many a maid, / Dancing in the chequered shade', and 'such sights as youthful poets dream' (*ll.* 26, 95–6, 129). 'Young and old come forth to play' (*l.* 97), but in 'Il Penseroso' a sober concern with 'the immortal mind' makes the pensive man forsake youthful pleasures. Consequently he seems to be, in Gary Stringer's phrase, 'L'Allegro grown older'.[34]

The Youth-Age theme is such a literary commonplace that it would be all too easy to indicate parallels between 'L'Allegro' and 'Il Penseroso' and other sixteenth- and seventeenth-century literature. But it is still worth noting that the long-observed parallel between Milton's poems and the pair of lyrics by Marlowe and Ralegh beginning 'Come live with me, and be my love' and 'If all the world and love were young' extends beyond the fact that they catalogue delights and have similar closing couplets.[35] The Marlowe and Ralegh lyrics were printed in *England's Helicon* in 1600 as a persuasion and reply, and in her reply to the shepherd's promise of future bliss the nymph pertinently concerns herself with the passage of time:

> If all the world and love were young,
> And truth in every Sheepheards tongue,
> These pretty pleasures might me move
> To live with thee and be thy love.

> Time drives the flocks from field to fold,
> When Rivers rage, and Rocks grow cold,
> And *Philomell* becometh dombe,
> The rest complain of cares to come.

The last verse of the lyric seems to express the point of view of Milton's pensive man towards the youthful delights of 'L'Allegro':

> But could youth last, and love still breede,
> Had joyes no date, nor age no neede,
> Then these delights my minde might move,
> To live with thee, and be thy love.

Marlowe's poem, like 'L'Allegro', offers apparently timeless delights, but 'Il Penseroso' joins Ralegh's in the conviction that these delights will not last. When Izaak Walton included the Marlowe and Ralegh poems in *The Compleat Angler* (1653) it was therefore tasteful of him to have a young milkmaid sing Marlowe's lines and her mother sing Ralegh's. The mother says, 'I learn'd the first part [the Marlowe poem] in my golden age, when I was about the age of my poor daughter; and the latter part . . . when the cares of the World began to take hold of me . . .'[36] 'L'Allegro' is aware of care's existence: Sport derides it (*l.* 31), the Lydian airs preserve against it (*ll.* 135–6), and the delights afforded by the upland hamlets are 'secure' (carefree). But the pensive man is gripped by cares; he feels time pass by.[37]

A symptom of the youthful *joie de vivre* in 'L'Allegro' is its bustling activity. Mirth is told 'haste thee' and 'trip it as you go' (*ll.* 25, 33), the cock 'scatters' the darkness (*l.* 50), and even the song of the lark is said to 'startle' the night (*l.* 42). The sounds of the hunt 'cheerly rouse the slumb'ring morn' (*l.* 54), and Orpheus is also wakened up (*ll.* 145–6). The goblin's cream-bowl is 'set' for him, but he sweats all night to earn it and eventually 'flings' out of doors (*l.* 113). Corydon and Thyrsis are temporarily 'set' at dinner, but Phillis leaves her bower 'in haste' to bind the sheaves (*ll.* 83–8). The phrase 'the busy hum of men' (*l.* 118) suggests the activity of swarming crowds. The ploughman whistles, the milkmaid sings, the mower whets his scythe, and there is music and dancing in the shade. The poem's content invites a reading that allows the octosyllabic couplet to trip it as it goes.

By contrast, 'Il Penseroso' is sedately contemplative. As Nan Cooke Carpenter says, 'The tone . . . is much soberer and the prevailing rhythm . . . far different, not only in the smoother verse-lines but in a different pattern of content.'[38] The speaker walks (*ll.* 65, 156), or sits (*l.* 170); his mind is 'fixèd' (*l.* 4); his goddess, whom he asks to 'fix' her eyes on the ground (*l.* 44), is clothed in 'staid wisdom's hue' (*l.* 16). Her power can 'raise' Musaeus (*l.* 104) – hardly the disturbance of music compelling Orpheus to 'heave his head / From golden slumber' in 'L'Allegro' (*ll.* 145–6). Throughout 'Il Penseroso' words such as 'still' (*ll.* 41, 78, 127), 'calm' (*l.* 45), 'gently' (*l.* 60), 'slow' (*l.* 76), and 'softly' (*l.* 150) check the possibility of any brisk movement. A line like 'Swinging slow with sullen roar' is carefully mimetic: balanced stressing ('swinging slow', 'sullen roar'), long vowels ('slow', 'roar'), and alliteration intervals marking the curfew's tolling combine to make the description solemnly evocative. In its sustained control of movement the introduction of Melancholy is masterly:

> Come pensive nun, devout and pure,
> Sober, steadfast, and demure,
> All in a robe of darkest grain,
> Flowing with majestic train,
> And sable stole of cypress lawn,   35
> Over thy decent shoulders drawn.
> Come, but keep thy wonted state,
> With even step, and musing gait,
> And looks commercing with the skies,

Thy rapt soul sitting in thine eyes: 40
There held in holy passion still,
Forget thyself to marble, till
With a sad leaden downward cast,
Thou fix them on the earth as fast.

Evenly distributed stresses endorse meaning in 'Sober, steadfast, and demure' (l. 32), and lines 31 and 38 are steadily proportioned. While the past-participial adjectives 'drawn', 'wonted', 'rapt', and 'held' preserve the nun's 'state', the present participles from 'flowing' (l. 34) to 'sitting' (l. 40), syntactically avoiding the diversions of subordinate clauses and also making time stand still, effect a dream-like metamorphosis. The pensive nun seems to change rather than move. The subject of 'flowing' may be the nun or her clothing, so that, with magical unobtrusiveness, she moves with her robe. 'Still' (l. 41) may be a temporal adverb, an adjective describing the pensive nun, or an adjective describing 'passion'; and the various readings, themselves held still, involve the reader in hypnotized lingering. In lines 42–4 it is not just the weight implied by 'marble' and 'leaden' that suggests that the sentence is dragged down, with Melancholy's eyes: the enjambment of line 42, leading into the four strong stresses of 'sad leaden downward cast', retards the verse movement. By the time that the last line of the passage is reached, the reader's attention, like Melancholy's eyes, is fixed fast. It is odd, in a way, that Stanley Fish should have only philosophical and mythological associations in mind when he comments that the figure of Melancholy 'displays less and less energy, but at the same time she is being energized from within by the meanings *we* attach to her dress and actions'.[39] She is being energized from within by the poetry. Beguiling ambiguities and mimetic movements entrance the reader into empathy with Melancholy, and indeed with the speaker whose disposition she represents.

Dreams are mentioned only once in 'L'Allegro', in a simile (ll. 129–30), and it remains very much a waking poem. But 'Il Penseroso' constantly suggests that a state of relaxed dreaminess is conducive to contemplation. Even in the dismissive simile which likens Mirth's 'vain deluding Joys' to 'hovering dreams / The fickle pensioners of Morpheus' train' (ll. 9–10), 'hovering', a word used elsewhere by Milton in contexts describing uncertainty or delusion,[40] sensitively catches the insubstantial yet real presence of dreams just at the moment of waking. Gently soporific moods are induced throughout the poem, whether by the continuously calming stroke of the present participle in 'Smoothing the rugged brow of night' (l. 58), or by the implication in 'entice the dewy-feathered Sleep' (l. 46) that oncoming sleep is like seduction. The bellman's 'charm' (l.83), which may be either the benediction he recites or the lulling sound of his bell, is 'drowsy'

17

('inducing sleepiness', *OED*). The vision in lines 147–50 is spellbindingly impressionistic:

> And let some strange mysterious dream,
> Wave at his wings in airy stream,
> Of lively portraiture displayed,
> Softly on my eyelids laid.

The dreaminess suggested by alliteration, assonance, and rhyme is increased here by ambiguously fluctuating syntax. Is the 'strange mysterious dream', or are the 'wings', 'in airy stream'? Do the words 'of lively portraiture displayed' describe 'dream' or 'wings' – or 'wings in airy stream'? What is laid on the speaker's eyelids – the 'dream', the 'wings', the 'airy stream', or the 'lively portraiture displayed'? Such questions may be asked, but any attempt to give definitive answers is frustrated by the beguiling ambiguousness of the syntax. The past participle 'laid' seems to give the dream a kind of completion, and yet to leave it hanging uncertainly in the air, a fascinating effect also achieved by the syntax: normally, the line 'Wave at his wings in airy stream' would follow the two lines which, in the poem, follow it; so that the reading would be 'And let some strange mysterious dream of lively portraiture displayed, softly on my eyelids laid, wave at his wings in airy stream'. But by reordering the lines so that an expected main verb after 'laid' never materializes, Milton leaves us with the dream's mystery. Coleridge is disappointing when he sees nothing more than a 'confused and awkwardly arranged period'[41] in these subtle lines. When Thomas Warton advises the reader not to seek for 'precise meanings of parts' but to 'acquiesce in a general idea resulting from the whole',[42] he at least shows his willingness to place the poetic function of the language before the claims of neat, orthodox parsing.

The preceding analysis of the poetic effects achieved mainly by pronouns, adverbs, and verbs in 'L'Allegro' and 'Il Penseroso' shows the care with which Milton has adapted his style to suit each poem's subject. As might be expected in the case of a highly deliberate artist, there is still more evidence of the skill with which he has selected and arranged stylistic detail. 'Il Penseroso', being a poem about the pensive man, is concerned with mental activities. Bridget Gellert Lyons has remarked on the 'sense of possibility rather than of actuality'[43] that pervades its presentation of experience. And Stanley Fish points to the word 'therefore' in the lines 'And therefore to our weaker view, / O'erlaid with black staid wisdom's hue' in order to show that readers of 'Il Penseroso' are required constantly to revise their opinion of what they have just read.[44] The stylistic evidence for the impression that 'Il Penseroso' is a comparatively philosophical poem, one that is more sophisticated in thought than 'L'Allegro', may be represented by the following table:

Feature	'L'Allegro'	Contexts	'Il Penseroso'	Contexts
'let' + Vb.	1	*l.* 125	5	*ll.* 85, 97, 147, 155, 161
'may' + Vb.	2	*ll.* 138, 145	5	*ll.* 87, 140, 164, 167, 170
'might' + Vb.			2	*ll.* 18, 104
'would have'	1	*l.* 148		
'but'	1	*l.* 11	7	*ll.* 11, 17, 37, 51, 103, 125, 155
'if' clause	4	*ll.* 37, 89, 132, 151	2	*ll.* 77, 116
'unless' clause			1	*l.* 56
'save' + noun			1	*l.* 82
'beside' + noun			1	*l.* 116
'yet'			1	*l.* 22
'though'			1	*l.* 101
'perhaps'	1	*l.* 79		
Totals	10		26	

The function and meaning of the words and constructions in the table may vary. For instance, 'but' may introduce an alternative rather than a qualification ('But come thou goddess fair and free', 'But hail thou goddess sage and holy'). Kester Svensden has interpreted 'but' in the lines 'But let my due feet never fail, / To walk the studious cloister's pale' (*ll.* 155–6) as 'in any event'.[45] Two of the 'if' clauses in 'L'Allegro' occur in direct addresses to Mirth (*ll.* 37, 151), and so differ in function from those occurring in the speaker's accounts of pleasant experience. The closing lines of 'Il Penseroso' – 'These pleasures Melancholy give, / And I with thee will choose to live' – state a condition without using 'if' at all.[46] Nevertheless, it is true, and appropriate, that 'Il Penseroso' concentrates more than 'L'Allegro' does on what is possible or hoped for, and that it qualifies its statements and places conditions upon its speaker's commitment, whereas 'L'Allegro' presses on from one experience to another.

These differences in the language of the two poems become still more marked when the distribution of the connectives 'and', 'then', and 'or' is considered:

Connective	'L'Allegro' (152 lines)	'Il Penseroso' (176 lines)
'and'	53	45
'then'	6	
'or'	7	20

Together, 'and' and 'then' indicate the vigorous, wide-ranging progression typical of 'L'Allegro'. On four occasions in the poem 'and' occurs twice in a single line: ''Mongst horrid shapes, and shrieks, and sights unholy', 'Quips and cranks, and wanton wiles, / Nods, and becks, and wreathed smiles', 'And young and old come forth to play' (*ll.* 4, 27–8, 97). Line 127 exuberantly manages three 'ands': 'And pomp, and feast, and revelry'.

'Il Penseroso' does not aim to match the élan of such rapid presentation. The table for connectives shows that its significant equivalent to 'and' and 'then' is preponderantly 'or'. Again, the word's functions need to be carefully interpreted. Robert Graves, for instance, notes 'or' in the account in 'L'Allegro' of 'neat-handed Phillis' going off to work:

> And then in haste her bower she leaves,
> With Thestylis to bind the sheaves;
> Or if the earlier season lead
> To the tanned haycock in the mead. (*ll.* 87–90)

He comments: 'Phyllis . . . scurries discreetly off in pretended haste, saying that she has to bind the August sheaves, or perhaps cart the June hay, she isn't sure which.'[47] The accuracy of Graves's entire description is suspect, for in these lines Phillis pretends nothing, and feels no obligation, whether it be to act discreetly, say something, or work. Graves interprets 'or' as evidence of her indecision (and of Milton's muddle-headedness). But Phillis could be indecisive only if the binding of the sheaves took place at the same time as the carting of the hay; which, naturally, it does not. The poem makes it clear that there will be a 'tanned haycock in the mead' in 'the earlier season'. Graves errs, as he does regarding the happy man at the window, by not attending carefully to the time scheme in 'L'Allegro'. 'Or' in the passage he cites betrays no indecision on Phillis' part; it merely introduces the suggestion that she may have a different job to do at another time of year.

In 'Il Penseroso' 'or' indicates the speaker's awareness of alternatives that can be chosen from a wealth of experience. 'Prince Memnon's sister' might suit black, he reflects, 'or that starred Ethiop queen . . .' (*ll.* 17–21). 'Or' also arranges his thoughts in a way that traces his mind's reflective drift, disclosing predilections and patterns of association. When he thinks of tragedies, for instance, his mind seems to leaf through his past reading: 'Thebes, or Pelops' line, / Or the tale of Troy divine. / Or what (though rare) of later age, / Ennobled hath the buskined stage' (ll. 99–102). 'Or' is again used with psychological delicacy to help represent mystical feeling:

> What worlds, or what vast regions hold
> The immortal mind that hath forsook
> Her mansion in this fleshly nook:
> And of those demons that are found
> In fire, air, flood, or under ground,
> Whose power hath a true consent
> With planet, or with element.   (ll. 90–6)

The speaker's mind ranges throughout the universe here, and though it settles nowhere, it is not felt to be restless. With cool impartiality 'or' keeps the potentially bewildering experience under rational control, while allowing the meditative mind to be shown accepting vast uncertainty with a calm, seemingly indifferent, awe.

Sometimes the speaker in 'Il Penseroso' is more committed to a choice among alternatives – when he plans what to do should bad weather prevent his walk in the moonlight, for instance: 'Or if the air will not permit, / Some still removed place will fit' (ll. 77–8). And at the spiritual climax of the poem (ll. 155–76), when the speaker envisages religious ecstasy and the delights of solitary meditation, his commitment is implied by the absence of the word 'or': in this ultimate vision his flitting reflective mind has found repose.

The significant differences between the conjunctions used in 'L'Allegro' and 'Il Penseroso' should not be allowed to obscure the fact that many conjunctions are used in each poem. It is partly for this reason that the poems have been recognized as catalogues of delights.[48] Cataloguing, and frequently shifting the area of attention, are activities motivated by a desire to cover representative aspects of Mirth and Melancholy. The extent to which the poems generalize becomes clear from several points of style:[49]

Feature	'L'Allegro' (152 lines)		'Il Penseroso' (176 lines)	
indefinite N. (pl.)	52		45	
'many a' + N. (sg.)	4	ll. 95(2), 101, 139		
'all' (quantifier)	2	ll. 111, 143	3	ll. 4, 81, 166
'such (. . .) as'	4	ll. 28–30, 129–30, 138–40, 148–50	3	ll. 17–18, 105–8, 145–6
'some' (+ adj.) + N.	3	ll. 5, 55, 79	7	ll. 5, 75, 78, 86, 139, 147, 153

simile	1	*ll.* 8–9	4	*ll.* 7–10(2), 67–70, 71–2

If the figures for conjunctions indicate that 'L'Allegro' ranges more freely than 'Il Penseroso', the first two figures in this table indicate the corollary, that 'Il Penseroso' examines experience in greater detail. The only passage in 'Il Penseroso' where indefinite plural nouns conglomerate is the brief account of romance literature (*ll.* 116–20), and this is hardly a conspicuous context when compared with the fairly consistent generalization throughout 'L'Allegro'. The four similes in 'Il Penseroso' are more precise in observation than the one simile in 'L'Allegro', and this (when one considers that constructing a simile involves mental correlation) increases meditative penetration. The simile in 'L'Allegro' compares the raggedness of 'low-browed rocks' to Melancholy's 'locks'. 'Low-browed' scarcely sanctions the comparison of rocks to hair, and the comparison remains sufficiently tenuous to complement the mock-irascible tone of the poem's opening: an angry mind appears as a careless one. Contrast this with the similes in 'Il Penseroso': Mirth's 'fancies fond with gaudy shapes' are said to be 'as thick and numberless / As the gay motes that people the sunbeams, / Or likest hovering dreams . . .'; and the 'wandering' moon, 'like one that had been led astray / Through the heaven's wide pathless way', is seen 'stooping through a fleecy cloud'. These similes bear the stamp of the fixed contemplative mind in their detail. It is only in its use of the quantifier 'some' that 'Il Penseroso' appears to be more vague than 'L'Allegro', but the blurring function of 'some' in the phrases 'some wide-watered shore', 'some still removed place', and 'some high lonely tower' aids the realization of the speaker's emotional disposition: atmosphere is what he has a feeling for, not sharply outlined description. But, even allowing for this stylistic detail, the evidence tabulated for 'L'Allegro' and 'Il Penseroso' shows that the pensive man, by acts of recollection, has processed experience more than his counterpart has done. In 'L'Allegro', matter predominates over mind; in 'Il Penseroso', mind over matter.

The similes, and the increase in detail, throughout 'Il Penseroso' suggest that T. S. Eliot's complaint that 'the imagery in *L'Allegro* and *Il Penseroso* is all general'[50] needs to be more discriminating. Generalized statements abound in both poems, but this does not preclude detail in their imagery. The table on page 174 shows that both poems contain a high frequency of adjectives (13.3 per cent of the words in 'L'Allegro'; in 'Il Penseroso', 15.2 per cent), and it is easy to select phrases in which adjectives sharpen the focus on images: from 'L'Allegro', 'brooding Darkness spreads his jealous wings', 'wrinkled Care', 'the twisted eglantine', 'russet lawns, and fallows grey', 'the nibbling flocks', 'labouring clouds', 'the neat-handed Phillis', 'the tanned haycock', 'the chequered shade', 'the spicy nut-brown ale', and 'shadowy flail'; from 'Il Penseroso', 'the fiery-wheeled throne', 'the dry smooth-shaven green', 'a fleecy cloud', 'drew iron tears down Pluto's cheek', 'minute drops from off the eaves', 'archèd walks of twilight groves', 'shadows brown', 'the bee with honied thigh', 'the dewy-feathered Sleep', 'a dim religious light', 'the hairy gown and mossy cell'. 'Labouring' in the phrase 'labouring clouds' suggests the slow, cumbersome gathering of clouds. 'Tanned' is used with originality to describe a haycock. And 'shadowy' is rich in implication: the goblin's flail is 'shadowy' in that it is mysterious, but since the goblin works in a room where a fire is burning, and since he works at superhuman speed, the flail is 'shadowy' in that its blur as the goblin wields it is scarcely distinguishable from the shadows in the room. In 'Il Penseroso' the adjectives often concentrate the mind on small objects, such as droplets of rain falling at minute intervals from the eaves, or the leg of a bee sticky with honey. Sometimes an adjective makes its impact by suggestion rather than by explicit description: in the account of the wonderful 'iron tears' that Orpheus' music 'drew' down Pluto's cheek, for instance, the paradoxical combination of 'iron' and 'tears' represents, in physical terms, the yielding of an unyielding nature. The adjectives in both poems, then, and in 'Il Penseroso' the similes and the precise evocations of the 'pensive nun', the moonlit stroll, or the poetic sleep – any of these challenges Eliot's view that the imagery is 'all general'.

If Eliot is criticizing 'L'Allegro' and 'Il Penseroso' for being generalized on the grounds that they contain a large number of indefinite plurals, his statement still needs to be modified, for 'Il Penseroso' contains fewer indefinite plurals than 'L'Allegro'. Eliot does not credit the poems with such significant and apt variation. The poems reveal the universals Mirth and Melancholy through their particular manifestations, so that even detailed images exist in a wider symbolic context. As Phyllis Mackenzie has suggested:

We should regard the natural details as a Platonist looks at the parts of the universe. They are the multiple bodyings-forth of an Idea in the mind of the poet. Part of the pleasure for the reader, therefore, is derived from the excitement of watching visual details spring to life, luxuriant and apparently real, which, none the less, bend and taper into the emergent design of the evolving whole.[51]

The images are 'general' in the sense that they form part of a general scheme. Had the images been too specific, they would have taken on a degree of individuality that would have upset the unity of this overall design. They would also have tended to become individualized in a way that would have disturbed what Tillyard calls the 'subtle friendliness' and 'perfect social tone'[52] of the poems. It is essentially the technique of the poems to sketch in outlines and leave the reader to fill in imaginative detail: in Macaulay's words, the poems 'are indeed not so much poems as collections of hints'.[53] If Eliot will not take a hint, he is bound to reject a vast quantity of poetry, from the early Renaissance onwards at least; for, as Coleridge notes, a tendency to generalize is very common indeed.[54] But, is Eliot not being merely inconsistent? He can hardly uphold a principled dislike of 'general' imagery and still regard Johnson's 'The Vanity of Human Wishes' as 'great poetry'.[55] And a glance at his own poems, even only at 'Preludes' or 'Morning at the Window', will confirm the truth of Kenneth Muir's remark that 'it is curious that Mr. Eliot should object to Milton's use of a method he frequently employs himself.'[56]

The main trouble with Eliot's comment regarding 'general' imagery is that it is itself too general: as so often in Eliot's criticism, the meaning is frustratingly unclear. Is his complaint about 'general' imagery perhaps a facet of his other complaint that Milton's imagery is not 'visual'? Or, even if 'L'Allegro' and 'Il Penseroso' contain 'visual' images (and it has been demonstrated earlier in this chapter that they do), is Eliot still right in saying that the images are 'general': are 'visual' and 'general' necessarily incompatible characteristics?

F. W. Bateson cites lines 71–2 of 'L'Allegro' – 'Russet lawns, and fallows grey, / Where the nibbling flocks do stray' – as evidence of visual imagery in the poems, and his comments raise interesting issues about the 'general' nature of the imagery:

[The two lines constitute] a masterpiece of concentrated observation. The sheep have broken through the temporary fence round the parish's fallow field, no doubt because the common pastures are 'Russet', the short-rooted grass having been 'burned', as farmers say, in the hot dry weather. 'Russet' is decidedly not the epithet one would have expected for 'Lawns' (the later Milton would have preferred 'green' or perhaps 'verdurous') – nor is 'Gray' what one would have expected for 'Fallows'. Milton must have had his eye on a real field. Most fallows after the summer ploughing are brown, but this field, perhaps because the subsoil was chalk, was grey. Milton is quite as specific about it as Wordsworth could have been.[57]

This expert commentary admirably establishes the visual accuracy of the adjectives 'russet' and 'grey'. But are Milton's lines as 'specific' as is being suggested? The poem speaks of 'lawns', 'fallows', 'flocks', 'mountains', 'clouds', and so on, whereas Bateson speaks of 'the sheep', 'a real field', and 'this field'. And nowhere does the poem mention 'the temporary fence round the parish's fallow field'. Milton, no doubt, observed a real field before he could write down his accurate observation; but in the poem the observation is applied generally. It is not the case, as Stanley Fish argues, that 'Milton wanted to keep the reader's eye from going to the trouble of envisioning a real field':[58] the reader is required to identify reality in 'L'Allegro', and he is particularly encouraged to do so by adjectives as specific as 'russet' and 'grey'. The soundness of Bateson's reading of Milton's words does not equal that of his field work. The observation behind the lines is specific, but the lines themselves are generalized.

Eliot cites 'L'Allegro', lines 63–8, in order to support his allegation that the imagery is 'general'. They are lines that have provoked considerable critical debate:

> While the ploughman near at hand,
> Whistles o'er the furrowed land,
> And the milkmaid singeth blithe,
> And the mower whets his scythe,
> And every shepherd tells his tale
> Under the hawthorn in the dale.

Eliot comments: 'It is not a particular ploughman, milkmaid, and shepherd that Milton sees (as Wordsworth might see them); the sensuous effect of these verses is entirely on the ear, and is joined to the concepts of ploughman, milkmaid, and shepherd.'[59] More recently, Leslie Brisman has expressed the view that 'the local habitation and a name which . . . makes imaginary beings "be", is more persuasive in the opening lines [of the poem] than in these more general descriptions.'[60] F. W. Bateson's answer to Eliot is that 'in this passage Milton is providing a list of morning *sounds* – exactly comparable, as it happens, with the two catalogues of sounds in Wordsworth's *An Evening Walk* – and if there are no details about the ploughman, etc., that is because the Cheerful Man is only concerned with them as *noise-producers*.'[61] Rosemond Tuve gives a different answer: 'Eliot will not find here his "particular milkmaid", for this one must instead be all milkmaids who ever sang.'[62] Hence the common pattern in literary criticism of assertion and counter-assertion again emerges. But which critic is right, and why?

In this case, where there are no moral complications, being right is a question of descriptive accuracy: which critic most faithfully represents what the poem says? It is sad to notice that none of these critics carries out a close textual analysis to convince the other, but proceeds with his or her own assertion. Eliot selects one aspect of lines that are not overtly onomatopoeic, their effect on the ear, and detaches this from the actual meaning of the words. But it is Eliot's obsession with aural effects that creates the breakdown, for sound and meaning in the poem are clearly one. Bateson overlooks meaning and alleges that Milton's emphasis on sound is deliberate. But the grammar of the lines cited pervades the poem, and does so in sections that have nothing to do with sound-production. Milton, then, cannot be interested only in the sounds made by the ploughman or milkmaid. Rosemond Tuve ignores or overlooks Eliot's mention of the concept of a milkmaid: would her milkmaid who represented all milkmaids who ever sang *not* be a conceptualized figure? Leslie Brisman, like Eliot, is judging according to personal taste, rather than analysing the poetic language: he finds the opening lines of 'L'Allegro' 'more persuasive' because he admires specificness. Just how the opening lines are – or can be – more persuasive, is not clear. The opening lines use the grammar that prevails throughout the poem ('Stygian cave forlorn', 'horrid shapes, and shrieks, and sights unholy', 'some uncouth cell', 'the night-raven', 'ebon shades', 'low-browed rocks'). Indeed, it is the very vagueness of these descriptions that gives them their macabre mock-terror. Grammar and vocabulary function differently in the ploughman passage, of course; but both passages cited by Brisman are generalized.

The most striking feature in the lines from 'L'Allegro' quoted by Eliot is the definite article, which occurs six times: 'the ploughman', 'the furrowed land', 'the milkmaid', 'the mower', 'the hawthorn', and 'the dale.' This constitutes an unusually high frequency of occurrence, for Milton's period, for Milton, and for 'L'Allegro' and 'Il Penseroso' themselves. In a sample of 27,000 words of poetry from Spenser to the Restoration, George Rostrevor Hamilton has found that 2,400, or slightly over 4 per cent, are definite articles.[63] His figure for Milton is 6 per cent, which is high compared to other authors.[64] A count for 'L'Allegro' and 'Il Penseroso' reveals that 6.5 per cent of the words in the former, and 4.5 per cent of those in the latter, are definite articles. The figure for the ploughman passage is 18 per cent, which exceeds even Hamilton's high figure of 15 per cent for some nature poetry.[65] Clearly, an understanding of the function of the definite article in lines 63–8 of 'L'Allegro' will be of considerable help in understanding what Milton is trying to achieve there.

When a speaker (or writer) uses the definite article before a noun, he assumes that the noun's referent exists, and that the hearer (or reader) knows that it exists.[66] For example, when Milton speaks of 'the ploughman' and 'the milkmaid', he assumes that the reader knows that ploughman and milkmaid exist. Thus, a contract of understanding is established between writer and reader. Sometimes this contract is strengthened, when the speaker sets up what Paul Christophersen calls a 'situational basis'[67] for the use of the definite articles. The speaker in 'L'Allegro' is made to do this several times, in the passage describing the cock, for example:

> While the cock with lively din,
> Scatters the rear of darkness thin,

And to the stack, or the barn door,
Stoutly struts his dames before.   (ll. 49–52)

Having mentioned 'the cock', the speaker continues, without preface, to
mention 'the rear of darkness thin', 'the stack', and 'the barn door'. All of
these things are associated by him in the situation he imagines. The speaker
also assumes that the reader shares his patterns of association, that he will
follow his rumination and enter into it imaginatively. The vignettes in
'L'Allegro' and 'Il Penseroso' are often so vivid because of definite articles
used in a 'situational basis' like this. Stanley Fish is not quite right in saying
that the details of the landscape in the poem 'refer to nothing beyond themselves and . . . ask from us no response beyond the *minimal* and literary
response of recognition' or that the patterns of alliteration and assonance
in the poetic language 'carry us along but do not move us to acts of
association or reflection'.[68] The definite articles invite the reader's recognition of what is being spoken of; but they do this by assuming the reader's
imaginative familiarity with the speaker's gradually developing thoughts.
The reader cannot avoid reflection: the very mode by which the poem
communicates demands it. In associating the details of the speaker's
reminiscences with each other, he is drawn – he cannot but be drawn –
into like-mindedness.

In merely alleging, or implicitly conceding, that the imagery of the
ploughman passage is 'general', T. S. Eliot, F. W. Bateson, and Leslie
Brisman overlook these subtleties of communication in the style. They also
miss an important ambiguity in the definite articles; the fact that they are
not quite 'general', but generic. That is to say, when Milton speaks of 'the
ploughman', 'the milkmaid', or 'the mower', the articles function symbolically: the ploughman represents all ploughmen, and, as Rosemond
Tuve insists, the milkmaid 'must . . . be all milkmaids who ever sang'.[69]
That the articles are generic in this way is conclusively established by the
last couplet of the ploughman passage:

And every shepherd tells his tale
Under the hawthorn in the dale.

Every shepherd; not *each* shepherd. 'Every', as Zeno Vendler points out,
stresses completeness and exhaustiveness, whereas 'each' would draw attention to the individuals 'as they appear, in some succession or other, one by
one'.[70] The last line contains two definite articles ('the hawthorn', 'the
dale'), and these must be generic, unless we are prepared to envisage all the
shepherds in the dale huddled under one hawthorn bush. 'And the most
undifferentiating conjunction, holds the whole passage together ('and the

milkmaid ... and the mower ... and every shepherd'). Therefore, the definite article must be generic throughout the passage.

A purely generic use of the article does not require a 'situational basis' in order to function successfully. That is to say, a sentence like 'the cat is a quadruped' (meaning all cats are quadrupeds) needs no specific setting. But Milton provides a setting for his ploughman, milkmaid, mower, and shepherds, and, as in the passage describing the cock and the barn-yard, the reader is prompted to imagine the setting. The ploughman is 'near at hand', whistling as he crosses 'the furrowed land' (also presumably nearby); the shepherds are 'under the hawthorn in the dale' ('You, the reader, know the dale I mean', is the speaker's assumption). Thus the concepts of plough-man, milkmaid, and so on, are brought to life and given a degree of individualization by the merest suggestion of locale. The milkmaid is therefore not merely a symbol of all milkmaids, but bears the illusion of individuality. Indeed, this subtle combination of the specific and generic is essential to the poetic technique of 'L'Allegro' (and, to a slightly lesser degree, of 'Il Penseroso'). It is the means by which the reader feels 'experience as lived through and as imagined, the experiences meanwhile typifying what is universally pleasurable and universally desired by men'.[71]

Generic articles and present tenses ('whistles', 'singeth', 'whets', 'tells') make the images permanent, but not static: the ploughman never stops whistling, and the milkmaid always sings. Nevertheless, G. Wilson Knight finds the images 'pictorially still, a sequential arrangement of tiny solids with no sense of any dynamic, evolving energy'.[72] For him, 'L'Allegro' and 'Il Penseroso' are 'mosaics of impression' that show little feeling for 'organic, pulsing life'.[73] But if the poems are mosaics of *impression*, then surely they must contain more psychological realism than a mere arbitrary sequence would do? And is it not precisely this kind of realism that is developed through the subtle functions of such aspects of their language as tense-sequences, conjunctions, and articles? The poems give appropriate structures for Mirth and Melancholy by adhering sensitively to the mental processes of a happy and a pensive man. It is in following these habits of mind, and in inducing similar mental processes in the reader, that the poems possess 'dynamic, evolving energy'.

Wilson Knight's objection that the poems do not possess 'organic, puls-ing life' seems to be paralleled by Cleanth Brooks's observation that 'though we see people going to work, we never see them *at* their work ... Nobody sweats in the world of "L'Allegro" – except the goblin'.[74] What Brooks means is that for the land to be 'the furrowed land' the ploughman would need to have ploughed it; but that he is not presented doing the ploughing. Instead of an observed sequence of actions undertaken, carried through, and completed, there would appear to be only a series of glimpses from a 'detached spectator'.[75] Brooks focuses on the settings of 'L'Allegro' and on the experiences described in the poem, and finds an 'aesthetic distance' constantly maintained between these settings and experiences and the happy or pensive man.[76] But the 'I' of the poems is himself a dramatic device for suggesting that the experiences are realistic and occur in actual settings: the ploughman is to be 'near at hand'. But, as has been shown, the grammar in a passage like the one featuring the ploughman, the milkmaid, and the mower, may indicate that the descriptions of the imagined settings are generic. Being generic, they are conceptualized descriptions. Therefore the speaker, the 'I' in the poems, is detached *mentally* from the experiences he is made to perceive as actual and specific. The poems are not so much about external settings as about the disposition of a happy or a pensive man. Indeed, is this not why they are entitled 'L'Allegro' and 'Il Penseroso'? The reader, by following the mental processes of the happy or pensive man, is meant himself to feel happy or pensive. And for this reason the descriptions of the external settings cannot be too particularized: the speaker's state of mind, inevitably individual to some degree, is to be publicly communicated; the private is to elicit a sympathetic response in other minds; the particular must always be universal too. Had the speaker in 'Il Penseroso' (or, indeed, in 'L'Allegro') mingled with the crowds in actual, rather than in imagined, conceptualized settings, the poems would have changed from being sketches to being complete pictures. Their universality would have been severely confined, if not lost altogether. Milton allows just enough detail into the poems to awaken the reader's imagination to happiness or pensiveness.

It is perhaps because of the degree of generalization in their style that 'L'Allegro' and 'Il Penseroso' relate so readily to other literature, such as the Theophrastan 'character' literature of the late sixteenth and early seventeenth centuries.[77] A study, say, of their relation to pastoral convention would only reveal their traditionalness further. But Milton's meticulously applied skill in devising appropriate structures for Mirth and Melancholy guarantees the uniqueness of his poems. He evidently thought highly enough of them to develop and adapt their style in 'Comus', in 'Lycidas', and in the descriptions of Eden in *Paradise Lost*.[78] Later poets have also held them in esteem: the style of 'L'Allegro' and 'Il Penseroso' may be traced throughout the nature poetry of the eighteenth century. Literary critics, with the exception of those mentioned at the beginning of this chapter, have also valued the poems, though often without supplying the necessary analysis of precisely what it is that they have valued. But analysis of the language of Milton's two superb miniatures does reveal why critical acclaim has been so thoroughly deserved.

29

NOTES

1. *Images and Themes in Five Poems by Milton* (1957), p. 36.
2. *English Poetry and Prose, 1540–1674*, ed. Ricks (1970), p. 280.
3. *5 Pens in Hand* (1958), pp. 34, 43.
4. ibid., pp. 34, 41.
5. *The Common Pursuit* (1952), p. 35.
6. 'Thy Darling in an Urn', review of *The Well Wrought Urn* by Cleanth Brooks, *Sewanee Review*, **55** (1947), 691.
7. J. B. Leishman, ' "L'Allegro" and "Il Penseroso" in their Relation to Seventeenth-Century Poetry', *ESEA* (1951), rpt. in *Milton's Minor Poems* (1969), pp. 129–30; D. C. Allen, *The Harmonious Vision* (1970 edn), pp. 10, 17; Maren-Sofie Røstvig, *The Happy Man: Studies in the Metamorphoses of a Classical Ideal* (2nd edn, 1962), **1**, 100; John Carey, *Milton* (1969), p. 39; A. S. P. Woodhouse, *The Heavenly Muse: A Preface to Milton*, ed. Hugh MacCallum (1972), p. 44; Stanley E. Fish, 'What It's Like to Read *L'Allegro* and *Il Penseroso*', *MS*, **7** (1975), 89–90.
8. Fish (ibid., 94) feels that there is a certain 'absence of mind' in 'L'Allegro', and Bridget Gellert Lyons associates such an absence with 'a process of self-distraction to ward off melancholy' (*Voices of Melancholy: Studies in Literary Treatments of Melancholy in Renaissance England* (1971), p. 153).
9. 'From Delusion to Illumination: A Larger Structure for *L'Allegro-Il Penseroso*', *PMLA*, **86** (1971), 37.
10. *Milton* (1969), p. 39.
11. For summaries of the various arguments, see Carey and Fowler, pp. 134–5, and *Variorum Commentary*, **2**, 279–84.
12. *MS*, **7** (1975), 77.
13. ibid., 81.
14. *5 Pens in Hand*, p. 39.
15. *MS*, **7** (1975), 84.
16. *Voices of Melancholy*, p. 154.
17. *Milton*, p. 38.
18. *MS*, **7** (1975), 82.
19. loc. cit.
20. *Voices of Melancholy*, p. 154.
21. Sense-perception may be voluntary or involuntary – one may look or see, listen or hear. The *OED* records constructions for the eye catching something, and for something catching the eye, before 'L'Allegro' (*catch* (Vb.) VIII.35, IX.37.b). In a sermon probably preached in 1630 John Donne makes a relevant comment on sight in seventeenth-century optics: 'No man knows so, as that strong arguments may not be brought on the other side, how he sees, whether by reception of species from without, or by emission of beames from within' (*The Sermons of John Donne*, ed. G. R. Potter and E. M. Simpson (1953–61), **9**, 247).
22. *Milton* (1930; rev. edn, 1966), p. 306.

23. loc. cit.
24. *The Harmonious Vision*, p. 5.
25. *Milton: A Biography* (1968), **1**, 103.
26. *Voices of Melancholy*, pp. 151–2.
27. ibid., pp. 154–9.
28. Donald C. Dorian, 'The Question of Autobiographical Significance in *L'Allegro* and *Il Penseroso*', *MP*, **31** (1933), 176, traces the false 'ideal day' theory to Masson, and presents several arguments against the theory. Rosemond Tuve (*Images and Themes in Five Poems by Milton*, p. 23) and William Riley Parker (*Milton: A Biography*, **1**, 99, **2**, 770) scatter the fragments of the exploded idea.
29. George L. Geckle, 'Miltonic Idealism: *L'Allegro* and *Il Penseroso*', *TSLL*, **9** (1967), 463.
30. 'The Unity of "L'Allegro" and "Il Penseroso" ', *TSLL*, **12** (1970), 221–9.
31. Cf. David M. Miller, 'From Delusion to Illumination: A Larger Structure for *L'Allegro-Il Penseroso*', *PMLA*, **86** (1971), 34: 'It is significant that Il Penseroso reads, rather than views, the plays . . . It is internal vision that he seeks.'
32. *Voices of Melancholy*, p. 154.
33. *Lives of the English Poets*, ed. G. B. Hill (1905), **1**, 167.
34. 'The Unity of "L'Allegro" and "Il Penseroso" ', *TSLL*, **12** (1970), 226.
35. See J. B. Leishman, *Milton's Minor Poems*, pp. 126–7.
36. *The Compleat Walton*, ed. Geoffrey Keynes (1929), p. 62.
37. George L. Geckle detects a 'sense of mortality and transience' in 'Il Penseroso' ('Miltonic Idealism: *L'Allegro* and *Il Penseroso*', *TSLL*, **9** (1967), 473). Stephen C. Behrendt, 'Bright Pilgrimage: William Blake's Designs for *L'Allegro* and *Il Penseroso*', *MS*, **8** (1975) reveals Blake's insight: the designs for 'L'Allegro' are 'essentially stationary in time', while those for 'Il Penseroso' show Milton's 'clear progression from wanderer "led astray" . . . to aged visionary prophet'. Edward Le Comte provides a useful general survey of Milton's developing attitude to time in *Milton's Unchanging Mind* (1973), pp. 5–68, though he gives surprisingly little attention to 'L'Allegro' and 'Il Penseroso'.
38. 'The Place of Music in *L'Allegro* and *Il Penseroso*', *UTQ*, **22** (1953), 365.
39. *MS*, **7** (1975), 90.
40. See 'Fair Infant', *l.* 38, and *PL*, V.140–1, IX.639.
41. *Coleridge on the Seventeenth Century*, ed. Roberta Florence Brinkley (1955), p. 566.
42. *Poems upon Several Occasions . . . by John Milton* (2nd edn, 1791), pp. 88–9.
43. *Voices of Melancholy*, p. 156.
44. *MS*, **7** (1975), 88.
45. 'Milton's *L'Allegro* and *Il Penseroso*', *The Explicator*, **8** (1950) item 49.
46. John Carey comments that 'if thou canst give' in 'L'Allegro' 'dilutes the address to Mirth with doubt, as against the sturdy "These pleasures Melancholy give" ' in 'Il Penseroso' (*Milton*, p. 39).
47. *5 Pens in Hand*, p. 42.
48. J. B. Leishman, *Milton's Minor Poems*, p. 126.

49. Indefinite plural nouns are those not preceded by an article or a possessive pronoun, those in 'L'Allegro', *ll.* 27–8, 75–9, for example.
50. 'A Note on the Verse of John Milton', *ESEA*, **21** (1936), 34.
51. 'Milton's Visual Imagination: An Answer to T. S. Eliot', *UTQ*, **16** (1946–7), 19.
52. *The Miltonic Setting, Past and Present* (1938), p. 11. See also Tillyard's *The Metaphysicals and Milton* (1956), pp. 12–28.
53. *Macaulay's Essay on Milton*, ed. Charles Wallace French (1898), p. 19.
54. *Biographia Literaria*, ch. 16. See also Rosemond Tuve, *Elizabethan and Metaphysical Imagery* (1947), pp. 42–3.
55. *On Poetry and Poets* (1957), p. 180. Christopher Ricks points out a similar inconsistency in F. R. Leavis's criticism of Milton and Johnson (*Milton's Grand Style* (1963), p. 4).
56. *John Milton* (2nd edn, 1960), p. 30.
57. *English Poetry: A Critical Introduction* (1950), p. 159.
58. *MS*, **7** (1975), 98.
59. 'A Note on the Verse of John Milton', *ESEA*, **21** (1936), 34.
60. ' "All Before Them Where to Choose": "L'Allegro" and "Il Penseroso" ', *JEGP*, **71** (1972), 231.
61. *English Poetry: A Critical Introduction*, p. 159.
62. *Images and Themes in Five Poems by Milton*, p. 20.
63. *The Tell-Tale Article: A Critical Approach to Modern Poetry* (1949), p. 5.
64. ibid., p. 6. Hamilton's other figures are: Spenser, 4.66 per cent; Donne, 1 per cent; Herrick, 4 per cent; Crashaw, 3 per cent; Marvell, 6 per cent; Dryden, 5.25 per cent. Unfortunately, Hamilton does not state which poems by these authors constitute his sample.
65. ibid., p. 20.
66. See Paul Christophersen, *The Articles: A Study in their Theory and Use in English* (1939), p. 28; and Zeno Vendler, *Linguistics in Philosophy* (1967), p. 69.
67. op. cit., p. 30.
68. *MS*, **7** (1975), 85.
69. *Images and Themes in Five Poems by Milton*, p. 20. Christophersen, *The Articles*, p. 31, and Christine Brooke-Rose, *A Grammar of Metaphor* (1958), pp. 28–33, discuss some symbolic uses of the article.
70. *Linguistics in Philosophy*, p. 78.
71. Rosemond Tuve, op. cit., p. 15.
72. *The Burning Oracle: Studies in the Poetry of Action* (1939), p. 64.
73. ibid., pp. 60, 59.
74. *The Well Wrought Urn* (1949), pp. 48, 49.
75. This is Brooks's expression, though Dr Johnson observes that the pensive man 'mingles as a mere spectator' with crowds (*Lives of the English Poets*, ed. G. B. Hill, **1**, 167).
76. op. cit., p. 48.
77. See my short article ' "L'Allegro" and "Il Penseroso" and Theophrastan Character Literature', *N & Q*, NS **27** (1980), 333–4.

78. See pp. 53–4, 56–7, 59–60, 88, below, on 'Comus' and 'Lycidas'. See also
    PL, IV.261–8, VII.309–31, for example.

CHAPTER TWO

The 'Nativity Ode' and 'Comus'

In 'L'Allegro' and 'Il Penseroso' Milton represents Mirth and Melancholy by appropriately contrasted symbolic structures. The structuring extends beyond a near-symmetrical arrangement of parallel, opposed images to include significant details in each poem's grammar and vocabulary. In the 'Nativity Ode' and 'Comus' a similar principle of organization seems to prevail. Though obviously different from 'L'Allegro' and 'Il Penseroso', and from each other, they present symbolic confrontations through boldly contrasted images and carefully organized language. But although Milton seems not to reveal a preference for the disposition of 'L'Allegro' or of 'Il Penseroso', in the structure of the 'Nativity Ode' and 'Comus' moral commitment is evident: both works celebrate the triumph of order over disorder.

In the 'Nativity Ode', order (represented by the 'Heaven-born child') and disorder (represented by the pagan gods) are viewed as self-contained, mutually exclusive states. It would seem that Christian and pagan powers cannot coexist or make concessions to each other: the pagan gods must go because God's Son has been born. The poem emphasizes that worship of the false gods is not merely wrong, but futile: 'In vain the Tyrian maids their wounded Thammuz mourn', 'In vain with cymbals' ring, / They call the grisly king', 'In vain with timbrelled anthems dark / The sable-stolèd sorcerers bear his worshipped ark' (*ll.* 204, 208–9, 219–20). Doom-laden negatives render the impotence of the pagan gods complete:

The oracles are dumb,
No voice or hideous hum
Runs through the archèd roof in words deceiving.
Apollo from his shrine
Can no more divine,
With hollow shriek the steep of Delphos leaving.

No nightly trance, or breathèd spell,
Inspires the pale-eyed priest from the prophetic cell.[1]

Order and disorder are associated with sharply contrasted images of light
and darkness, sound and quiet, harmony and discord, and arrival and departure.[2] So well-defined is this structure that one critic has commented that
'details are subdued to an over-all clarity of outline and movement' in a
kind of 'vital symbolic geometry'.[3] This may be seen in the use of colour in
the poem. If words like 'burning', 'cloudy', and 'dark' are taken to be colour adjectives, only four of the thirty-nine in the poem denote colours other
than black or white: 'olive green', 'red fire', 'furnace blue', and 'yellow-
skirted fays' (*ll.* 47, 159, 210, 235). Even then, the furnace and the fays are
engulfed in a general gloom, the 'red fire' is accompanied by 'smould'ring
clouds', the 'olive green' of Peace's wand is overlaid by its significance, and
the 'sun in bed' is 'curtained with cloudy red' (*ll.* 229–30). Colour is
characteristically reduced to a stark chiaroscuro, with a polished radiance,
glittering, gleaming, beaming, or burning on one side, and a dim, dusky,
cloudy atmosphere associated with pallor on the other.[4] As William Riley
Parker has remarked, 'Even when something colourful is introduced, it is
felt as black and white.'[5]

The symbolic structure of the 'Nativity Ode' is kept clear-cut by a pervasively active enchantment: magical influence makes the enactment of any
real struggle or confrontation between the infant Christ and the false gods
unnecessary.[6] The visit of the magi, the curtailment of the 'old dragon',
and the departure of the gods, all follow automatically from the establishment of heavenly rule on earth. The poem becomes 'a moment of astonishment . . . about a moment of astonishment',[7] its only conquest 'a schematic
conquest . . . not of transformation . . . or of love over law, but of arrangement'.[8] Movement is repeatedly curbed into images: of standing ('The
hookèd chariot stood / Unstained with hostile blood', 'The stars with deep
amaze / Stand fixed in steadfast gaze', *ll.* 56–7, 69–70); of the babe lying in
the manger (*ll.* 31, 151, 238); of the birds of calm, the shepherds, Mercy,
and the angels sitting (*ll.* 68, 87, 144, 244); of fixing ('Heaven's youngest
teemèd star, / Hath fixed her polished car', *ll.* 240–1); and of holding ('She
knew such harmony alone / Could hold all heaven and earth in happier
union', *ll.* 107–8). The winds are 'with wonder whist' (*l.* 64), the
shepherds' souls are taken in 'blissful rapture' (*l.* 98), and the air 'still pro-
longs each heavenly close' of the angelic music (*l.* 100). When Peace,
Truth, Justice, and Mercy descend, they slide gently and smoothly, like
masque figures (*ll.* 45–52, 141–6). Peace waves a wand, and stars bend
'their precious influence' (*ll.* 51–2, 71). Figures are drilled into neat groups:
the 'sun's team' pulls its chariot across the sky (*l.* 19); 'flocking shadows
pale, / Troop to the infernal jail' (*ll.* 232–3), and, with equal discipline,

'each fettered ghost slips to his several grave' (*l.* 234). The angels are always 'in order serviceable' (*l.* 244) – as a 'spangled host' of 'squadrons bright' in 'glittering ranks' (*ll.* 21, 114), or as a 'quire' (*ll.* 27, 115). The very shepherds sit in a 'rustic row' to have a chat (*l.* 87).

The artful tidiness of the 'Nativity Ode', resulting from the control of action, is complemented by a high degree of conceptual contrivance. Traditional nativity-poem paradoxes are only in evidence in the phrases 'wedded maid' and 'virgin mother' (*l.* 3),[9] but there is extensive animation and humanization of nature.[10] Nature is made to change her clothes, woo the air, hear the heavenly music, almost think her part done (*ll.* 29–44, 101–8), and, like the sun and the night (*ll.* 80, 111), feel embarrassment (*ll.* 40–4). The winds kiss the ocean and whisper to it, the ocean forgets to rave, stars refuse to move until told, and the new star waits on its master (*ll.* 69–76, 240–2). Nature's response to the birth of Christ signifies a reversal of the Fall: firm government is restored. But it is in the spirit of the 'happy morn' celebrated that, as a result of consistent stylistic contrivance, nature's compliance seems so congenial. This at least tones down the grimness of the picture of 'the bitter cross' (*l.* 152) on which redemption will eventually be achieved. However, one other consequence of the personification of nature is that the poem does not focus very much on the natural, 'nativity' aspect of the Incarnation. John Broadbent has shown that there is a movement throughout the poem 'from the incarnate towards the ideate',[11] and Winifred Maynard finds that what is presented is 'not . . . a domestic scene, but . . . a symbolic action'.[12] In the last stanza of the poem, the child is placed in the manger by his mother, but in the previous stanza the reader has been faced with the least natural of the poem's conceits – the 'rather charming, but also a little absurd'[13] image of the sun in bed. The poem's concerns seem to be diverted repeatedly from the naturalness of the nativity towards the imposed fixities of symbol and scheme.

The elaborate and systematized prosopopoeias are symptomatic of the poem's self-conscious, witty cleverness in language. But the virtuosity commands respect. In stanza V of the Hymn, for instance, alliteration, onomatopoeia, rhythm, and rhyme are attuned to the most serene lullaby:

> But peaceful was the night
> Wherein the Prince of Light
> His reign of peace upon the earth began:
> The winds with wonder whist,
> Smoothly the waters kissed,
> Whispering new joys to the mild ocean,
> Who now hath quite forgot to rave,
> While birds of calm sit brooding on the charmèd wave.

The whole stanza seems to flow like a charmed wave. At the other extreme, stanza XII dramatizes stern rule:

> While the creator great
> His constellations set,
> And the well-balanced world on hinges hung,
> And cast the dark foundations deep,
> And bid the welt'ring waves their oozy channel keep.

'Set' is placed in firm control of the seemingly uncontrollable polysyllable 'constellations'. 'Hung' implies a simple mechanical act: the creator hangs the world with the same proficiency as, say, that with which a carpenter might hang a door. And the even stress on 'well-balanced world' and the alliteration on 'hinges hung' combine to strike the balance being described. Adjectival and syllabic weight is amassed by the phrase 'dark foundations deep', so that 'cast' becomes a feat of strength. And if 'bid' seems momentarily challenged by 'welt'ring', 'keep' at the line end, the last of the simple monosyllabic verbs in the stanza, ensures obedience. Milton brilliantly imitates the engineering of the creator.

Several of the adjectives in the 'Nativity Ode' function mimetically. The adjectival phrase in 'Typhon huge ending in snaky twine' (*l.* 226), for instance, drags behind like a tail. Most remarkably, the adjectives throughout the description of the departing pagan gods are placed after their nouns, in order to preserve a sense of lingering ritualistic mystery: 'words deceiving', 'altars round', 'service quaint', 'temples dim', 'shadows dread', 'furnace blue', 'lowings loud', '[timbrelled] anthems dark', 'Typhon huge', and '[flocking] shadows pale' (*ll.* 175–232).

Adjectives play a fundamental role in the style of the 'Nativity Ode'. Their frequency is high, as in many of Milton's early poems.[14] Furthermore, over one third of the adjectives are implicitly or explicitly verbal, often arresting movement into posture. This may be observed in stanza XI of the Hymn:

> At last surrounds their sight
> A globe of circular light,
> That with long beams the shame-faced night arrayed,
> The helmèd cherubim
> And sworded seraphim,
> Are seen in glittering ranks with wings displayed,
> Harping in loud and solemn quire,
> With unexpressive notes to heaven's new-born heir.

Angels with 'displayed' wings herald the 'new-born' child; the cherubim are 'helmèd'; the seraphim, 'sworded'. Though in one respect the angels may not be consistently visualized – harpists in armour might produce all too 'unexpressive' sounds – they are certainly paraded, as though for a military inspection. 'Surrounds their sight' transfers attention from the 'shepherds on the lawn' to the heavenly host, and 'are seen' objectifies cherubim and seraphim. 'Harping' becomes more a fixed attitude than an action. The only thing that moves is the superbly-modulated stanza form, swelling aptly with the 'long beams', the 'glittering ranks with wings displayed', and the 'unexpressive notes', and engulfing the angels in their harmony.[15]

The 'rustic row' of the 'shepherds on the lawn' is dwarfed by the ravishing symbols of heavenly music and light: their souls are taken; their sight is surrounded. In fact, the 'Nativity Ode' subordinates humans to symbols consistently, and to the symbol of music in particular, by making the symbols active: 'In urns, and altars round, / A drear and dying sound / Affrights the flamens at their service quaint' (*ll.* 192–4); and though on the night of Christ's birth 'the trumpet spake not to the armèd throng' (*l.* 58), at the last judgement 'first to those ychained in sleep, / The wakeful trump of doom must thunder through the deep' (*ll.* 155–6). In stanza XIII of the Hymn the speaker reveals the full significance of the music's power:

> Ring out, ye crystal spheres,
> Once bless our human ears,
> (If ye have power to touch our senses so)
> And let your silver chime
> Move in melodious time;
> And let the base of heaven's deep organ blow,
> And with your ninefold harmony
> Make up full consort to the angelic symphony.

The spheres ring out, the silver chime moves in time, the bass of heaven's organ blows, the ninefold harmony joins the angelic song – and all independently of human agency. The parenthesized reservation '(If ye have power to touch our senses so)' expresses doubt about the possibility of the sphere-music even reaching human ears, as well as about the fitness of human ears to hear it. At best humans will be able to hear the music 'if such holy song / Enwrap our fancy long' (*ll.* 133–4). And even if this happens, another series of events will begin that again requires no human intervention:

> Time will run back, and fetch the age of gold,
> And speckled vanity
> Will sicken soon and die,
> And lep'rous sin will melt from earthly mould,

And hell itself will pass away,
And leave her dolorous mansions to the peering day.   (*ll.* 135–40)

Truth, Justice, and Mercy will 'down return to men', and heaven will 'open wide the gates of her high palace hall' (*ll.* 141–8). And it is not mankind that prevents this from happening sooner: 'But wisest fate says no, / This must not yet be so' (*ll.* 149–50). Of course, theologically, the redemptive scheme does assign a part for men to play; but the grammar of the 'Nativity Ode' represents the scheme as self-operating.

When grammatical agents are omitted altogether in the poem, a blank awesomeness is felt:

No war, or battle's sound
Was heard the world around
The idle spear and shield were high up hung. . .   (*ll.* 53–5)

A voice of weeping heard, and loud lament. . .   (*l.* 183)

The parting genius is with sighing sent. . .   (*l.* 186)

Nor is Osiris seen
In Memphian grove, or green.   (*ll.* 213–14)

No-one appears to hear the sound of battle or hang up the weapons. And this facelessness contributes to the desolation attending the departure of the false gods. Non-human or omitted agents, and of course the complementary humanizing of nature, together implicitly magnify the poem's omnipotent symbols. Human beings contemplate, wait in hushed vigilance, or are surprised; but they are everywhere subject to supernatural influence.

These features of the language of the 'Nativity Ode' intimate that mankind has only a small part in the redemptive plan. The Incarnation is significant for mankind, but is not limited to it or by it. Everything is centred on the symbolic significance of the moment when God's Son is born. That moment is fixed and projected into eternity throughout the poem by present-participial adjectives, a large number of which refer, understandably, to heavenly light and fire: 'far-beaming blaze of majesty', 'everlasting day', 'glimmering orbs', 'burning axle-tree', 'the peering day', 'smould'ring clouds' (*ll.* 9, 13, 75, 84, 140, 159). (Moloch's fire is left in shadow – 'His burning idol all of blackest hue' (*l.* 207) – and 'burning' is made to suggest that the idol that formerly burned children now burns itself up.) Participles, past or present, tend throughout the poem to be descriptive rather than active:

While birds of calm sit brooding on the charmèd wave. . .   (*l.* 68)

> The stars with deep amaze
> Stand fixed in steadfast gaze,
> Bending one way their precious influence. . .
> (ll. 69–71)

> Mercy will sit between,
> Throned in celestial sheen,
> With radiant feet the tissued clouds down steering. . .
> (ll. 144–6)

> Heaven's youngest teemèd star,
> Hath fixed her polished car,
> Her sleeping Lord with handmaid lamp attending.
> (ll. 240–2)

Verbs and participles combine to cast an entranced stillness over such descriptions.[16] What happens cannot satisfactorily be called action: Frank S. Kastor's phrase 'suspended animation'[17] is more accurate, for the reader sees not action but images of action.

The stillness in the descriptions is significant. The all-important moment of Christ's birth makes time seem to halt, so that, as Winifred Maynard says, 'It is the first Christmas, and it is Christmas 1629.'[18] Sometimes tense-changes in verbs make this suggestion:

> But he her fears to cease,
> Sent down the meek-eyed Peace,
> She crowned with olive green, came softly sliding
> Down through the turning sphere
> His ready harbinger,
> With turtle wing the amorous clouds dividing,
> And waving wide her myrtle wand,
> She strikes a universal peace through sea and land.
> (ll. 45–52)

The smooth movement in the verb sequence from past ('sent') to present ('strikes') indicates that peace is ever-present from the moment at which God sent it down. Further, the graceful advent and spreading influence of peace are suggested by the repetition of the words 'peace' (echoed by 'peaceful' and 'peace' in the lines that follow those quoted) and 'down'. The participles 'sliding', 'turning', 'dividing', and 'waving' lubricate the smooth descent, while also preparing for the dramatic 'strikes'. The syntax is appropriately fluid: lines 47–8 may be divided into a series of self-sufficient sense units ('She crowned with olive green came | softly | sliding | down'), but the various possible strands of meaning do not disturb the sentence's serene glide. The present tense of 'strikes' casts a retrospective influence, transforming the actions described by the preceding participles into postures fixed by, and for, contemplation. The movement of the lines, like that of many others, is spellbinding: it is no surprise that Brooks and Hardy should see the whole poem as 'a kind of dream vision'.[19] But though the poem allows meditative, enraptured states to be realized, and induced in the reader, its symbolism and overall structure remain bold and clear. In the fullest sense the 'Nativity Ode' is a composition.

'Comus' resembles the 'Nativity Ode' in several ways, without matching its witty compactness. The opposition between heavenly and false earthly powers may not be presented as directly as it is in the 'Nativity Ode' – understandably, since 'Comus' is concerned with the trial of human virtue – but a bold symbolic contrast between virtue and vice is still easily detectable. J. C. Maxwell observes that though 'virtue reveals itself in different contexts, as chastity, as virginity, as temperance, as continence', virtue remains the work's 'main theme'.[20] A. E. Dyson would extend the list of manifest forms of virtue to include such qualities as 'self-control, insight and moral balance', but he too sees integrity in the Lady's stance 'not for a particular virtue but for Virtue itself'.[21] The Lady has virtuous confederates: her two brothers, the Attendant Spirit, Sabrina, and, indeed, the Ludlow audience, in the main masque. And she confronts vice in the form of the antimasque comprising Comus, son of Bacchus and Circe, and his rout of ugly-headed monsters.

The moral status and characteristic attitudes of the masque and antimasque figures are revealed through several image patterns, some of which will be familiar from the 'Nativity Ode'. Moral issues are presented throughout 'Comus' with considerable boldness: the reader is as sure as he is in the 'Nativity Ode' which side of the central conflict he is meant to be on. But it is true only in the loosest sense that 'the moral conflict is limned in black and white',[22] and misleading to speak of 'the struggle between good and evil, light and dark'.[23] The relation established throughout 'Comus' between an image and its moral significance is more complex than such statements suggest. The antimasque is sometimes associated with light, for instance: Circe is 'daughter of the sun' (*l.* 51); Comus and his rout claim, however preposterously, to 'imitate the starry quire' (*l.* 112); and the drink with which he eventually tempts the Lady is an 'orient [i.e. shining] liquor in a crystal glass' that 'flames, and dances' (*ll.* 65, 672). The distinction to be carefully made, by the reader as by the Lady,[24] is between the true light of heaven (*ll.* 1–17, 80, 212–13, 330–4, 975–80, 1002) and the false, deceiving lights in the dark wood (*ll.* 37–8, 61–2, 93–142, 277) through which the aspiring virtuous soul must pass.[25] Comus's light is manufactured ('the secret flame / Of midnight torches', *ll.* 129–30). The starlight he imagines, irrespective of the vividness with which he imagines it, is a fantastically unnatural light caused by a terrestrial upheaval that thrusts diamonds up to the earth's surface:

The sea o'erfraught would swell, and the unsought diamonds
Would so emblaze the forehead of the deep,

And so bestud with stars, that they below
Would grow inured to light, and come at last
To gaze upon the sun with shameless brows.

(*ll.* 731–5)

Of course, the intention behind his imaginative display and the 'dazzling fence' (*l.* 790) of his rhetoric remains a shady one: as Jon S. Lawry has said, 'In Comus' stance, evil seeks the dark but tries to dazzle.'[26] On the other side, the masque is concerned with showing that the light of reason guides a virtuous life; but this does not mean that light beams down continuously on the Lady, and that her every problem is immediately solved. She develops spiritually as her virtue is tested. When John Carey judges that the Elder Brother's belief that virtue can see by its own light 'does not tally with his sister's complaints about the darkness . . . or with the success of Comus's dust in cheating her eye with "blear illusion" ',[27] he is assuming that the Lady is perfect rather than that she aspires towards perfection. She realizes her virtue's power as the masque proceeds: Comus's dust does not blur her physical sight for long when her spiritual insight becomes keener. True light in 'Comus' is associated with chaste human perception. Rosemond Tuve hints at this psychological subtlety when she notes that 'the same moon that was Hecate to Comus makes the sable cloud itself become the Lady's help.'[28] It may be remembered that the benighted Lady sees the reassuring silver lining of the cloud immediately after recalling to her mind 'pure-eyed Faith, white-handed Hope . . . hovering angel girt with golden wings' (*ll.* 194–224). Heavenly light guides those on earth whose minds are pure enough to detect it and live by it. The earth may be dark, but light pierces through to those who will eventually live in light; just as haemony is an apparently unattractive plant of 'darkish' leaf on earth that opens out to 'the morning ray' and bears a 'bright golden flower' in heaven (*ll.* 621–32). At the end of 'Comus' darkness remains because, as Sears Jayne has indicated, 'the whole action of the achievement [of Platonic *castitas*] takes place in the realm of natural providence . . . while the soul is still in the body.'[29] But the ascendancy of virtue over vice is signalled by the comment of the Attendant Spirit that 'the stars grow high' (*l.* 955).

The opposition of masque and antimasque figures in 'Comus' is revealed mainly through their often subtle response to light and darkness. Other imagery is used to contrast the two groups further. That of song and dance, so central to any masque performance, makes clear the differences that actual singing and dancing at Ludlow would have dramatized. Though it seems likely that the Ludlow performance contained more music than the five songs explicitly indicated in the text of 'Comus', and though it is not certain that Comus did *not* sing,[30] the imagery strongly suggests that the antimasque was given no song. The sounds made by Comus and his rout are those of 'riot, and ill-managed merriment', 'the tumult of loud mirth', and the 'roar' of 'barbarous dissonance' (*ll.* 171, 201, 548–9). Song, implying controlled, orderly beauty, is related by a philosophy that is itself 'musical as is Apollo's lute' (*l.* 477) to heavenly harmony (*ll.* 240–2); and it would appear to be the prerogative of the Lady, Sabrina, and the Attendant Spirit (Henry Lawes in disguise). John Broadbent's comments on the verbal music of the verse spoken by Comus and the Lady is consistent with the implicit directions given by the imagery: 'His music is jazz, lulling or frenzied, opiate or Dionysiac; it spellbinds, drugs, ensnares . . . the Lady's song reflects the rational Olympian light that guides her.'[31] The dancing of the antimasque matches their anarchic sounds: they have no organized movements, only a 'tipsy dance', an unruly stomp in which they 'beat the ground' (*ll.* 104, 143–4). As Richard Neuse has said, Comus 'recognizes no season, *mesure* or rhythm other than the rhythm of his own self-intoxication'.[32] So clear is the contrast between masque and antimasque that, just as Comus can detect the 'chaste footing' and 'different pace' of the Lady moving with 'due steps' to heaven (*ll.* 145–6, 12), so his 'hateful steps' (*l.* 92) can be readily discerned by the Attendant Spirit. In the dance of the Ludlow rustics (*ll.* 957–64), which is strongly reminiscent of the 'dancing in the chequered shade' in 'L'Allegro', 'Comus' presents a third rhythmic movement.[33] This high-spirited merrymaking is tolerated by the Attendant Spirit until it becomes inappropriate to the 'other trippings to be trod' by the masquers and audience. And the masque ends with this formal 'victorious dance' celebrating harmony and order (*ll.* 960, 973–4).

Of the images used in 'Comus' those of light and darkness and song and dance are the most obvious. But there are others, often subtly structured. G. Wilson Knight takes up a strand of labyrinthine imagery from the descriptions of the wood (*ll.* 37, 180, 277, 568), and by following it makes the observation that Echo, addressed in song by the Lady, lives by the river Meander: in the one image he sees 'labyrinthine distress'; in the other, 'labyrinthine harmony'.[34] The wood, suggestive of the psychological complexities of life, particularly as they are felt by adolescents,[35] is certainly a treacherous labyrinth, full of snares (*ll.* 151, 164, 566, 699, 908) and baits (*ll.* 162, 536). Comus's dazzling spells are 'lime-twigs' (*l.* 645) – designed to catch the Lady, a 'poor hapless nightingale' who speaks of the 'love-lorn nightingale' in a song that is said to float 'upon the wings / Of silence' and smooth 'the raven down / Of darkness' (*ll.* 565, 233, 248–51).[36] Comus is consistently associated with tangles: his father Bacchus has 'clustering locks, / With ivy berries wreathed' (*ll.* 54–5); he exhorts his bestial rout to 'braid' their locks 'with rosy twine' and to 'knit hands, and beat the ground' (*ll.* 105, 143); and his rites are devised in order to join hellish forces 'in triple knot' (*l.* 580) against the Lady. An ominous entangling inwardness is implicit in the use of such words as 'immured', 'imbrute', 'embodied', and 'embowered' in descriptions of Comus.[37] But the Lady, though 'immanacled' (*l.* 664), will not be 'enthralled' (*l.* 589): he cannot trap her mind and spirit.

Tangles in 'Comus' are not always dangerous: like the images of light, they may be ominous or pleasant. The image of Comus's ensnaring wood contrasts with the following description by Thyrsis:

> This evening late by then the chewing flocks
> Had ta'en their supper on the savoury herb
> Of knot-grass dew-besprent, and were in fold,
> I sat me down to watch upon a bank
> With ivy canopied, and interwove
> With flaunting honeysuckle, and began
> Wrapt in a pleasing fit of melancholy
> To meditate my rural minstrelsy,
> Till fancy had her fill . . .
>
> (*ll.* 539–47)

The words 'knot-grass . . . ivy canopied . . . interwove . . . flaunting' suggest innocent pastoral tangles. There is no deceit or threat in them: they are associated with basic feeding, natural cover, and peacefulness. (Comus, of course, knows such associations well enough, but uses them deceitfully: it is only to gain the Lady's confidence that he mentions her brothers plucking fruit for her 'under a green mantling vine' that 'crawls' along a hillside, *ll.* 293–5.) In Thyrsis' description mental contentment is felt to derive from contemplating nature's pleasing twists and turns: 'wrapt' (*l.* 545) precisely signifies the involvement of the meditative mind. Later in the masque, the account of Sabrina 'in twisted braids of lilies knitting / The loose train of [her] amber-dropping hair' (*ll.* 861–2), contrasting with the account of Comus and his rout dropping wine from their braided hair during orgiastic rites (*ll.* 105–6), once again sets controlled natural beauty against twisted unnaturalness. And the Lady's most natural attribute, her chastity, is given symbolic protection against Comus's lures by the militant figure of Minerva holding a 'snaky-headed Gorgon shield' (*ll.* 446–8).

Lines 539–47 present the pastoral correlatives of the Lady's 'well-governed and wise appetite' (*l.* 704): the 'chewing flocks', reminiscent of the 'nibbling flocks' of 'L'Allegro', take supper and are put in fold; and the musing shepherd contemplates only until fancy has its 'fill'. Comus, of course, is associated with 'savage hunger' and 'swilled insolence' (*ll.* 357, 177), and takes the moment when the flocks are put in fold as his signal that riotous revelling can start (*ll.* 93–104). He is cunning enough to try to gain the Lady's trust by mentioning the 'swinked hedger at his supper' (*l.* 292), but in reality he would probably think such fare worthy of 'lean and sallow Abstinence' (*l.* 708): he argues for the necessity of 'refreshment after toil, ease after pain' (*l.* 686) only by way of forcing a debauching drink on the Lady; and, far from being a time of rest after a day's work, night is for him a time with 'better sweets to prove' in the form of a 'feast' (*ll.* 123, 102). The main masque does not advocate asceticism, but moderation. Beauty is like 'the fair Hesperian tree / Laden with blooming gold', but it is necessary for good men 'to save her blossoms, and defend her fruit / From the rash hand of bold Incontinence' (*ll.* 392–6). In the Younger Brother's boyish fantasy, philosophy is 'a perpetual feast of nectared sweets', but a feast 'where no crude surfeit reigns' (*ll.* 478–9). The Elder Brother predicts that through intemperance evil will ultimately be 'self-fed, and self-consum'd' (*l.* 596).

Imagery of natural growth and nursing is associated with this imagery of appetite and feeding. The Egerton children are themselves 'fair offspring nursed in princely lore' (*l.* 34), educated to regard Contemplation as Wisdom's 'best nurse' (*l.* 376). Again, Comus twists the idea in flattery aimed at deceiving the Lady: when he first meets her he reasons that, since the wood did not 'breed' her, she must be a goddess who protects its 'prosperous growth' (*ll.* 264–9). His notion of growth is in fact expediently sensual and short-lived:

> here be all the pleasures
> That fancy can beget on youthful thoughts,
> When the fresh blood grows lively, and returns
> Brisk as the April buds in primrose season. (*ll.* 667–70)

He thinks, moreover, that he holds a patent on growth: 'And first behold this cordial julep here' (*l.* 671), goes his slick sales-talk. His apparently disinterested philosophizing is prompted by his selfish physical appetite. When he argues that beauty 'withers on the stalk' (*l.* 743) unless it is plucked, he is thinking of physical growth and of his self-gratification. Pure natural beauty, delightful in itself and not to be greedily used up, is represented by Sabrina's river, 'where grows the willow and the osier dank' (*l.* 890). This is the physical correlative of the spiritual growth that 'Comus' extols. The Egerton children are returned to their parents at the end of the masque as 'three fair branches' that have 'so goodly grown', for by then their virtue has been tested (*ll.* 965–74). They have avoided the spiritual malady that afflicts those who keep up a 'frail, and feverish being' (*l.* 8) in ignorance of virtue's rewards; and, more particularly, they have not yielded to the lust which admits 'defilement to the inward parts' and 'contagion' to the soul (*ll.* 465–6). Natural protection is available to the Brothers in haemony, a 'healing herb' with 'med'cinal' properties (*ll.* 620,

635), and the Lady who refuses the drink offered by Comus as a restorative receives Sabrina's 'precious cure' (*l*. 912).

Intoxicating wine and heat (suggestive of sexual ardour) are associated with Comus; clear water and coolness (suggestive of purity) with the Lady and Sabrina.[38] 'Misused wine' (*l*. 47), dropping from the hair of Comus and his rout, is condemned; as, of course, is Comus's drink. When the two brothers search for sustenance for their sister, they try to find 'cooling fruit' and a 'cool friendly spring' (*ll*. 185, 281). They imagine her alone on a 'cold bank' covered with 'chill dew', the prey of 'savage heat' (*ll*. 351–2, 357). Comus, once again, deceives the Lady by claiming that his drink is the kind of refreshment sought by, and associated with, the virtuous when he tells her that it is 'cool to thirst' (*l*. 677). But he over-advertises its qualities, and his claim is strongly contradicted by the appearance of the syrupy liquid flaming in its glass (*ll*. 671–3). His drink is about as refreshing as a liqueur. Eventually it is Comus, not the Lady, who is afflicted by extremes of temperature: the sweat brought on by the influence of chastity is a 'cold shuddering dew' that 'dips [him] all o'er' (*ll*. 801–2) – an ironic baptism indeed. His spell is broken; his powers are reversed. His 'marble venomed seat / Smeared with gums of glutinous heat' (natural coldness mysteriously heated, like the chill marble that 'seems to sweat' in the 'Nativity Ode', line 195) is touched by the 'chaste palms moist and cold' of a nymph who lives 'under the glassy, cool, translucent wave' (*ll*. 915–17, 860). Transcendent beauty is reflected in the image of the rainbow, again associated with water (and with heavenly light): the Attendant Spirit's 'sky robes' are 'spun out of Iris' woof' (*l*. 83), and the rainbow liberally 'waters the odorous banks' and drenches flowers with 'Elysian dew' (*ll*. 991–7).

Images of wealth are used in 'Comus' to clarify the values associated with heavenly light, harmonious song and dance, and cool purity. The Second Brother thinks that a helpless maiden alone in the wood is as vulnerable as a miser's treasure spread out near an outlaw's den (*ll*. 397–402); and Comus, easily identified as the outlaw in question, gives his assurance to the Lady that 'Beauty is Nature's coin, must not be hoarded, / But must be current, and the good thereof / Consists in mutual and partaken bliss' (*ll*. 738–40). Comus feels that treasure *should* be spread out; the Second Brother fears what may happen if it is. It is not quite the case, then, that the Second Brother's comparison of vulnerable treasure to the vulnerable Lady 'concedes a view of the affair which fits better with Comus's . . . than with the Lady's'.[39] As Roger B. Wilkenfeld reminds us, 'Everything Comus says must be reinterpreted in terms of the Lady's condition';[40] and, viewed in this way, Comus's statements look less like fair-minded hypotheses and more like camouflage for his selfish desires. Comus does not exactly want the Lady to place her treasure near him: he has already secured this much by deceiving her. He wants her to hand her treasure over, and to him. Given the Lady's predicament, his account of how Nature 'hutched the all-worshipped ore, and precious gems / To store her children with' in her own loins (*ll.* 717–19) carries the implication that such riches in general, and the Lady's virginity in particular, are there for the taking. Clearly, too, he thinks that he will be the one to receive such wealth. But the Lady, as one of Nature's children, is already well stored with natural wealth, and has no need of more. Comus is not, therefore, telling her how blest she is with natural bounty; in effect, he is telling her that because they are both Nature's children she must give him her possessions! In his greed, he overlooks two important issues: the possibility that other aggressors besides himself may compete for the Lady's treasures; and the prerequisite of the Lady's love, or at least consent. His chop-logic tends single-mindedly towards the conclusion that because Nature 'lent' her soft limbs they are for *his* 'gentle usage' (*ll.* 679–80). To hear him accuse the Lady of being an 'ill borrower' who has inverted the 'covenants' of her 'trust' (*ll.* 681–2), one would think that he, and not nature, was the source of her wealth. His general speculation about the 'all-giver' ultimately being made to appear 'a penurious niggard of his wealth' (*l.* 725) relates quite specifically to the Lady's refusal of a debauching drink. And she is clearly aware of this: when she outlines her scheme for having the all-giver's praise 'due paid' (*ll.* 775) she is careful to deflate the specious generality of Comus's idea by her acutely personalizing references to 'every just man', 'moderate and beseeming share', and 'unsuperfluous even proportion' (*ll.* 767–8, 772). By detecting his 'base forgery' (*l.* 697) the Lady preserves the mould of 'reason's mintage' – the 'express resemblance of the gods' (*ll.* 528–9, 68–9). Comus's selfish, appetitive attitude towards nature is contrasted with the attitude of Thyrsis, who 'pursed . . . up' haemony and yet 'little reckoning made' of its value to him (*l.* 641). And it is this attitude of Thyrsis that the masque finally advocates: in the bejewelled splendour of Sabrina's setting, nature's riches, her truly 'unsought diamonds' (*l.* 731), are available as a source of help to the Lady, and as a source of spiritual delight to the mind that ponders them.

It becomes clear from this analysis of the image structure of 'Comus' how Milton 'concentrates the psychological movements of drama in terse symbols' and clarifies the central ideological conflict 'not so much by argumentation but by contrasting and most delicately attuned poetic images'.[41] Comus and the Lady take up opposing stances in the 'central debate'; but though their arguments stand to be scrutinized as arguments, the major images of the masque are the chief means by which the truth is revealed. William J. Grace is right to describe the images as 'most delicately attuned', for though 'Comus', like any masque, deals with large, commonplace ideas,[42] its mode of presenting the ideas is sophisticated and often subtle. Analysis of the image structures inevitably involves the collection and reorganization of material scattered throughout the masque, but this merely indicates that the significance of the images is not unambiguously prescribed from the start, but is gradually learned by the reader, and by the Lady, as the masque proceeds.[43] By the end, however, the opposition of masque and antimasque has been revealed through the imagery with striking definition.

As might be expected from a work in which imagery is prominent, 'Comus' is written in a highly adjectival style. Adjectives constitute 14 per cent of its words – a higher frequency sustained over 1022 lines than that found over the 193 lines of 'Lycidas'.[44] The adjectives are frequently grouped so as to accentuate and clarify the image structure. First, there are groups in which adjectives in series are placed before a noun: 'bright aerial spirits', 'long levelled rule', 'wild surrounding waste' (*ll.* 3, 339, 402), etc. There are forty-four such groups in 'Comus', comprising eighty-nine, or 8.7 per cent of all the adjectives. (The odd number results from the three adjectives in the phrase 'glassy, cool, translucent wave' in line 860.) Some of these groups serve to thicken the prevailing sensuous atmosphere of the masque: 'cloudy ebon chair', 'fair silver-shafted queen', 'rich distilled perfumes', 'bright golden flower', 'cold shuddering dew' (*ll.* 134, 441, 555, 632, 801). When a group combines sensory and moral terms, the reader is required to feel his way towards virtue, or away from vice, by sensory association: 'bleak unkindly fog', 'cool friendly spring', 'black usurping mists', 'sandy perilous wilds' (*ll.* 268, 281, 336, 423). Sometimes the reader is told more blatantly what he is to think by adjectives whose heavy emphasis simplifies moral issues: 'fond intemperate thirst', 'loose unlettered hinds', 'aidless innocent Lady', 'good venturous youth', 'unsuperfluous even proportion', 'besotted base ingratitude', 'fair unspotted side' (*ll.* 67, 173, 573, 608, 772, 777, 1008). Such adjective formations are familiar from Spenser: a count reveals that in the first four cantos, or 1755 lines, of *The Faerie Queene* there are thirty-eight groups comprising eighty adjectives. But the groups are more frequent in 'Comus', and not always used in a Spenserian manner. As Ronald David Emma maintains, Milton in general does not use synonymous or near-synonymous adjectives, often alliterating, as Spenser does: 'faithfull true', 'solemne sad', 'most perfect pure, and guiltlesse innocent' (*FQ*, I.i.2.7–8; VI.iii.18.3).[45] The adjective groups in 'Comus' do make valid distinctions between the adjectives, though the very accumulation of adjectives achieves something of the 'Gothic' style noted by Emma in Spenser.[46] When Spenser's courtly disgust is provoked, as it is during the episode at Error's den, for instance (*FQ*, I.i.12–22), both adjectives in series and conjoined adjectives proliferate: 'most lothsom, filthie, foule, and full of vile disdaine', 'her huge long taile', 'ugly monstrous shapes', 'fruitfull cursed spawn', 'the place unknowne and wilde', 'a floud of poyson horrible and blacke'. Milton tames the aggressive amplification of such writing and displays a cooler precision; but the examples from 'Comus' manifest a similar tendency to that found in the Spenser groups: to inflate drama into melodrama and simultaneously simplify moral issues.

These adjective groups may contain something of the 'big-bad-wolf' element of fairly-tale writing, which is appropriate to the slightness of the masque fable and to the Egerton children.[47] It must not be forgotten that, for all its careful construction and its morality, 'Comus' is legitimately to be regarded as an entertainment provided for a celebrating audience. The stout philosophical pronouncements of the little boys (aged eleven and nine) are made to sound decidedly academic and pompous by their wilder, irrational fantasies about 'black usurping mists', 'sandy perilous wilds', 'blue meagre hag, or stubborn unlaid ghost', or a 'dark sequestered nook' (*ll.* 336, 423, 433, 499). Their telling exaggeration would doubtless amuse an adult audience. However, the comic side of 'Comus' must not be too heavily stressed. When, for instance, D. M. Rosenberg says that 'the decorum of the masque transports the audience to an improbably comic nursery tale forest with its concomitant unrealities of comic romance, a place of miraculous adventures, disguises, white and black magic, and apparent disaster',[48] he belittles the fearsome difficulty of the wood to the children, its serious symbolic significance, and, above all, the grotesque sexual threat of the lurid and loud antimasque. If, as he says, the Ludlow audience 'behold the idyllic world of the pastoral masque through the experienced and saddened eyes of the fallen adult',[49] then 'Comus' cannot be simply comic for them. Milton entertains, but he also instructs.

Groups of conjoined adjectives resemble the groups of adjectives in series in their function throughout 'Comus'. The senses are obviously engaged by such combinations as 'calm and serene air', 'confined, and pestered', 'rich, and various gems inlay', and 'thick and gloomy shadows damp' (*ll.* 4, 7, 22, 469); and a sensuous morality is taught by 'frail, and feverish being', 'low / But loyal cottage', 'soft and solemn-breathing sound', and 'chaste palms moist and cold' (*ll.* 8, 318–19, 554, 917). So consistently does Milton make sense perception the vehicle of moral symbolism in 'Comus' that it is unprofitable to insist on strict distinctions between the two. But several adjective groups do inculcate the morality alone: 'sacred, and home-felt delight', 'less warranted ... or less secure', 'lewd and lavish act of sin', 'degenerate and degraded state', 'well-governed and wise appetite', 'mutual and partaken bliss', 'moderate and beseeming share', and 'the sage / And serious doctrine of virginity' (*ll.* 261, 326, 464, 474, 704, 740, 768, 785–6).

It is no surprise that conjoined parts of speech, chiefly adjectives and nouns, are to be found in Milton's prose as well as in his poetry. The main functions of conjoining in his style may be illuminated by considering both types of discourse. Ronald David Emma has already suggested that the presence of more conjoined adjectives in a sample of Milton's prose than in a sample of his poetry 'invites the conclusion that Milton found the usage more suitable for polemic than for poetry'.[50] But is all prose, and no poetry 'polemic'? Is there no contextual variation? Emma's samples are far too small to support the kind of conclusion he wishes to draw;[51] and, in any case, the stylistic effects of conjoining matter more than the general medium in which it occurs. The opening paragraph of Milton's first pamphlet, *Of Reformation in England* (1641), contains a high enough frequency of conjoinings for their stylistic effect to be pinpointed:

Adjectives	Nouns
deep and retired thoughts	ways and works
foul and sudden corruption	religion and works
wonderful and happy reformation	height and temper
winnowed and sifted [gospel]	time and place
weak and fallible office	ushers or interpreters
outward and customary eye-service	grossness and blindness
[make God] earthly and fleshly	purity or impurity
[make themselves] heavenly and	God and the soul
spiritual	necessity and obligement
exterior and bodily form	palls and mitres
deformed and fantastic dresses	gold and gewgaws
visible and sensuous colleague	his motions and his postures
broken and flagging [pinions]	his liturgies and his lurries
dull and droiling carcass	God and holy things
adoptive and cheerful boldness	the custom and the worm [of
servile and thrall-like fear	conscience]
	pangs and gripes
	piebald frippery and ostentation

By the even distribution of stress over the phrases, and frequently also by alliteration, near-synonymy, and close association, an impression of stout, measured deliberateness is given. There is no obscurity, no evasiveness, no guarded preciousness about the writer's meaning; he intends to sound decisive and clear. The style is therefore suited to exposition, and, since it gives the impression of a speaker who does not lose his temper, it is able to make invective particularly trenchant.

In 'Comus' conjoining is used mainly in expository passages, seventeen times by the Attendant Spirit (nine in his opening speech), six times by the Brothers (four by the Elder Brother), and once by Sabrina. Almost every one of these conjoined groups contains words that relate directly to the masque's main image patterns, so that conjoining complements the function of adjectives in series in spelling out meaning and simplifying it. Comus's language contains five instances of conjoining; the Lady's, six:

Comus	The Lady
l. 261 'a sacred, and home-felt delight'	*l.* 199 'the misled and lonely traveller'
ll. 318–19, 'a low / But loyal cottage'	*l.* 202 'rife, and perfect [tumult]'
l. 708 'the lean and sallow Abstinence'	*ll.* 325–6 'a place / Less warranted than this, or less secure'
l. 710 'full and unwithdrawing hand'	*l.* 704 'a well-governed and wise appetite'
l. 740 'mutual and partaken bliss'	*l.* 768 'a moderate and beseeming share'
	ll. 785–6 'the sage / And serious doctrine of virginity'

Such groups are used to intensify the clash of rival philosophies, especially at lines 704–10. But this is not the only function of conjoining in the language of the protagonists. If all the conjoinings are taken into account, and if the confrontation between Comus and the Lady is viewed in three stages corresponding to their first appearances (*ll.* 93–242), his meeting her and deceiving her (*ll.* 243–329), and his final temptation and her resistance (*ll.* 658–812), several stylistic traits emerge more clearly:

Conjoining

	Comus					The Lady				
	N.	Adj.	Vb.	Total	No./ 10 lines	N.	Adj.	Vb.	Total	No./ 10 lines
stage 1	14	1	13	28	3.7	12	2	10	24	3.3
stage 2	9	2	11	22	3.7	3	2	3	8	2.9
stage 3	10	6	26	42	4.6	7	3	10	30	3.2

Conjoining is more characteristic of Comus's style than of the Lady's: there are four conjoinings in an average ten lines of his speeches, and fractionally over three in ten of hers. More important, however, is the fact that conjoining becomes increasingly characteristic of his style, especially in the final stage of the temptation, when he tries to overwhelm the Lady by sheer profusion. In particular, the dramatic rise in the number of conjoined verbs at this stage betrays his emphasis on her acting in accordance with his persuasion. (She, of course, remains cool and constant.) At this stage too, when Comus urges his case more hectically and the Lady temperately rejects its terms, the opposition of conjoined groups is rich in potential for parody. Comus insists, however irrelevantly, on 'gentle usage, and soft delicacy', 'odours, fruits, and flocks', 'the all-worshipped ore, and precious gems', 'courts . . . feasts, and high solemnities', and 'love-darting eyes, or tresses like the morn' (*ll.* 680, 711, 718, 745, 752). And the Lady pertinently translates his amoral description into moral terms when she retaliates with 'truth and honesty', 'vizored falsehood, and base forgery', 'sober laws, / And holy dictate of spare temperance', 'crams, and blasphemes', and 'the sublime motion, and high mystery / That must be uttered to unfold the sage / And serious doctrine of virginity' (*ll.* 690, 697, 765–6, 778, 784–6). In Comus's last, desperate attempt to overthrow the Lady, conjoining is really a symptom of his fevered obsession with abundance: his speeches teem with plural nouns, with verbs like 'pour', 'covering', and 'thronging' (*ll.* 709–12), with broad statements ('all' occurs in lines 713, 719, and 722), and with sweeping rhetorical denials and exaggerations ('no corner . . . nothing wear but frieze . . . not half his riches known . . . like Nature's bastards, not her sons', *ll.* 716–26). His generalizing ranges wide of the mark, and his thought turns nervously inconsequential:

> here be all the pleasures
> That fancy can beget on youthful thoughts,
> When the fresh blood grows lively, and returns
> Brisk as the April buds in primrose season.   670
> And first behold this cordial julep here
> That flames, and dances in his crystal bounds
> With spirits of balm, and fragrant syrups mixed.

His quackery is exposed by the ugly transition to 'and first behold' in line 671. Again, when he accuses the Lady of dealing harshly –

> like an ill borrower
> With that which you received on other terms,
> Scorning the unexempt condition
> By which all mortal frailty must subsist,   685
> Refreshment after toil, ease after pain,

> That have been tired all day without repast,
> And timely rest have wanted, but fair virgin
> This will restore all soon –

his platitude (*ll.* 685–6), the clear insinuation of the omitted subject in line 687 that *she* is being referred to, his general unctuousness ('timely rest . . . fair virgin . . . restore all soon'), and the abruptness of 'but fair virgin' make his offer decidedly unattractive. To critics who deplore the Lady's reply to him ('' Twill not, false traitor') one should perhaps say, 'Would *you* take a drink from this man?'

Comus remains essentially unchanged since his opening speech:

> The star that bids the shepherd fold,
> Now the top of heaven doth hold,
> And the gilded car of day,   95
> His glowing axle doth allay
> In the steep Atlantic stream,
> And the slope sun his upward beam
> Shoots against the dusky pole,
> Pacing toward the other goal   100
> Of his chamber in the east.
> Meanwhile, welcome joy, and feast,
> Midnight shout, and revelry,
> Tipsy dance, and jollity.
> Braid your locks with rosy twine   105
> Dropping odours, dropping wine.

The headlong octosyllabics, assisted by simple conjoining and by present participles that deftly avoid the possible diversions of subordinate clauses ('pacing', 'dropping', 'dropping'), represent his habit of vigorous, excited accumulation. His tone is unselfconsciously optimistic; eagerly, even relentlessly, enthusiastic. The verse nimbly, yet bewilderingly, shifts attention from shepherd and fold to the top of heaven, from the sinking sun to the dusky pole, from the east to the orgy. Time virtually stands still for Comus: verbs are present tense; 'meanwhile' (*l.* 102) is the slightest of time-markers; and he seizes on 'now' (*l.* 94), a word significantly repeated throughout his opening speech (*ll.* 107, 116, 124). The echo of the 'light fantastic toe' from 'L'Allegro' in his final injunction to his rout –

> Come, knit hands, and beat the ground,
> In a light fantastic round –   (*ll.* 143–4)

confirms what has been rhythmically and grammatically inculcated: that his language, though adapted to describe macabre rites, is a version of the 'L'Allegro' style.[52]

This morally debased style reflects Comus's true nature, before he adopts the Lady's medium of blank verse to try to deceive her. By contrast with Comus's romping, alcoholic lines, the Lady's verse moves with tentative sobriety. This is partly in response to her plight – she is lost and trying to find her way – but also because she is serious-minded and alert:

> This way the noise was, if mine ear be true,
> My best guide now, methought it was the sound
> Of riot, and ill-managed merriment . . .   (*ll.* 169–71)

Her most saving virtue, self-awareness, is emphasized in these lines: 'mine ear', 'my best guide', 'methought'. In fact, her self-possession is repeatedly in evidence throughout her long first speech: 'my unacquainted feet', 'my thoughts', 'my listening ear', 'my life and honour', 'my new-enlivened spirits / Prompt me' (*ll.* 179, 191, 202, 219, 227–8). She is conscious of time passing: 'this way the noise was', 'my best guide now'. Throughout her speech such words as 'now' (*ll.* 191, 215), 'when' (*ll.* 174, 181, 187), 'then' (*l.* 187), and 'late' (*l.* 178) constantly reveal this. Being aware of time, she is sensitive to new experiences and thus critical of her response to them: 'if mine ear be true', ''tis likeliest / They had engaged their wand'ring steps too far', 'as well as I may guess', 'they perhaps are not far off' (*ll.* 169, 191–2, 200, 228). She asks many questions (*ll.* 178–80, 194–9, 204, 220–1, 235–6), and often thinks speculatively, as the words 'if' (*ll.* 169, 218, 237), 'perhaps' (*l.* 228), 'may' and 'might' (*ll.* 204, 209, 241), and 'would' and 'should' (*ll.* 176, 195, 218) clearly show. Only in a moment of insecurity, possibly induced by Comus's magical influence, does the style characteristic of his speech take over her mind:

>   A thousand fantasies
> Begin to throng into my memory
> Of calling shapes, and beckoning shadows dire,
> And airy tongues, that syllable men's names
> On sands, and shores, and desert wildernesses.   (*ll.* 204–8)

But she soon regains her characteristic rational composure and, with it, her faith:

> These thoughts may startle well, but not astound
> The virtuous mind . . .   (*ll.* 209–10)

Idealistic, and committed to a quasi-religious philosophy, she certainly is; but her behaviour as she preserves her ideals shows her to be the most prudent of empiricists. She is the one who says 'I see ye visibly, and now believe' (*l.* 215), and one remembers this during her gradual exposure of Comus's treachery. In lines 220–4 what at first seems padded-out writing –

> Was I deceived, or did a sable cloud
> Turn forth her silver lining on the night?
> I did not err, there does a sable cloud
> Turn forth her silver lining on the night –

in fact testifies dramatically to her qualities of mind: caution, critical awareness, and balance. If Comus's language before he meets the Lady appears to be a perverted version of the 'L'Allegro' style, her language consistently indicates her spiritual affinities with 'Il Penseroso'.[53]

Several critics have felt that, because the central confrontation between Comus and the Lady results in a stalemate, 'Comus' presents rejection rather than temptation.[54] Of course, if 'temptation' is defined as a psychological experience of the person tempted, rather than as an act by a tempter, and if there is little psychological evidence, it is easy to conclude that no real 'temptation' has taken place. But in 'Comus' there is an act of temptation – critics who find Comus tempting can hardly deny it. But it is an unsuccessful act; and not because the Lady is mindless, but because she detects her tempter's deceit. Those who yield to temptation – Samson, for instance – no doubt prove to be of greater psychological interest than those who say no. But is Comus really presented as being so tempting that the Lady should wrangle with her convictions over him? To expect the Lady, fifteen-year-old Alice Egerton, to be shown giving Comus a try, 'engaging' more with him, is not only unreasonable in view of her age and the presence of her celebrating family and friends;[55] it would transform the most obvious temptation to bestial debauchery into a wine-tasting. As Balachandra Rajan reminds us, 'She has been ensnared by an enchanter pretending to be a helpful shepherd, imprisoned in a chair, threatened with transformation into a statue and offered a drink which she has no reason to believe is other than poisonous.'[56] It is little wonder that the Lady comes to no crisis of conscience over Comus's offer of a drink. Nor is it the case that 'since enthralment is symbolized by the effects of Comus's potion, the logical thing to do would have been to show the Lady *accepting* the drink but, unlike those who lack virtue, suffering no change from human to animal, from chastity to lustfulness'.[57] The Attendant Spirit makes it clear at the start of the masque that those who accept the potion are immediately transformed into humans with animal heads (*ll.* 66–72). Therefore enthralment lies in accepting the drink. If the potion had no effect on the virtuous there would be no threat whatsoever to the Lady and those like her, and Comus would be pathetically impotent. Besides, if the Lady did yield at all to Comus, the whole figurative device of the masque would be destroyed.[58]

Another common criticism of the confrontation between Comus and the Lady is that his poetry is better than hers. This is a twentieth-century view, which originates in Charles Williams's remark that 'Comus himself is, no doubt, a black enchanter, but he talks the most beautiful poetry'.[59] Some later critics stress the implications of 'but' more than Williams himself does: for them, the very fact that Comus is given powerful lines damages the foundations of the masque's structure. David Wilkinson, for instance, argues that 'the Lady has said nothing *poetically* strong enough to reduce Comus, the Comus of the great "green shops" speech, to . . . collapse. It is a failure of the combatants to engage poetically . . . and we cannot but be left unpersuaded, with the potent speech of Comus unresolved . . . Milton has merely asserted a moral preference, and has left his preference poetically somewhat ill-supported.'[60] John Carey praises Comus's language in similar terms: it wears 'a Shakespearian fabric of metaphor, constantly depending on the junction of unlikely elements', and it carries nothing less than 'the unifying charge of poetic language'.[61] In his view, the Lady is 'labouring under a crude moral vocabulary', and since reason is thus 'drably unprovided with sensuous imagination', the 'poetic fluency' of Comus 'cannot be resisted'.[62]

The concept of poetry applied evaluatively by these critics is so narrow that its validity must be questioned. Though they supply only the sketchiest outline of what they mean by the words 'poetry', 'poetic', and 'poetically', their definitions clearly exclude certain attributes of poetry which are particularly important for a work like 'Comus': controlled structuring of language, the stylistic dramatization of symbolic attitudes and of character, and, indeed, the suitability of language to context. It is ironic that applying 'the unifying charge of poetic language' as a criterion of value should split a symbolic drama down the middle. These critics are not considering the function of style or its significance in the masque. F. R. Leavis's critical principles lapse with theirs when he praises the 'green shops' speech of Comus: he judges the language by saying, 'If one could forget where one had read it, and were faced with the task of assigning it to its author . . .';[63] and yet he goes on to talk about the 'total effect' of the style, insisting that it is 'not to be analysed in abstraction from the meaning'.[64] 'Meaning' and 'total effect' are clearly of crucial importance when judging poetic language; but surely they are discoverable only when the language is viewed in its context? Comus's language is attractive: given that he is a tempter, this is no surprise. But whether it is attractive, and uniformly so, in quite the ways that its admirers suggest, is open to question.[65] Is it at all adequate for a literary critic to admire Comus's style *as style*, and then to denigrate the Lady for not speaking as he does?

When Comus first appears, the verse he speaks is in the 'L'Allegro' style.[66] But it is identifiably in a debased form of the style: metrics and grammar are very similar to 'L'Allegro', but the content is so different that the whole function and meaning of the verse must be revalued. It becomes necessary to ask what the style is doing, what the language fully discloses. And this principle applies throughout Comus's speeches: the reader, like the Lady, must decide what the significance of the style in context really is, and what moral status is consequently to be attributed to Comus. What is distressing is that, by overlooking the constraints of character and situation upon style, David Wilkinson and John Carey seem perilously committed to thinking that the Lady should have yielded to Comus because of his eloquence. At one level, Comus's 'poetic fluency' need not be resisted, either by the reader or by the Lady. She herself credits his language with the virtuosity of skilled swordplay when she calls it a 'dazzling fence' (*l.* 790). But when the entire context is taken into account, resisting Comus ultimately involves resisting his style. And building up the context in which Comus's words acquire their full significance is one of Milton's sustained poetic concerns in the masque.

The critics who prefer Comus's language to the Lady's overemphasize the extent to which it is sensuous, just as they focus on the Lady's words of final rejection and misrepresent the moral content of her verse in general. Comus is made to emerge as an alert intuitive intelligence, a 'poet', tingling at the finger-ends with sensory life; while the Lady appears as a dimwitted moralist and, no doubt, a bit of a spoilsport too. But, as might be expected from a tempter, Comus often speaks a heavily 'moral' language. This may be found even among the justly admired stylistic displays of the 'green shops' speech:

> O foolishness of men! that lend their ears
> To those budge doctors of the Stoic fur,
> And fetch their precepts from the Cynic tub,
> Praising the lean and sallow Abstinence. . .   (*ll.* 705–8)

> But all to please, and sate the curious taste. . .   (*l.* 713)

>   if all the world
> Should in a pet of temperance feed on pulse,
> Drink the clear stream, and nothing wear but frieze,
> The all-giver would be unthanked, would be unpraised,
> Not half his riches known, and yet despised,
> And we should serve him as a grudging master,
> As a penurious niggard of his wealth,
> And live like Nature's bastards, not her sons . . .   (*ll.* 719–26)

The unmistakable tone of cynical railing achieved through this verse – its presumptuous 'come, come' manner – reveals Comus's character as much as his sensuous verse does. Indeed, it is because of the uneasy combination of moral stridency and sensuous intensity in his temptation speeches that his treachery stands to be exposed. When Comus makes his final appeal to the Lady, Milton again reveals character through the verse:

> List Lady be not coy, and be not cozened
> With that same vaunted name virginity,
> Beauty is Nature's coin, must not be hoarded,
> But must be current, and the good thereof
> Consists in mutual and partaken bliss,
> Unsavoury in the enjoyment of itself
> If you let slip time, like a neglected rose
> It withers on the stalk with languished head.
> Beauty is Nature's brag, and must be shown
> In courts, at feasts, and high solemnities
> Where most may wonder at the workmanship;
> It is for homely features to keep home,
> They had their name thence; coarse complexions
> And cheeks of sorry grain will serve to ply
> The sampler, and to tease the housewife's wool.
> What need a vermeil-tinctured lip for that
> Love-darting eyes, or tresses like the morn?
> There was another meaning in these gifts,
> Think what, and be advised, you are but young yet. (*ll.* 736–54)

Comus's unreliability is suggested by the stylistic range encompassed in this speech. He sounds, by turns, a bully, a flatterer, and a patronizing uncle. At some points his tone is blatantly hectoring: 'List Lady be not coy, and be not cozened . . . think what, and be advised'; 'must not be hoarded . . . must be current . . . must be shown'. At other points, his insincerity is disclosed by the conventionality of his language: the style lapses into the simile, familiar from *carpe diem* lyrics, of beauty withering like a neglected rose; into florid compound epithets ('vermeil-tinctured', 'love-darting'); and into mere rhetorical caricature – of homeliness – calculated to highlight the already exaggerated beauty attributed to the Lady. Comus is fluent, optimistic, plausible-sounding. But on closer inspection all is false and hollow. Meaning is suspiciously thin: a degree of near-redundancy is built into the series of phrases 'homely features', 'coarse complexions', and 'cheeks of sorry grain'; and after 'to ply / The sampler', 'to tease the housewife's wool' makes substantially the same point. Of course, Comus is operating not logically but psychologically, gradually implanting ideas in the Lady's mind. But his techniques are there to be seen through, and the Lady, because of her predicament, must see through them. His two statements about Beauty are particularly off-putting: 'Beauty is Nature's coin' is an expression that hints at his appetitiveness; and 'Beauty is Nature's brag' is utterly loveless. Comus intends to debauch the Lady, and when argument and persuasion have failed, his bullying becomes more aggressive:

> Come, no more,
> This is mere moral babble, and direct
> Against the canon laws of our foundation;
> I must not suffer this, yet 'tis but the lees
> And settlings of a melancholy blood;
> But this will cure all straight, one sip of this
> Will bathe the drooping spirits in delight
> Beyond the bliss of dreams. Be wise, and taste . . .   (*ll.* 805–12)

By now his inconstancy, stylistic and moral, is clear – even comically so.
He has not long finished praising the Lady's beauty in the most unctuous
terms; now he dismisses her 'mere moral babble' and tells her that she is
suffering from 'the lees / And settlings of a melancholy blood'. The very
metaphor of 'lees' and 'settlings' is a reminder of Comus's own proneness
to intoxication. The drink with which he tries to drug the Lady is adver-
tised as so attractive ('cure all straight . . . beyond the bliss of dreams') that
it sounds decidedly suspicious. His language stands to be criticized by the
Lady. By detecting his untrustworthiness in his speech she is able to see that
the man who posed as a shepherd who would help her is really an enchanter
who would assault her.

The critics who misrepresent the unity of Comus's language by concen-
trating narrowly on his few bursts of overt sensuous brilliance inevitably
exaggerate the degree to which he is winsome, potent, or dignified.
Comus's language, taken as a whole, shows him to be an insincere oppor-
tunist. Even superb lines about 'millions of spinning worms, / That in
their green shops weave the smooth-haired silk' or about 'the winged air
darked with plumes' should be kept firmly in perspective by his 'list Lady
be not coy' manner. And it is not the case that Milton writes badly in order
to make Comus weak. Comus appears as he does because Milton manages a
virtuosic range of style in his speeches, successfully adapting language to
representations of cynicism, intense sensuous experience, insincere praise, and
hard-headedness. This achievement is a more consistently poetic one than
the critics who praise (parts of) Comus's language have acknowledged.

But what of the Lady's language? Again, it is important to avoid
misrepresentation of her speeches as a whole. When she finally rejects
Comus she speaks a 'moral' language, understandably. But to mention
only that language is to oversimplify her character. As already noted, the
style of her speeches when she first appears intimates her rational wariness
and her spiritual relation to 'Il Penseroso'.[67] It also intimates her
vulnerability:

> My brothers when they saw me wearied out
> With this long way, resolving here to lodge
> Under the spreading favour of these pines,

Stepped as they said to the next thicket-side
To bring me berries, or such cooling fruit   185
As the kind hospitable woods provide.
They left me then, when the grey-hooded Even
Like a sad votarist in palmer's weed
Rose from the hindmost wheels of Phoebus' wain.
But where they are, and why they came not back,   190
Is now the labour of my thoughts, 'tis likeliest
They had engaged their wand'ring steps too far,
And envious darkness, ere they could return,
Had stole them from me, else O thievish Night
Why shouldst thou, but for some felonious end,   195
In thy dark lantern thus close up the stars,
That Nature hung in heaven, and filled their lamps
With everlasting oil, to give due light
To the misled and lonely traveller?

She is self-aware (*ll*. 181, 187, 191, 194), and attentive to time (*ll*. 181, 187, 191, 193). Her mind is critical, and she makes careful distinctions: 'as they said . . . berries, or such cooling fruit . . . but where they are, or why they came not back . . . 'tis likeliest . . . else O thievish Night'. But there is a change in tone and pace at line 190. The verse till then moves with composure towards the restful melancholy of lines 188 and 189, but from line 190 it progresses more fitfully, with jolts in the middle of lines. The syntax becomes less controlled: ''tis likeliest' and 'else O thievish Night' come with a rush. The verse works to suggest that there is anxiety in the Lady's caution. In the face of difficult circumstances she is seen to be neither terrified nor complacent. The strongest impression given by her lines is of innocent candour. Her personifications of nature reveal that she conceives of her surroundings as being either entirely kind to her ('the spreading favour of these pines . . . the kind hospitable woods . . . the grey-hooded Even / Like a sad votarist in palmer's weed') or entirely malevolent ('envious darkness . . . thievish Night'). Even the placing of nearly every adjective in the speech before its noun contributes to the impression of her uncomplicated, trusting attitude to the world: 'long way . . . spreading favour . . . cooling fruit . . . kind hospitable woods' – the description comforms to fairy tale in its simplicity. In contrast to Comus's disintegrated style, her style when she first appears is gently harmonious, except only in a few moments of panic. And harmony is established by her song to Echo:

SONG

Sweet Echo, sweetest nymph that liv'st unseen
Within thy airy shell
By slow Meander's margent green,
And in the violet-embroidered vale

> Where the love-lorn nightingale
> Nightly to thee her sad song mourneth well.
> Canst thou not tell me of a gentle pair
> That likest thy Narcissus are?
> O if thou have
> Hid them in some flowery cave,
> Tell me but where
> Sweet queen of parley, daughter of the sphere.
> So mayst thou be translated to the skies,
> And give resounding grace to all heaven's harmonies.

The words are quietly attuned to a mood of tender melancholy. There are apt echoes in rhymes and in repetitions ('sweet...sweetest...sweet'; 'nightingale / Nightly'). The style is expansive, swelled by sensory adjectives, including the 'ornate' compounds in 'violet-embroidered vale' and 'love-lorn nightingale'.[68] (As already noted, the meaning of such compounds is altered by Comus when he uses them not in disinterested description but in flattery.) The syntax is uncomplicated, fittingly so, for the Lady is not experienced in the subtle ways of the world. Throughout the masque Milton contrasts the Lady's innocence with Comus's experience. It is merely in order to deceive her into thinking him sympathetic to her plight that Comus speaks the language associated with her:

> Two such I saw, what time the laboured ox
> In his loose traces from the furrow came,
> And the swinked hedger at his supper sat;
> I saw them under a green mantling vine
> That crawls along the side of yon small hill,
> Plucking ripe clusters from the tender shoots ...   (*ll.* 290–5)

> I know each lane, and every alley green
> Dingle, or bushy dell of this wild wood,
> And every bosky bourn from side to side
> My daily walks and ancient neighbourhood,
> And if your stray attendance be yet lodged,
> Or shroud within these limits, I shall know
> Ere morrow wake, or the low-roosted lark
> From her thatched pallet rouse ...   (*ll.* 310–17)

And the Lady, not yet knowing his real nature, answers him graciously in evocative speech:

> Shepherd I take thy word,
> And trust thy honest-offered courtesy,
> Which oft is sooner found in lowly sheds
> With smoky rafters, than in tap'stry halls
> And courts of princes ...   (*ll.* 320–4)

Several points should be made regarding the Lady's language at this stage. First, her vocabulary is not overtly 'moral'; much less, crudely so. Second, Milton has not left his moral preferences ill-supported poetically. Third, and most important of all, to read the Lady's language with a view to concluding that Comus's is more to one's taste is to fail to detect the significance of style in the masque's symbolic structure. And this is scarcely a literary-critical procedure that commands respect: it overlooks too much.

Later in the masque Comus's style changes, and the Lady's changes in response to it and to her circumstances. Comus the swain of Elizabethan pastoral turns out to be Comus the courtly machiavel of Jacobean drama. It is understandable that the Lady's language becomes 'moral'. But this does not mean that it inevitably becomes 'unpoetic'. W. W. Robson has pointed out that 'it is not always true that Milton fails to make "good" characters speak good poetry',[69] quoting as illustration the following lines from the Lady's final speech:

> Yet should I try, the uncontrolled worth
> Of this pure cause would kindle my rapt spirits
> To such a flame of sacred vehemence,
> That dumb things would be moved to sympathize,
> And the brute Earth would lend her nerves, and shake,
> Till all thy magic structures reared so high,
> Were shattered into heaps o'er thy false head.
>
> (*ll*. 792–8)

He comments: 'The motive force here is obviously an impassioned moral fervour . . . the words, the phrasing, the run of the verse, all seem to "sympathize" with it. We feel that invoked "shaking" in the reading, and the "structures" (finely placed word) already unsubstantial and tottering before the last line brings them down in ruins (the alliteration of "shake" and "shattered" contributes to this effect of a continuous process) . . . the passage . . . employs the method of poetry, in using language to carry the mind to what it says.'[70]

This commentary shows how impassioned and dramatic Milton makes the Lady's rejection of Comus. It is much-needed commentary, too, since critics who have lamented the complete scorn with which the Lady greets Comus's offer of the debauching drink have tended to overlook the energy with which Milton has represented her conviction and indignation. Viewed in context, her resistance and her tone when addressing Comus can hardly be surprising: as Geoffrey Rans has pointed out, she gives 'a just response to a not very pleasant suggestion, at a time when the language of moral contention was not exactly polite'.[71] The Lady is by no means invariably discourteous or scoldingly 'moral' towards Comus: she shows her moral side justly, and with spirit, to overcome danger.

By no means every critic has found Comus tempting. Gale H. Carrithers, Jr acknowledges the 'extraordinarily vivid lines' in the 'green shops' speech, but is careful to point out that Comus throughout that speech views the world 'in consumer-technocratic terms' and recognizes 'only a weltering race between appetites and the occasions and fruits of appetite'.[72] Franklin R. Baruch, referring to the same speech, observes that Comus's concept of a scale of being extends only from stones to man, so that 'there is no spirit, no soul.'[73] Roger B. Wilkenfeld finds Comus 'grossly materialistic', one who distorts the 'principle of plenitude' into a 'principle of licence'.[74] The logical fallacies in Comus's arguments have been exposed by several critics.[75] And Balachandra Rajan points out how Comus's rhetoric becomes 'strangled in its waste fertility'[76] as his temptation dwindles. These criticisms possess various merits: they implicitly acknowledge the guidance provided by the masque's imagery in their interpretation of Comus's language and character; they do not pretend to be able to separate style from meaning; by taking the whole masque into consideration they do not distort the character of Comus or of the Lady; and they recognize symbolic structure as created by significant dramatic language. Such criticisms are therefore superior to the criticisms by those who simply prefer Comus's style to the Lady's, in that they do not suggest that style in Milton, or indeed outside of Milton, is free from moral significance or constraint.

It is strange to find anyone who asserts that Milton has not supported his moral preferences poetically in 'Comus' also ignoring the Sabrina episode of the masque, for the writing in that episode is related to the poetry of virtue. The Lady's virtue is free, but, as Brooks and Hardy point out, ' "free" does not mean *independent*.'[77] It is not that the Lady's release by virtue's white magic from Comus's black magic implies that she is morally inadequate:[78] she figures forth virtue, and Sabrina's liberating power is available to her as a devotee of virtue. Sabrina and the Lady are united by the same 'divine philosophy', and so the style throughout the Sabrina episode re-establishes, and transcends, the gracefully ordered language spoken by the Lady before she needed to reject Comus. Placid harmony, delicate beauty, and control are reinstated:

> By scaly Triton's winding shell,
> And old soothsaying Glaucus' spell,
> By Leucothea's lovely hands,
> And her son that rules the strands,
> By Thetis' tinsel-slippered feet,
> And the songs of Sirens sweet,
> By dead Parthenope's dear tomb,
> And fair Ligea's golden comb,

> Wherewith she sits on diamond rocks
> Sleeking her soft alluring locks . . .   (*ll.* 872–81)

Comus's false copiousness is replaced by orderly sensuous plenitude. The verbal exactness of the invocation of Sabrina is like that of a spell: as Thomas B. Stroup has said, it is 'a long incantation worded according to proper formulary'.[79] Every name and every adjective seems to be needed, to reflect the beauty through which Sabrina will be summoned. And when Sabrina answers, her words reveal a magical yet controlled sensibility:

> By the rushy-fringèd bank,
> Where grows the willow and the osier dank,
> My sliding chariot stays,
> Thick set with agate, and the azurn sheen
> Of turkis blue, and emerald green
> That in the channel strays,
> Whilst from off the waters fleet
> Thus I set my printless feet
> O'er the cowslip's velvet head,
> That bends not as I tread,
> Gentle swain at thy request
> I am here.   (*ll.* 889–900)

'Rushy-fringèd' announces orderliness in nature: the fringe may be the ordinary edge of the river, but also an ornamental border.[80] Indeed, the whole passage manifests graceful coherence, neatly pairing adjective and noun. Paradoxes are accommodated harmoniously, to magical effect: a 'sliding' chariot 'stays' (and stays sliding); the fixed solidity of 'thick set' is dissolved by 'strays'; and 'set' and 'tread' are erased by 'printless'. But, by contrast with Comus's lurid fantasies, the words of Sabrina's speech reflect the delights of the observable world. Coleridge makes this abundantly clear:

The word 'strays' *needed* a Note – and therefore it is the only part of the sentence left unnoticed. First of all, Turquoises and Emeralds are not much addicted to *straying* anywhere; and the last place, I should look for them, would be in channels; and secondly, the verb is in the singular number and belongs to Sheen, i.e. Lustre, Shininess, as it's nominative case. It may therefore bear a question, whether Milton did mean the wandering flitting tints and hues of the Water, in my opinion a more poetical as well as a much more appropriate Imagery. He particularizes one precious stone, the Agate, which often occurs in brooks and rivulets, and leaves the *substance* of the other *ornaments* as he had of the chariot itself undetermined, and describes them by the effect on the eye thickset with agate and that transparent, or humid, shine of (turquoise-like) Blue, and (emeraldine) Green that strays in the channel. For it is in the water immediately above the pebbly Bed of the Brook, that one seems to see these lovely glancing Water-tints.[81]

Without matching his enviable illumination of natural detail, Brooks and Hardy are in substantial agreement with Coleridge: '[The] "sliding chariot" is simply the water, and "stayes", waits for her, beside the bank, only in the paradoxical sense that there is always the flowing water there. The jewels that adorn it are only the names of gems applied to the colours of the water.'[82]

Brooks and Hardy offer a sound enough interpretation of the diction in lines 889–900, but the repeated word 'only' in their commentary betrays neglect of, or a rationalist insensitivity to, the syntax by which Milton suggests a beauty that is as imperishably firm as the precious stones and yet naturally free like the water. Coleridge resolves the syntax one way by taking 'sheen' as the subject of 'strays'. But is it not the case that Milton has left the syntax enchantingly unresolved? The chariot 'stays, / Thick set with agate', but also 'stays, / Thick set with agate, and the azurn sheen / Of turkis blue' and 'stays, / Thick set with agate, and the azurn sheen / Of turkis blue, and emerald green': the independent units of sense are fused into one another; the syntax is made to stray. The conjoining of 'agate' and 'azurn sheen' implies that the very glint of the colours is solidly real, and the 'thick set' chariot 'strays'. One may take 'thick set with agate, and the azurn sheen / Of turkis blue, and emerald green' as an adjective phrase built on to 'my sliding chariot stays'; but the words 'that in the channel strays' are placed so as to imply that only the 'emerald green' strays in the water – the azurn sheen / Of turkis blue, and emerald green / That in the channel strays'. One may agree with Coleridge that 'sheen' is the orthodox grammatical subject of 'strays'; but plural subjects with singular verbs are common enough in Spenser and Shakespeare,[83] and can be found in later writers,[84] especially when the subjects form one conception, as they do in Milton's sentence. Therefore, while Milton's syntax may be construed in a conventional way, it also implies that, individually, the 'agate', the 'turkis blue', and the 'emerald green' stray in the channel. The indeterminate movement implied by 'strays' also becomes apt. 'Turkis' and 'emerald' may be nouns (denoting precious stones) or adjectives (denoting tints of the colours 'blue' and 'green'). The ultimate fusion of solid and liquid is thus suggested, and the 'sliding chariot stays . . . that in the channel strays'. The essence of Sabrina's statement is, 'My sliding chariot stays . . . whilst . . . I am here.' But, like her chariot, she moves while staying still: 'Whilst from off the waters fleet . . . I set my printless feet . . . I am here.' Her movement is magically imperceptible, as if to suggest that her resources are ever-present in nature wherever they may be needed. Her words are bewitching, but not in an evil sense: they abound in that ambiguity which, in Angus Fletcher's words, 'is one condition of mystery.'[85]

Throughout the closing section of 'Comus' (say, after line 859) Milton relies on verse-movement rather than on syntactic ambiguities for the creation of a sense of enchantment and harmony. One means by which he keeps the verse elegant and smooth is the placing of adjectives after their nouns. Of the twenty-seven adjectives so placed in 'Comus' thirteen occur in the last 128 lines. In addition to those in the passage just analysed, 'Sabrina fair', 'Sirens sweet', 'goddess dear', 'office best', 'fountain pure', 'tresses fair', 'Lady bright', and 'slumber soft' also occur (*ll*. 858, 877, 901, 907, 911, 928, 965, 1000). These adjectives are all monosyllabic and highly conventional, and are required only to blend unobtrusively into the glide of the lines. 'Slumber soft' and 'tresses fair' are rhythmically more caressing than 'soft slumbers' and 'fair tresses'.

Quite apart from the ways in which Milton uses adjectives throughout 'Comus', the sustained high frequency of adjectives (14 per cent of the words over 1022 lines) is remarkable.[86] A comparison of the verse of 'Comus' with the verse of other seventeenth-century masques only adds weight to the significance of this figure:[87]

Masque	*Date*	*Adjs.*	*Wds.*	*Adj./Wd.*
Daniel: *The Vision of the Twelve Goddesses*	1604	135	1474	9.2%
Campion: *The Lord's Masque*	1613	179	1997	9.0%
Beaumont: *The Masque of the Inner Temple & Gray's Inn*	1613	95	1262	7.6%
Browne: *The Masque of the Inner Temple (Ulysses & Circe)*	1615	131	2285	5.8%
Middleton: *The Inner Temple Masque (Masque of Heroes)*	1619	152	2307	6.6%
Shirley: *The Triumph of Peace*	1634	163	2738	6.0%
Nabbes: *The Spring's Glory*	1638	136	2084	6.6%
Davenant & Jones: *Salmacida Spolia*	1640	109	1268	8.6%
Shirley: *Cupid and Death*	1653	221	3974	5.6%

The average adjective frequency in these masques is 6.9 per cent of the words, less than half that of 'Comus'. The conclusion that Milton's style is distinct is further established by a survey of the verse in Ben Jonson's masques:[88]

Masque	*Adjs.*	*Wds.*	*Adj./Wd.*
Masque of Blacknesse	145	1435	10.1%

Masque of Beauty	122	1477	8.3%
Hymenaei	393	3888	10.1%
The Haddington Masque	148	1966	7.6%
The Golden Age Restored	75	1352	5.6%
The Vision of Delight	85	1576	5.4%
The Fortunate Isles	175	2915	6.0%

The average adjective frequency in these masques is 7.9 per cent, just over half that of 'Comus'. Even when Jonson amplifies his normally restrained masque style, as he does in 'The Masque of Blacknesse' and 'Hymenaei' to increase their splendour, he nowhere sustains the level of adjectival saturation found in 'Comus'.

This stylistic evidence establishes that the style of 'Comus' is virtually unique within the masque tradition. It therefore relates to the debate whether 'Comus' is a masque at all.[89] Considering that authorities no less than Milton and Henry Lawes called it 'A Mask', the whole issue may appear rather perverse, as John Demaray has argued,[90] and the peril of contradicting Milton and Lawes is increased by the fact that the masque form 'had always been infinitely mutable; indeed . . . novelty and variety were . . . virtues'.[91] 'Comus' undeniably shares many features with other masques. Its fable and plot are slight; it is enacted in a pastoral setting; it honours a specific occasion; it pays compliments to the figures in the main masque and in the assembled audience; and it unites masquers and audience in a final celebratory dance.[92] It honours the Jonsonian precedent in combining intellectual and moral idealism with entertainment through its central 'debate', its Platonism, and its symbolic songs and dances; and it arranges its figures in strict masque and antimasque formation. Its action is largely controlled by magic,[93] for both masque and antimasque possess superhuman powers, and this tends to ritualize behaviour.[94] 'Comus' is not a naturalistic stage-drama. It contains dramatically written speeches, but it lacks action and pace. In a sense, then, Dr Johnson in the 'Life of Milton' is right to say that 'as a drama it is deficient': everybody who has judged 'Comus' according to criteria drawn from stage-dramas has found it so. (What is perhaps surprising is the persistence with which such critics wish to find themselves thwarted.)

These characteristics of 'Comus' substantiate Woodhouse's opinion that it should be read 'in relation to the masque form'.[95] Of course, it has been said – rightly – that 'Comus' is no ordinary masque.[96] The text alone cannot adequately indicate what any complete masque would have been like in performance, but the scholarly view, though necessarily coloured by some speculation, is that 'Comus' differed from most masques in that it was not extravagant, in stage machinery, scenic spectacle, or costume.[97] It certainly differs from most masques in being more structured, more consistently unified, and more concerned with dialogue and doctrine.[98] But this does not mean that 'the purely descriptive poetry . . . although a great source of pleasure, is only incidental: the central thing is the philosophic debate':[99] ideas are pervasively allied to the senses by sophisticated image structures, and the poetry is carefully organized throughout. Neither does Milton's emphasis on the poetry of the masque constitute a break with masque tradition: didn't Ben Jonson wish to be free as a poet from Inigo Jones's staging devices?[100] If Milton changes some points of emphasis in masque form, this hardly means that 'Comus' is not a masque at all. Rosemond Tuve's insight is still worth attending to: 'Milton touched no form that he did not remould, yet he did this from within, working on the basis of a profound and respectful knowledge of the essential nature – but also of the full capacities – of ode, elegy, epic or masque.'[101]

It is possible to see some relevance in the remarkably increased adjective frequency in the verse of 'Comus' to the masque tradition, if it is borne in mind that only the verse of other masques is being compared to that of 'Comus': if the detailed descriptions of scenery, props, and costumes which frequently accompany masque texts were taken into account, there is little doubt that the disparity in adjective frequency between these masques and 'Comus' would be reduced. But this is just the point: 'Comus' incorporates such description in its text. Scenery, sounds, movements, magic, ritual – in fact, the sensuous plenitude that is the very soul of masque – all this is realized in the poetry. Dr Johnson remarks that 'a work more truly poetical is rarely found; allusions, images, and descriptive epithets, embellish almost every period with lavish decoration.'[102] In effect, Milton makes the masque truly literary by elevating the status of the words from that of programme notes to that of permanent poetry. In so doing he also gives morality a more central part in the masque ritual, which perhaps makes it less surprising that a 'Puritan', or at any rate a person of Milton's developing seriousness and dedicatedness, should associate himself with a genre traditionally swollen with courtly indulgence.[103] In a sense, Milton's poetic amplification of masque makes 'Comus', in John Demaray's words, 'more of a masque than any single work offered in comparison'.[104] It also makes 'Comus', as T. S. Eliot remarked, 'the death of the masque'.[105] But, then, is not every masterpiece final?

NOTES

1. Stanza XIX. See also *ll*. 202, 213, 216, 218, 224, 226.
2. See Arthur E. Barker's influential article, 'The Pattern of Milton's Nativity Ode', *UTQ*, **10** (1941), 167–81, and the more recent accounts of the symmetrical structure of the poem by Maren-Sofie Røstvig ('Elaborate Song: Conceptual Structure in Milton's "On the Morning of Christ's Nativity" ') and by H. Neville Davies ('Laid Artfully Together: Stanzaic Design in Milton's "On the Morning of Christ's Nativity" ') in *Fair Forms: Essays in English Literature from Spenser to Jane Austen*, ed. Røstvig (1975), pp. 54–84, 85–117. Lawrence W. Kingsley has pointed out that the poem's imagery is developed in such a way that Christian mythology incorporates and modifies pagan mythology, producing a 'rectified iconography': 'Mythic Dialectic in the Nativity Ode', *MS*, **4** (1972), 163–76.
3. Isabel G. MacCaffrey, ed., *John Milton: 'Samson Agonistes' and the Shorter Poems* (1966), p. xvii.
4. G. Stanley Koehler points out that Milton 'shows a preference for effects of light and dark rather than of colour' throughout his poetry: 'Milton's Use of Colour and Light', *MS*, **3** (1971), 55–81.
5. *Milton: A Biography*, **1**, 62.
6. Ralph Waterbury Condee, *Structure in Milton's Poetry: From the Foundations to the Pinnacles* (1974), p. 52.
7. Laurence Stapleton, 'Milton and the New Music', *UTQ*, **23** (1953–4), rpt. in *Milton: Modern Essays in Criticism*, ed. Arthur E. Barker (1965), p. 39.
8. J. B. Broadbent in *The Living Milton*, ed. Frank Kermode (1960), p. 28.
9. ibid., pp. 20, 26.
10. M. M. Mahood, *Poetry and Humanism* (1950), p. 175, identifies this as a characteristic of 'Baroque' style in the poem.
11. *The Living Milton*, ed. Kermode, p. 23. Broadbent's view is supported by Louis L. Martz, *The Poetry of Meditation* (rev. edn, 1962), pp. 164–5, and by Christopher Ricks, *English Poetry and Prose, 1540–1674* (1970), p. 271.
12. *John Milton: Odes, Pastorals, Masques*, ed. Broadbent *et al.* (1975), p. 9.
13. *Poems of Mr. John Milton*, ed. Cleanth Brooks and J. E. Hardy (1952), p. 102. Tillyard (*Milton* (rev. edn, 1966), p. 32) and Parker (*Milton: A Biography*, **1**, 64) find the image 'grotesque'. Mother Mary Christopher Pecheux, 'The Image of the Sun in Milton's "Nativity Ode"', *HLQ*, **38** (1975), 315–33, detects an implicit parallel between 'sun' and 'son' throughout the poem. But she is unconvincing when she sees 'the image of the bridegroom sun issuing from his curtained bridal chamber' (Psa. 19:4–6) in the image of the 'sun in bed'. The sun is *in* bed, not coming from it, the 'bed' is not specifically in a bridal chamber in Milton's poem, and in Psalm 19 the chamber is not 'curtained'. The very charming absurdity of Milton's image might be thought to preclude any such weighty interpretation.
14. See the table on p. 174.
15. It is strange that Rosemond Tuve should regard the shepherds as the only

69

icon in the poem (*Images and Themes in Five Poems by Milton*, p. 55). The shepherds are described less than the angels are, and the two descriptions use similar grammar.

16. John Carey observes a similar stylistic technique in *Paradise Regained*: Carey and Fowler, pp. 1071–2.

17. 'Miltonic Narration: "Christ's Nativity" ', *Anglia*, **86** (1968), 351.

18. *John Milton: Odes, Pastorals, Masques*, ed. Broadbent *et al.*, p. 8. See also Kathleeen M. Swaim, ' "Mighty Pan": Tradition and an Image in Milton's Nativity Hymn', *SP*, **68** (1971), 491. Lowry Nelson, Jr, *Baroque Lyric Poetry* (1961), p. 51, concludes from several tense-changes in the poem that 'the Christian ideas of the circularity of time and the simultaneity of all moments under the aspect of eternity' underlie the 'innermost structure' of the 'Nativity Ode'. He has been supported by Lawrance W. Hyman, 'Christ's Nativity and the Pagan Deities', *MS*, **2** (1970), 110–11, by David B. Morris, 'Drama and Stasis in Milton's "Ode on the Morning of Christ's Nativity" ', *SP*, **68** (1971), 207–22, and by Mother Mary Christopher Pecheux, 'The Image of the Sun in Milton's "Nativity Ode" ', *HLQ*, **38** (1975), 324–6, 329.

19. *Poems of Mr. John Milton*, ed. Brooks and Hardy, p. 104.

20. 'The Pseudo-Problem of *Comus*', *Cambridge Journal*, **1** (1947–8), 380.

21. 'The Interpretation of *Comus*', *ESEA*, NS **8** (1955), 91.

22. R. H. Bowers, 'The Accent on Youth in *Comus*', *SAMLA Studies in Milton*, ed. J. Max Patrick (1953), p. 76.

23. John Broadbent, *Milton: Comus and Samson Agonistes* (1961; rpt., 1964), p. 12.

24. See Stanley Fish, 'Problem Solving in *Comus*', *Illustrious Evidence: Approaches to English Literature of the Early Seventeenth Century*, ed. Earl Miner (1975), pp. 115–31.

25. See Balachandra Rajan, *The Lofty Rhyme* (1970), pp. 28, 153 n25.

26. *The Shadow of Heaven: Matter and Stance in Milton's Poetry* (1968), p. 74.

27. *Milton*, pp. 46–7.

28. *Images and Themes in Five Poems by Milton*, p. 148.

29. 'The Subject of Milton's Ludlow Masque', *PMLA*, **74** (1959), rpt. in *Milton: Modern Essays in Criticism*, ed. Barker, p. 94.

30. See Eugene Haun, 'An Inquiry into the Genre of *Comus*', *Essays in Honour of Walter Clyde Curry*, ed. Hardin Craig (1954), pp. 223–4, 233, and Louis L. Martz, 'The Music of *Comus*', *Illustrious Evidence*, ed. Miner, pp. 93–113, for discussion of the musical content of 'Comus'.

31. *Milton: Comus and Samson Agonistes*, p. 20.

32. 'Metamorphosis and Symbolic Action in *Comus*', *ELH*, **34** (1967), rpt. in *Critical Essays on Milton from ELH* (1969), p. 98.

33. Philip Brockbank, 'The Measure of *Comus*', *ESEA*, NS **21** (1968), 60, notes the third rhythm of the rustic dance, but he regards it as a rival measure to that of the Lady and of Comus. Comus and the Lady tread rival measures; but is the dance of the Ludlow rustics not simply an innocent entertainment of the kind found so often in masques?

34. *The Burning Oracle*, p. 65.

35. See A. S. P. Woodhouse, '*Comus* Once More', *UTQ*, **19** (1950), 220; R. H. Bowers, 'The Accent on Youth in *Comus*', *SAMLA Studies in Milton*, ed. J. Max Patrick, p. 76; Rosemond Tuve, *Images and Themes in Five Poems by Milton*, p. 118; Terry Kidner Kohn, 'Landscape in the Transcendent Masque', *MS*, **6** (1974), 146; and Thomas O. Calhoun, 'On John Milton's *A Mask at Ludlow*', ibid., 166–7.

36. The bird image is appropriate to the aspiring soul: the Elder Brother speaks of Wisdom pluming her feathers and letting her wings grow by contemplation (*ll.* 374–9). By contrast, bestiality is associated with the lower, earth-bound natures of Comus and his rout (*ll.* 601–4, 693–4, 775, etc.), and especially with the effects of Comus's drink (*ll.* 68–71, 77, 524–9).

37. Roger B. Wilkenfeld, 'The Seat at the Centre: An Interpretation of *Comus*', *ELH*, **33** (1966), rpt. in *Critical Essays on Milton from ELH*, p. 139.

38. See W. B. C. Watkins, *An Anatomy of Milton's Verse* (1955), p. 28; G. Wilson Knight, *The Burning Oracle*, p. 68; C. L. Barber, '*A Mask Presented at Ludlow Castle*: The Masque as a Masque', *The Lyric and Dramatic Milton*, ed. Joseph H. Summers (1965), p. 62. A. S. P. Woodhouse, '*Comus* Once More', *UTQ*, **19** (1950), 222, sees Sabrina's sprinkled water as 'an infusion of divine grace'. Jon S. Lawry, *The Shadow of Heaven*, pp. 79, 90, regards Comus's cup as a parody of the holy communion, and notes the redemptive function of Sabrina's sprinkling. And John Carey, *Milton*, p. 48, comments that 'her triple sprinkling recalls baptism and the Trinity.'

39. John Carey, *Milton*, p. 47.

40. *Critical Essays on Milton from ELH*, p. 141.

41. William J. Grace, *Ideas in Milton* (1968), pp. 131, 133.

42. Herford and Simpson, eds., *Ben Jonson*, **2** (1925), 299; Dolora Cunningham, 'The Jonsonian Masque as a Literary Form', *ELH*, **22** (1955), 108; Stephen Orgel, *The Jonsonian Masque* (1965), pp. 123–4.

43. See Rosemond Tuve, *Images and Themes in Five Poems by Milton*, p. 153, and Stanley E. Fish, 'Problem-Solving in *Comus*', *Illustrious Evidence*, ed. Miner, pp. 115–31, especially 125–31.

44. See the table on page 174.

45. *Milton's Grammar* (1964), p. 70. See also Herbert W. Sugden, *The Grammar of Spenser's Faerie Queene* (1936; rpt., 1966), pp. 82–3.

46. loc. cit.

47. The fairy-tale element is stressed by John G. Demaray, *Milton and the Masque Tradition: The Early Poems, 'Arcades' and 'Comus'* (1968), p. 89; Harry Levin, *The Myth of the Golden Age in the Renaissance* (1969), p. 136; Terry Kidner Kohn, 'Landscape in the Transcendent Masque', *MS*, **6** (1974), 153; and Peter Mendes in *John Milton: Odes, Pastorals, Masques*, ed. Broadbent *et al.*, p. 99. These writers are concerned with plot rather than with style, however. John Broadbent acutely observes 'the obvious adjectives and trite insistent rhythms of pantomime' in the Attendant Spirit's opening speech (*Milton: Comus and Samson Agonistes*, p. 13).

48. 'Milton's Masque: A Social Occasion for Philosophic Laughter', *SP*, **67** (1970), 251.

49.   ibid., p. 249.

50.   *Milton's Grammar*, p. 72.

51.   See pages 167–8, below.

52.   George Williamson, *Milton and Others* (1965), p. 35, comments that 'the jollity of *L'Allegro* becomes less innocent' with Comus, and Edward Le Comte, *Milton and Sex* (1978), p. 15, finds the style of 'L'Allegro' and of Comus's lines 'metrically similar but morally different'. Robert Wilcher, 'Milton's Masque: Occasion, Form, and Meaning', *CQ*, **20** (1978), pp. 8, 12, sees the contrasting image structures of 'L'Allegro' and 'Il Penseroso' in the structure of 'Comus', pointing out that 'Comus [like L'Allegro] operates in a world of physical presences; the Lady [like Il Penseroso] centres her being on the world of the mind.'

53.   See pages 3, 8, 19, above.

54.   David Wilkinson, 'The Escape from Pollution: A Comment on *Comus*', *EC*, **10** (1960), 37–8, 42; Thomas Wheeler, 'Magic and Morality in *Comus*', *Studies in Honour of John C. Hodges and Alwin Thaler*, ed. R. B. Davis and J. L. Lievsay (1961), p. 43; John Carey, *Milton*, p. 51, and cf. ibid., p. 130.

55.   Geoffrey Rans, 'Mr. Wilkinson on *Comus*', *EC*, **10** (1960), 368, asks pertinently, 'How could she answer in Comus's terms, unless she were to become like Eve?' William Leahy, 'Pollution in *Comus*', *EC*, **11** (1961), 111, presents the not-in-front-of-the-family case. John G. Demaray, *Milton and the Masque Tradition*, p. 93, argues that physical and spiritual purity are 'morally essential' to Lady Alice's state in life. The necessity of the Lady's unflinching resistance to Comus is stressed also by Barbara Breasted, '*Comus* and the Castlehaven Scandal', *MS*, **3** (1971), 201–24: in this article '*Comus*' is viewed as a 'ritual purification' of the Bridgewater family after the sexual misdemeanours of the Earl of Castlehaven had come to light.

56.   *The Lofty Rhyme*, p. 36.

57.   Richard Kell, 'Thesis and Action in Milton's *Comus*', *EC*, **24** (1974), 52.

58.   See Rosemond Tuve, *Images and Themes in Five Poems by Milton*, p. 142.

59.   Introduction to *The English Poems of John Milton* (World's Classics, 3rd edn, 1946), p. x.

60.   'The Escape from Pollution: A Comment on *Comus*', *EC*, **10** (1960), 38–9.

61.   *Milton*, p. 54.

62.   ibid., pp. 51, 54.

63.   *Revaluation: Tradition and Development in English Poetry* (1936; rpt., 1972), p. 51.

64.   ibid., p. 52.

65.   Leavis himself notes that Comus's 'green shops' speech is 'not very like most of *Comus*' (loc. cit.).

66.   See pages 53–4, above.

67.   See pages 54–5, above.

68.   Compounds in Milton's style are discussed at length in my article 'Compound Words in Milton's English Poetry', *MLR*, **75** (1980), 492–506.

69.   'The Better Fortitude', *The Living Milton*, ed. Kermode, p. 127.

70.   loc. cit.

71. 'Mr. Wilkinson on *Comus*', *EC*, **10** (1960), 368.

72. 'Milton's Ludlow *Mask*: From Chaos to Community', *ELH*, **33** (1966), rpt. in *Critical Essays on Milton from ELH*, p. 116.

73. 'Milton's *Comus*: Skill, Virtue, and Henry Lawes', *MS*, **5** (1973), 301.

74. *Critical Essays on Milton from ELH*, p. 142.

75. See, for example, Philip B. Rollinson, 'The Central Debate in *Comus*', *PQ*, **49** (1970), 481–8; E. S. Le Comte, *Milton and Sex* (1978), p. 17; and Robert Wilcher, 'Milton's Masque: Occasion, Form, and Meaning', *CQ*, **20** (1978), 3–20, especially 12–15.

76. *The Lofty Rhyme*, p. 34.

77. *Poems of Mr. John Milton*, p. 232.

78. Thomas Wheeler suggests that this is implied: 'Magic and Morality in *Comus*', *Studies in Honour of John C. Hodges and Alwin Thaler*, ed. Davis and Lievsay, p. 44.

79. *Religious Rite and Ceremony in Milton's Poetry* (1968), p. 9. The invocation is to be contrasted with Comus's (*ll.* 93–144). There are contrasts within their image patterns, both are written in octosyllabic couplets, and there are exact verbal parallels between the two (cf. *ll.* 105–6 and 861–2, and *ll.* 117–19 and 882–3).

80. *OED*, 'fringe', 2, 1. Thomas Carew has 'With various Trees we fringe the waters brinke' and 'channels fring'd with flowers' in similar contexts: *The Poems of Thomas Carew with his Masque Coelum Britannicum*, ed. Rhodes Dunlap (1949; rpt., 1970), pp. 88, 177.

81. *Coleridge on the Seventeenth Century*, ed. Roberta Florence Brinkley (1955), pp. 567–8.

82. *Poems of Mr. John Milton*, p. 225.

83. See Herbert W. Sugden, *The Grammar of Spenser's Faerie Queene* (1936; rpt., 1966), p. 160, and the works referred to there, especially Abbott and Franz.

84. See Otto Jespersen, *A Modern English Grammar on Historical Principles* (1909–49; rpt., 1961), **2**, 169, 174–5, 179.

85. *The Transcendental Masque: An Essay on Milton's 'Comus'* (1971), p. 111.

86. See the table on page 174.

87. The texts are those in *A Book of Masques in Honour of Allardyce Nicoll*, ed. T. J. B. Spencer and S. W. Wells (1967).

88. The texts are from *Ben Jonson*, ed. Herford and Simpson, **8**.

89. See *Variorum Commentary*, **2**, 740–55, for a summary of the main issues.

90. *Milton and the Masque Tradition*, p. viii.

91. Stephen Orgel, ed., *Ben Jonson: The Complete Masques* (1969), p. 37. I am indebted throughout my discussion of the masque form to Enid Welsford, *The Court Masque: A Study in the Relationship between Poetry and the Court Revels* (1972), and to the works already mentioned (by Rosemond Tuve, John G. Demaray, and Stephen Orgel).

92. Pastoral in the masque is noted by Tillyard (*Milton*, p. 58), D. M. Rosenberg, 'Milton's Masque: A Social Occasion for Philosophic Laughter', *SP*, **67** (1970), 249, and *Variorum Commentary*, **2**, 748. Ronald Bayne, 'Masque and Pastoral', in *The Cambridge History of English Literature*,

ed. Ward and Waller (1910), **6**, 328–72, is occasionally inaccurate but remains useful. John D. Cox, 'Poetry and History in Milton's Country Masque', *ELH*, **44** (1977), 622–40, argues that 'Comus' is unique in being 'a masque of the Country rather than the Court'. The social relationships of masquers and audiences are stressed by Gale H. Carrithers, Jr in *Critical Essays on Milton from ELH*, p. 104: he finds an 'ideal of community' in 'Comus', implicit in the fact that the Egerton children move 'from threatened isolation and from relative passivity, to relative activity and charitable commitment, attending "their Father's state" '. Thomas O. Calhoun, 'On John Milton's *A Mask at Ludlow*', *MS*, **6** (1974), 165–79, develops the idea of 'Comus' as a family drama.

93. Since Charles Williams's description of the action as 'an attempted outrage on a Mystery' (Introduction to *The English Poems of John Milton*, The World's Classics, p. x), magic in 'Comus' has received much attention. John M. Major, '*Comus* and *The Tempest*', *SQ*, **10** (1959), 177–83, finds a 'world of enchantment' common to both works. John G. Demaray, *Milton and the Masque Tradition*, p. 90, points out that instruments of magic with allegorical meanings were common in masques and entertainments. Nils Eñk Enkvist, 'The Functions of Magic in Milton's *Comus*', *NM*, **54** (1953), 312, 316, views the action of 'Comus' as a conflict between Comus's black magic and the Lady's white magic. He is followed by (among others) W. B. C. Watkins, *An Anatomy of Milton's Verse*, p. 6; Philip Brockbank, 'The Measure of Comus' *ESEA*, NS **21** (1968), p. 49 ('Comus' presents 'a choice of enchanted states'); and Angus Fletcher, *The Transcendental Masque*, p. xiii ('the central action . . . is the overthrow of one magician by another').

94. Thomas Wheeler, 'Magic and Morality in *Comus*', *Studies in Honour of John C. Hodges and Alwin Thaler*, ed. Davis and Lievsay, p. 44, complains that 'morality is not mysterious; it is merely difficult', and argues that 'when magic comes in the door morality flies out of the window.' But Wheeler is mistakenly assuming that morality can be represented only naturalistically. John Arthos, *On A Mask Presented at Ludlow-Castle by John Milton* (1954), p. 44, points out that 'the spells and magical instruments of the masque are mere conveniences of the will.' The ritualization of action in 'Comus' is stressed by Thomas B. Stroup, *Religious Rite and Ceremony in Milton's Poetry*, pp. 8–10.

95. *Variorum Commentary*, **2**, 741. See also Demaray, pp. 3, 26.

96. Robert L. Ramsay, 'Morality Themes in Milton's Poetry', *SP*, **15** (1918), 147–8; John M. Major, '*Comus* and *The Tempest*', *SQ*, **10** (1959), 178; Thomas O. Calhoun, 'On John Milton's *A Mask at Ludlow*', *MS*, **6** (1974), 176.

97. See Parker, *Milton: A Biography*, **1**, 129–30; Demaray, p. 96; Fletcher, *The Transcendental Masque*, p. 18; and *John Milton: Odes, Pastorals, Masques*, ed. Broadbent *et al.*, pp. 97, 172. Wheeler's suggestion that 'Comus' is a drama rather than a masque because Milton would not have written poetry to justify costly spectacle (op. cit., p. 45) is a shot in the dark. John Carey is oddly in-

consistent in saying that '*Comus* is strictly a lost work' and then saying that 'the middle of an elaborately-mounted masque is hardly the place to start preaching against luxury' (*Milton*, pp. 42, 46). Irony is certainly possible when Jonson banishes excess amid the costly spectacle and machinery of Inigo Jones's devising (Orgel, *The Jonsonian Masque*, p. 152); but not, as far as is known, in 'Comus'.

98. *Variorum Commentary*, **2**, 744–5; Roger B. Wilkenfeld in *Critical Essays on Milton from ELH*, pp. 123–50.

99. J. B. Leishman, *Milton's Minor Poems*, p. 208.

100. See *Ben Jonson*, ed. Herford and Simpson, **2**, 269–70; *Ben Jonson: The Complete Masques*, ed. Orgel, pp. 36–7.

101. *Images and Themes in Five Poems by Milton*, p. 121. This accords with Angus Fletcher's idea of 'transcendental form' (op. cit., p. 116).

102. *Lives of the English Poets*, ed. G. B. Hill (1905), **1**, 167–8.

103. Christopher Hill remarks that 'a masque appears at first sight rather a surprising thing for a Puritan to write', adding the qualification 'if we can properly call Milton a Puritan at this time' (*Milton and the English Revolution* (1977), p. 45). John Spencer Hill argues that Milton's Puritanism, as reflected in his sense of personal vocation, does not develop fully until the late 1630s or early 1640s (*John Milton: Poet, Priest and Prophet* (1979), chs. 1 and 2). However, Milton's Puritanism is not at odds with the kind of masque that 'Comus' is: the Lady advocates moderation; and Milton emphasizes the poetry rather than extravagant presentation.

104. *Milton and the Masque Tradition*, p. 143.

105. 'Ben Jonson', *Elizabethan Dramatists* (1963), p. 82.

CHAPTER THREE

'On the Death of a Fair Infant Dying of a Cough', 'The Passion', and 'Lycidas'

Milton wrote 'Lycidas' for inclusion in a Cambridge volume of commemorative verse after Edward King had drowned in the Irish Sea on August 10th, 1637. He headed his manuscript version of the poem 'Novemb: 1637'. 'Lycidas' is, then, an occasional poem. As such it potentially runs the risk of becoming a professional display-piece, instead of being a medium through which feeling is represented. To say this is not to voice what O. B. Hardison, Jr has called 'the romantic prejudice against occasional literature':[1] everything depends on the success with which the individual poem is suited to its occasion; and since 'Lycidas' is an elegy, the representation of feeling is particularly important. It is necessary to make a distinction between feeling and the poetic representation of feeling, between what Northrop Frye calls 'personal sincerity' and 'literary sincerity', for, as he says, 'one may burst into tears at the news of a friend's death, but one can never spontaneously burst into song, however doleful a lay.'[2] Feeling must be translated into feeling through words, and a feeling *for* words becomes indispensable to the poet. This whole question of sincerity is central to 'Lycidas' – it has certainly been central in debates about the poem. But it will help clarify the critical issue of the relation of style to sincerity if 'Lycidas' is approached via two of Milton's earlier poems in which poetically authenticated feeling was called for: 'On the Death of a Fair Infant Dying of a Cough' and 'The Passion'.

Dr Johnson in his commentary on 'Lycidas' provides a useful starting-point for discussion when he states the principle that 'where there is leisure for fiction there is little grief.'[3] This suggests that an expansive, amplificatory style is likely to seem insincere. Johnson elucidates his idea when, in the 'Life of Waller', he makes a comment on the style he considers appropriate to religious poetry: 'Repentance trembling in the presence of the judge is not at leisure for cadences and epithets.'[4] This implies that an adjectival element in a poem's style tends to give an impression of ostentation, and consequently of insincerity. The 'Fair Infant', 'The Passion', and 'Lycidas' are certainly all written in a highly adjectival style: adjectives constitute 12.7 per cent, 13.8 per cent, and 13.9 per cent of their words respectively. But what really matters is the use made of the adjectives, their place in the context of each poem. The observation of a tendency in style must not harden into a prejudice, or critical endeavour will fail to acknowledge the Johnsonian ideal and 'exalt Opinion to Knowledge': instead it will degenerate into 'the Tyranny of Prescription'.[5]

A close look at the 'Fair Infant' reveals that the poem's style is not always appropriate to its subject. This may be observed in stanza III:

> So mounting up in icy-pearlèd car,
> Through middle empire of the freezing air
> He wandered long, till thee he spied from far,
> There ended was his quest, there ceased his care.
> Down he descended from his snow-soft chair,
> But all unwares with his cold-kind embrace
> Unhoused thy virgin soul from her fair biding-place.

As the work of a seventeen-year-old, this is remarkably accomplished. Several features invite notice: the splendid artifice, matched by verbal contrivance in the compounds 'icy-pearlèd' and 'snow-soft'; the controlled progression from the cold, chiselled hardness of the 'icy-pearlèd car' through the 'freezing air' to a more comfortable 'snow-soft chair', and from a 'cold-kind embrace' to a 'biding-place'; the firm syntactic organization of movement between 'mounting up' and 'descended',[6] with the desolating pause after 'wandered long'; the menace in the potential transitivity of 'freezing'; the sensation of sighting an object achieved by advancing the position of 'thee'; and the restful, satisfied feeling of the repeated 'there' in a rhythmically and syntactically settled line. The tautology in 'down he descended' is nearly compensated for by the deliberate stateliness of the alliteration. In sum, the writing, like that in 'At a Solemn Music', shows the verse-paragraphing for which Milton was to become justly famous in his later poetry. But where is there evidence of grief for an infant dying of a cough? John Broadbent's comment on the middle of the poem is relevant here: 'Baby Anne gets totally lost in all this, as does her mother.'[7] The more the carefully polished details are admired, the more irrelevant they seem. The lack of heat in the writing imparts only cold comfort.

Later, when the speaker (revealingly) says –

> Yet can I not persuade me thou art dead
> Or that thy corse corrupts in earth's dark womb,

Or that thy beauties lie in wormy bed,

Hid from the world in a low-delved tomb –   (*ll.* 29–32)

the momentary realism of 'dead . . . corse corrupts . . . dark . . . wormy', intensified by the chilling suggestion that the child is born dead in earth's
womb, is dispelled by a feeble rhetorical question ('Could heaven for pity
thee so strictly doom?'), by a mere display of protest ('O no!'), and by a
compliment that avoids the fact of death ('something in thy face did
shine / Above mortality that showed thou wast divine'). The whole poem
abounds in signals of grief and ardent feeling – 'alas', 'alack', 'O say', 'O
tell me', 'but O' (*ll.* 7, 28, 41, 51, 64) – all of them flatly refusing to express a convincing depth of emotion. Even the adjective 'low-delved' in line
32, original though it is, betrays the poeticizing tendency also found in the
word 'envermeil' (*l.* 6), or in 'soft silken primrose fading timelessly' (*l.* 2)
with its cleverly lingering adjective phrase. Surely the poet feels more love
for his poem than for the dead infant and her grieving mother? In stanza III
the display of ethereal beauties constitutes a remote, spectacular diversion
from the grave where the small body corrupts. And the poem's efforts to
rationalize away the death serve only to reveal that it was caused by an uncomforting mythological blunder ('thought', 'all unwares', 'unweeting',
ll. 10, 20, 23). Paradoxes in 'blown but blasted', 'kiss / But killed', 'fatal
bliss', and 'cold-kind' (*ll.* 1, 6–7, 7, 20) studiously dwell on a gross mistake
that angers more than it consoles.

The 'Fair Infant' allows a process of elaboration to blur its focus on
death and grief, and to divert it toward self-absorbing delights.[8] Adjectives
are symptomatic of this tendency, as they amplify descriptions that are
largely off the point. The poem is concerned with the fabrication of an
elaborate but flimsy mythological world, and with asking questions (there
are eight in the first ten stanzas) that speculate tediously over the details of
the mythology ('wert', *ll.* 43, 53, 57; 'or', *ll.* 40, 47, 50, 53–5, 57). It is
preoccupied with a pedantic and irresponsible guessing-game, and its cre-
ative enterprise gravitates towards the whimsical but embarrassed uncertainty of 'some fair one', 'something in thy face', 'where'er thou
hoverest', 'some goddess', 'some good' (*ll.* 11, 34, 38, 48, 56), and,
weariest of all, 'any other of that heavenly brood' (*l.* 55). It would appear
that Milton when he wrote the poem possessed neither the emotional nor
the poetic maturity to respond appropriately to an infant's death. The style
of the 'Fair Infant' betrays a self-conscious, exhibitionist inclination to add
detail to what is already irrelevant, unconvincing, or uncomforting.[9]

'The Passion' has been regarded by the critics as Milton himself presumably regarded it when he abandoned it – as a failure. Nevertheless, failures
in a poet's career can be instructive. Several flaws that it is useful to notice
may be seen in stanza II of the poem:

> For now to sorrow must I tune my song,
> And set my harp to notes of saddest woe,
> Which on our dearest Lord did seize ere long,
> Dangers, and snares, and wrongs, and worse than so,
> Which he for us did freely undergo.
> Most perfect hero, tried in heaviest plight
> Of labours huge and hard, too hard for human wight.

The stanza, like the poem, is self-conscious, wordy, and lacking in emotional substance. Northrop Frye has pointed out the pervasive, and unproductive, obsession in the poem with 'my muse', 'my song', 'my harp', 'my Phoebus', and 'my roving verse';[10] and William Riley Parker, noting that in every stanza but the third the poet mentions himself in the process of composition, exclaims that *'he was writing a poem about himself writing a poem.'*[11] In stanza II the mechanical implication of tuning or setting an instrument discloses the lack of any real sorrow. The lines are repetitive and improvised: 'tune my song' is virtually synonymous with 'set my harp', 'sorrow' *is* 'saddest woe', and woe is sad by definition. The lack of verbal distinctions and of development of thought dramatizes the poet's inability to come to grips with his subject. The fourth line of the stanza is thin in meaning, undramatic, and, with 'worse than so', anti-climactic: David Aers asks pointedly, 'What *is* worse than so? Out of control already?'[12] Superlatives predominate in the stanza: 'saddest woe', 'dearest Lord', 'most perfect hero', 'heaviest plight'. In fact, one sixth of the adjectives in the poem are superlative. The 'Nativity Ode', by contrast, contains only two superlatives (*ll*. 207, 218). The 'Vacation Exercise' contains six, but it is a declamatory public poem, full of youthful idealism about the writing of poetry. 'The Passion' calls for quieter, devotional feeling. Its superlatives reveal that the poet is *in extremis*, straining to express the grandeur and momentousness he feels are appropriate to the crucifixion, but lacking the substance in which to represent such qualities. He speaks repeatedly of degree and worth, as though trying in general terms to assess the importance of his subject: 'worse than so', 'too hard for human wight', 'O what a mask was there, what a disguise!', 'yet more', 'too dark for day to know' (*ll*. 11, 14, 19, 20, 33). Only once does this mental trait look as though it could find poetic realization:

> Loud o'er the rest Cremona's trump doth sound;
> Me softer airs befit, and softer strings
> Of lute, or viol still, more apt for mournful things.   (*ll*. 26–8)

The mimetic sonority of the first line is quietened into an inward personal reflectiveness by the repeated 'softer' and by 'more apt'. The long vowels give way to shorter ones in 'softer', 'befit', 'strings', 'of', 'or', 'still', 'apt', and 'things'. Yet this brief instance of poetic awareness amounts to no more than striking of attitudes: the poet is not tackling his subject, the crucifixion. Several modals and subjunctives in the poetic language indicate his unsettled fancifulness: 'The leaves should all be black whereon I write', 'Yet on the softened quarry would I score / My plaining verse', 'The gentle neighbourhood of grove and spring / Would soon unbosom all their echoes mild, / And I (for grief is easily beguiled) / Might think . . .' (*ll.* 34, 46–7, 52–5). And when he says, 'Or should I thence hurried on viewless wing, / Take up a weeping on the mountains wild' (*ll.* 50–1), even a sobering allusion to Jeremiah 9:10 does not rescue the tone from sounding like that of a man who has just thought up a pleasant hobby for himself. A. S. P. Woodhouse thinks these lines 'beautiful', but has to add that they are 'exquisitely inappropriate'.[13] The poet's dilemma is an emotional one: he seems paralysed by his inability to say what he thinks he ought to be saying about a subject as moving as the crucifixion. When he digresses to mention Elijah's transportation to heaven, he, ever restless, is whisked off by 'some transporting cherub' to Salem, where he momentarily stops:

> There doth my soul in holy vision sit
> In pensive trance, and anguish, and ecstatic fit.   (*ll.* 41–2)

The sudden pensiveness, anguish, and ecstasy are introduced too readily for adequate realization. The regular placing of adjectives in the phrases 'holy vision', 'pensive trance', and 'ecstatic fit' achieves at most a rather routine elation. And the neat pivotal position of 'anguish', a word seemingly introduced as an emotional additive, serves to quell the expression of the very feeling announced. Milton's tears do, as he says, 'fitly fall in ordered characters' (*l.* 49). Only such self-knowledge and his appended statement that he is 'nothing satisfied' with 'The Passion' preserve hope for his future development.[14]

The emotional and stylistic indiscretions of the 'Fair Infant' and 'The Passion' reflect an inappropriate response to events which could, or should, elicit a convincing representation of feeling. The problem could potentially increase in 'Lycidas', for pastoral is a convention that can easily degenerate into shallow artifice, especially in elegy. Is 'Lycidas', then, another escapist poem, a patchwork of threadbare conventions pieced together by an ambitious young Cambridge poet eager to swell *Justa Edouardo King* to a decent length and promote his own reputation? Is the poem sincere?

Many of the poem's admirers will think such questions profane, but important questions are raised by them which cannot be ignored if the poem is to be thinkingly admired. Dr Johnson's criticism of 'Lycidas' is not to be dismissed entirely as staunch fashionable prejudice against the pastoral genre, especially when he says that the poem 'is not to be considered as the effusion of real passion; for passion runs not after remote allusions and obscure opinions. Passion plucks no berries from the myrtle and ivy, nor calls upon Arethuse and Mincius, nor tells of "rough satyrs and fauns with cloven heel". '[15] Johnson shows a concern for the representation of authentic emotion by poetically conventional means. His criticism is still echoed in the twentieth century. In his essay 'A Poem Nearly Anonymous' John Crowe Ransom argues convincingly that a time-honoured convention such as pastoral must be either absorbed or revolutionized by poets using it; but he thinks that Milton in 'Lycidas' is bound by convention. For Ransom, the poem afforded Milton 'little chance . . . to express the interests, the causes, which he personally and powerfully was developing' by being 'too occasional and too formal'.[16] More recently, John Carey has felt starved of 'vicarious emotion' by 'Lycidas': 'Grief cannot keep its sharpness in the classical air. Totting up the debts to Theocritus, Moschus and Virgil merely makes the grief seem second-hand . . . the poem mostly seems too preoccupied for tears, and the uncouth swain twitching his mantle free and making off (192) looks improperly cheerful.'[17] He finds the poem's ending 'improperly cheerful' because he places unrealistic demands on the rest of the poem: Lycidas is dead, he insists, 'and the poem, for all its trying, does not explain why.'[18] Can any poem explain why? Nor is the swain presented doing anything so hasty or escapist as 'making off': he moves on 'to fresh woods and pastures new', still in the world, but finally reconciled to it.

John Crowe Ransom's point is essentially a biographical one, but, good New Critic that he is, he underestimates the importance and relevance of Milton's biography. One of Milton's preoccupations before 'Lycidas', and one expressed repeatedly in his poems, is the passing of time.[19] The concern is absent from 'L'Allegro', but noticeably present throughout 'Il Penseroso'.[20] 'Sonnet VII' ('How soon hath time') expresses spiritual shock at a failure to reach 'inward ripeness' with age, and 'Sonnet IX' ('Lady, that in the prime of earliest youth') praises the Lady, not for her beauty, but for her virtue as a Wise Virgin who anticipates the coming of the Bridegroom 'at the mid-hour of night'. In 'On Time', Time is faced in a spirit akin to that with which Donne faces Death in 'Death, be not proud': the omnipotent abstraction is rendered impotent by the witty bravado of a direct address. But the conquest of Time remains a merely verbal one: Time remains 'envious Time' ($l.$ 1), and has to be redeemed by achievements that are not 'false and vain' ($l.$ 5). Parker notes that the poem possesses 'none of the zest for life, the sensuous joy, the humanistic air of well-being which had animated the earlier poems in Latin and English'.[21] 'Lycidas' represents the mature culmination of this passionate concern with time. In addition to significant tense-alternation in its verbs,[22] the poem contains thirty-eight temporal adverbs ('once more', 'no more', 'now', 'never', etc.), nineteen temporal adjectives ('mellowing', 'due', 'destined', 'rathe', etc.), six temporal nouns ('occasion', 'prime', 'evening', etc.), and two temporal prepositions ('before' and 'ere', *ll.* 5, 8). The shocking possibility of early death forces a review of the worth of virtue and fame on Milton, whereas previously he had assumed that there would be time for both to develop. In 'On Shakespeare. 1630' Shakespeare is a 'dear son of memory, great heir of fame' who has built himself a 'live-long monument' in his readers' admiration. In 'Lycidas' fame becomes uncertain because death may deny a young man the very opportunity of earning it.

Milton could hardly have been unfamiliar with death. His younger sisters, Sara and Tabitha, were buried as babies, and in the autumn of 1625, the year of King James's death, the plague claimed 35,000 victims.[23] The years 1625–6 saw the deaths of a considerable number of eminent figures in university and public life, and in 1637 itself, Milton's mother, Ben Jonson, and the Countess Dowager of Derby (for whom Milton wrote 'Arcades') all died. But with the exception of the Marchioness of Winchester, who died at the age of twenty three, Milton did not resemble others as he did Edward King. The deaths of older relatives, infants, established poets, and public figures could very well seem remote; but King, though probably no great personal loss, made tragically real to Milton the 'enigma of the youthful life, full of high promise, cut short almost before it is begun'.[24] As Edward Wagenknecht says, Milton 'was intensely interested in Edward King as a type of unfulfilment'.[25] It is not that Milton may have been unmoved by the other deaths, but that King's death came at a time when Milton's interest in being a religious poet was becoming particularly intense.[26] As far as may be known, death really shook Milton for the first time. Though, as Christopher Ricks insists, it is no licence for reading the poem as a series of cryptic Personal Column announcements,[27] it is no accident that so many critics have detected a 'personal element' in it.[28] Arthur E. Barker feels that the act of writing the poem 'performed a cathartic function for the poet himself' and was 'the very process through which a balanced calm was brought out of emotional disquiet'.[29] Rex Warner sees it as marking Milton's real coming of age.[30] No matter how successfully 'Lycidas' may handle the theme of premature death, there is little doubt that the theme itself allowed the working-out of Milton's personal and powerful interests in 1637. There was certainly enough passionate concern on his part to make a successful poem possible.

The criticisms of 'Lycidas' made by Dr Johnson, John Crowe Ransom, and John Carey justly emphasize the superior importance of the poem over the personal history behind it, though when considering Milton's choice of pastoral convention it is surely worth remembering that the personal history was *likely* to produce a representation of 'real feeling'. Dr Johnson is prejudiced against pastoral – he curtly dismisses one of the poems of Lyttle-ton with the remark, 'it is sufficient blame to say that it is pastoral'[31] – and this prevents his distinguishing carefully between individual ex-amples of the genre, which, of course, achieve varying success. As Martha H. Shackford points out, terms such as 'pastoral', 'idyll', 'eclogue', and 'bucolic' are used interchangeably for productions which range from 'exquisite poetry' to 'sustained doggerel'.[32] Dr Johnson is legitimately concerned with realism, however, and it is in this that he is joined by John Crowe Ransom and John Carey: all feel that conventional expression obscures genuine feeling in 'Lycidas'. But what Ransom calls 'great raw grief'[33] is an emotion, not a poem, and poems are not spontaneous speech acts, but representations of speech acts, recorded and reworked. Therefore, a convention presenting a toughly 'realistic' and apparently spontaneous outpouring of emotion in a twentieth-century idiom does not *per se* allow the expression of real grief any more than the pastoral convention of an earlier period does. As Arthur Miller has said, 'Realism, heightened or con-ventional, is neither more nor less an artifice, a species of poetic symboliza-tion, than any other form. It is merely more familiar in this age.'[34] It is true, as Frank Kermode has indicated, that the pastoral mode praised notably by the Elizabethans today suggests 'mannerism, triviality, lack of seriousness, possibly even the *ersatz*'.[35] But a conventional response to a literary convention impedes literary criticism: what matters is the use made of the convention in the individual poem.[36] Only a careful and detailed analysis of the poem's language will reveal this. Is it not significant that Ransom should confess, 'Of Milton's "style", in the sense of beauty of sound, imagery, syntax and dystax, idiom, I am quite unprepared to be very analytic'?[37]

Dr Johnson's axiom 'where there is leisure for fiction there is little grief' certainly applies tellingly to the 'Fair Infant' and 'The Passion', and in particular to their allusive, dilatory, adjectival style, which tends towards irrelevance. 'Lycidas', the poem to which he applies the axiom, is also a descriptive work, with an adjective-word frequency of 13.9 per cent. But, again, what matters is the nature and function of the description. This may be observed in the opening verse-paragraph, which establishes several patterns fundamental to the poem's structure:

> Yet once more, O ye laurels, and once more
> Ye myrtles brown, with ivy never sere,
> I come to pluck your berries harsh and crude,
> And with forced fingers rude,
> Shatter your leaves before the mellowing year.
> Bitter constraint, and sad occasion dear,
> Compels me to disturb your season due:

> For Lycidas is dead, dead ere his prime,
> Young Lycidas, and hath not left his peer:
> Who would not sing for Lycidas? he knew
> Himself to sing, and build the lofty rhyme.
> He must not float upon his watery bier
> Unwept, and welter to the parching wind,
> Without the meed of some melodious tear.

Adjectives constitute 19.3 per cent of these words – 5.4 per cent above the poem's high average figure. Josephine Miles notices that adjectives are common in the passage, but comments that 'the strongest content . . . consists in the brown, sere, harsh, crude, rude, mellowing, bitter, sad, dear, due, young, dead, dead, rather than in I come, shatter, compel, hath not left, would not sing, which are less frequent and less full of the significance of atmosphere.'[38] In short, she finds that adjectives are emphasized more than verbs. But her neat procedure of skimming off words into inflexible grammatical categories, and her application of a purely numerical criterion of 'strong' content, are seriously open to question. In poetry strength is not always in numbers; and even if it were, the first verse-paragraph of 'Lycidas' contains twelve verbs and four adjectives derived from verbs ('forced', 'mellowing', 'parching', 'unwept'). That is, 15.5 per cent of the words are markedly verbal in implication. Their force is strengthened by significant patterning: 'I come', 'shatter', and 'compels' are placed prominently at the beginnings of lines, the latter two verbs receive appropriately strong stress, and 'unwept' is made almost anxiously outstanding by syntax, verse-lining, and rhythm. 'Shatter' is violently destructive (Milton substituted it for the gentler, more horticultural 'crop' of the Trinity manuscript), and the contrast with the gradual natural clemency of 'mellowing' makes it the more so. The speaker's manifest purpose, to announce the reason for his utterance, depends crucially on emphasizing verbs, since his motivating conviction is that something must be *done*. The strange impersonality of the motivation, the feeling that Lycidas' death is somehow unreal, is suggested by the use of abstract nouns ('constraint', 'occasion') as subjects of the transitive verb 'compels'. The speaker's deliberate actions ('I come to pluck . . . and . . . shatter') parallel Lycidas' former positive actions ('He knew . . . to sing, and build') – ironically, since Lycidas' present helpless passivity ('float', 'welter') implies the existence of a destructive force in the world that threatens all creativity. Nature has to be disturbed, for it is indifferent equally to the cruelty of 'the parching wind' to Lycidas' body and to the gentleness of 'the mellowing year' to fruit. Positive action is seen as emotional compensation for the negation implicit in Lycidas' death: '[Lycidas] hath not left his peer' is countered by 'Who would not sing for Lycidas?', which implies rhetorically that anyone would take action and sing; and the double negatives in 'must not float . . . unwept . . . without the meed of some melodious tear' cancel each other out to enjoin remedial action. The intensity with which this action is urged surfaces in the severe adjectives: 'harsh', 'crude', 'forced', 'rude', 'bitter', 'dead', 'dead', and 'parching'. The reader is not asked to muse on a pleasant idyllic sadness of the kind suggested by Josephine Miles's phrase 'significance of atmosphere', but rather to feel the keen shock of death through the pointed words that plead for its reversal.[39]

'Lycidas' is a disturbed poem.[40] Its lines ebb and flow with an impassioned irregularity that suggests 'intense, formless agitation',[41] its rhyme scheme is innovatory and at first difficult to detect;[42] its diction alternates between the harsh and violent and the mild; its sentiment and vision oscillate between personal and public crises, between innocence and experience,[43] between the pagan and the Christian.[44] Rosemond Tuve finds in its structure 'great fundamental oppositions like growth and destruction, life and nothingness, union and sundering, fruition and annihilation'.[45] There are shifts from low to high,[46] geographical sweeps,[47] and changes from past to present.[48] However, the critics who have noticed these features in the poem have found them to be structurally significant. At the most abstract level of analysis, there is a discoverable rhyme scheme,[49] and numerologically 'Lycidas' has been taken to be 'one of the best built poems in our literature'.[50] Such analyses confirm the strong impression of many critics that, at less abstract and more important levels, what Ants Oras calls 'the symphonic structure of Lycidas'[51] does exist; that it is in the fullest sense 'a poem built out of conflict',[52] no mere conventional pastoral, but a work which renders concord significant by acknowledging the discords of powerful feeling; and that it does not assume, but rather achieves, a measure of assurance and sober optimism.[53]

Of course, the fact that 'Lycidas' contains opposed elements is not necessarily cause for praise. The most random juxtaposition of language units produces variety, contrast, and opposition. The art lies in how Milton has given form to the apparently formless, in how he has reconciled dissonances to produce a harmonious whole. His basic technique is repetition, which takes various forms. Pervasive alliterative and rhythmic patterns are, no doubt, psychologically influential in creating unity, but more determinable effects have been detected in the imagery. The image patterns include rising and falling, coming and going, growth and decay, death and resurrection, the solar cycle, flowers, water, song and singer, the stars, and eye, ear, and mouth images.[54] John Carey has detected a surprising legal strand in the words 'plea', 'felon', and 'dungeon',[55] and Josephine Miles indicates the patterning of the value terms 'high', 'fresh', 'pure', 'new', and 'sacred'.[56] Localized verbal repetition occurs throughout the poem (*ll.* 1–2, 8–11, 15–17, 23–8, 37–41, 58–60, 91, 108, 130–3, 165, 174, 190–1). The gesture of consolation makes some kind of repetition standard practice in elegies,[57] and Kathleen M. Lea has noted that 'repetition is found in uttering grief, as when there is no more to say.'[58] In 'Lycidas' repetition is particularly important to the voicing of the speaker's emotion. In lines 23–8 the gentle insistence of 'self-same hill . . . same flock' and 'together both . . . both together' distils pastoral peace and leisureliness; but sadly, for the implied mutual bonding of the two lives of the shepherds has been broken. The speaker's obsession with Lycidas' death is inculcated with mounting passion in the calling of his name –

> For Lycidas is dead, dead ere his prime,
> Young Lycidas, and hath not left his peer:
> Who would not sing for Lycidas? (*ll.*8–10)

– in the double blow of 'dead, dead'; and later in the languorous, desolate fixation of

> now thou art gone,
> Now thou art gone, and never must return! (*ll.* 37–8)

This is immediately disturbed by the more animated

> Thee shepherd, thee the woods, and desert caves,
> With wild thyme and the gadding vine o'ergrown,
> And all their echoes mourn (*ll.* 39–41)

and leads to the near-exasperated repetition of 'the muse herself' in the troubled syntax of

> Had ye been there . . . for what could that have done?
> What could the muse herself that Orpheus bore,
> The muse herself for her enchanting son . . . (*ll.* 57–9)

These variations on the theme 'Lycidas is dead' express a whole range of natural reaction, and impart a sad irony to the diligent search represented by 'He asked the waves, and asked the felon winds, / What hard mishap hath doomed this gentle swain?' (*ll.* 91–2). Disturbance and acceptance are modulated throughout within the same iterative schemes. The stirring exhortation 'begin . . . begin' in lines 15–17 that follows the anguished call for action in the opening paragraph is balanced by the plea 'return . . . return' (*ll.* 132–3) that follows the Pilot's vehement call for revolutionary action within the church. Even the disruptive figure of the Pilot appears in an ordered procession. The formalized inevitability of 'Last came, and last did go, / The pilot of the Galilean lake' (*ll.* 108–9) prepares for the awful finality of 'that two-handed engine at the door, / Stands ready to smite once, and smite no more' (*ll.* 130–1), and is also integrated

into the poem's calming larger rhythms of coming and going.[59] The last
repetition –

> And now the sun had stretched out all the hills,
> And now was dropped into the western bay –   (ll. 190–1)

is redolent of the calm of the accepted natural cycle. The simultaneous all-
seeing implied by 'and now . . . and now', the imperceptible motion in 'the
still morn *went out*', and the blurred time distinctions in the rapid succession
of 'morn', noon, evening, and 'tomorrow' (ll. 187–93) signal that the eter-
nal point of view has been taken up.[60] These repetitive devices quieten the
forcefulness of all previous repetitions, just as the final paragraph's *ottava
rima* quells the rebellious *canzone*.[61] In 'Lycidas', then, repetition gives
structure to moments of varied emotion by a process of acclimatizing both
speaker and reader to dramatic alternations of turbulence and calm. It traces
the process by which order is achieved, and thus emphasizes that poetry is
both the means of expressing feeling and of confronting the confusing, even
annihilating, forces in the world. In John Broadbent's words, the poem becomes 'a ritual gaze at, and defence against, chaos'.[62]

Just as repetition is not merely complacent, or conventionally elegiac
through being unvaried in tone, so, too, pastoral in 'Lycidas' is not an
untransmuted code. Dr Johnson, John Crowe Ransom, and John Carey
stress the tradition in which the poem is written, but without giving
due emphasis to its modification of the tradition. It is true that 'Lycidas'
'gathers into its compass the entire tradition of pastoral'[63] – the notes in the
Variorum Commentary will convince any unbelievers – but it is in its treatment of pastoral that it becomes most disruptive. The shattering of the
leaves symbolizes the necessity of writing prematurely because Lycidas is
dead 'ere his prime', but also the revolutionizing of the convention from
within.[64] Throughout the poem the speaker expresses an attitude to
pastoral. The swain touches 'the tender stops of various quills' (l. 188),
signifying the inclusion of different styles,[65] and revealing distinctions are
made between the 'higher mood' of Phoebus' speech, the lower style of the
pastoral 'oat', and the 'dread voice' of the Pilot (ll. 87–8, 132–3). In the
course of the poem the code of pastoral is cracked.[66]

Milton draws on the very traditionalness of pastoral to suggest continuity in the face of death. But death also calls for a fresh knowingness in
the poet, an internal revolution. This makes stylistic change obligatory.
'Lycidas' converts purely idyllic pastoral as represented in its third verse-
paragraph into a more realistic world picture. The style of the third paragraph is important as a basis for the style of the poem:

> Together both, ere the high lawns appeared
> Under the opening eye-lids of the morn,
> We drove a-field, and both together heard

> What time the grey-fly winds her sultry horn,
> Battening our flocks with the fresh dews of night,
> Oft till the star that rose, at evening, bright,
> Toward heaven's descent had sloped his westering wheel.
> Meanwhile the rural ditties were not mute,
> Tempered to the oaten flute,
> Rough satyrs danced, and fauns with cloven heel,
> From the glad sound would not be absent long,
> And old Damaetas loved to hear our song.

The passage is highly descriptive – 18.5 per cent of the words are adjectives, 4.6 per cent more than the poem's already high frequency of 13.9 per cent. The expansiveness of the pastoral way of life is what is celebrated. Sensory adjectives predominate: 'high', 'opening', 'sultry', 'fresh', 'bright', 'mute', 'oaten', 'rough', and 'cloven'. Syntax is uncomplicated, sound is pleasant. Adjectives derived from verbs are intransitive as far as the speaker is concerned – they do nothing to him, but preserve a tableau for his delighted observation: 'opening eye-lids . . . westering wheel . . . tempered'. Plural nouns, seven in all, leave the picture generalized. And there is a remarkable frequency of definite articles: 'the high lawns', 'the opening eye-lids of the morn', 'the grey-fly', 'the fresh dews of night', 'the star that rose at evening', 'the rural ditties', 'the oaten flute', and 'the glad sound'.[67] The verbs provide the key to their interpretation: by denoting repeated, frequent actions, they reveal the articles as generic, so that 'the oaten flute' represents all oaten flutes. But the articles also refer to known, identifiable, and associated objects in a picture composed from the speaker's memory. Thus, generic and specific functions are combined. The grammar of the noun phrase throughout the passage is that of 'L'Allegro'.[68] The crucial difference is that the main verbs of the third verse-paragraph of 'Lycidas' are in the past, not the present, tense. The illusory timelessness of the pastoral world is represented in the circumlocutory vagueness of 'what time', the present tense of 'battening', and the rapid linking of morning, noon, night, and evening, which suggests that time flies imperceptibly. But the main verbs place the idealized existence firmly in memory. The time-consciousness of 'Il Penseroso' has intruded on the carefree timelessness of 'L'Allegro'. The very possibility of an 'old' Damaetas, of young and old coming forth to play together ('L'Allegro', *ll*. 97–8), or even of the attainment of 'old experience' ('Il Penseroso', *ll*. 173–4), is deeply questioned: 'young Lycidas' is 'dead, dead ere his prime'. The academic putativeness of the earlier companion poems is threatened by the pressure of disturbing events in the real world.

The dramatic opposition of conventional pastoral and the real world may be traced in the use of several kinds of adjective in 'Lycidas'. The artificial permanence and self-absorbed activity typical of pastoral are characterized by past-participial forms ('enamelled eyes', 'the pansy freaked with jet', 'the well-attired woodbine', ll. 139, 144, 146), and, as noted in the third verse-paragraph, by intransitive present-participial adjectives ('the gadding vine', 'smooth-sliding Mincius', 'gushing brooks', 'the glowing violet', ll. 40, 86, 137, 145). 'Sounding seas' introduces a slight change to this picture of a potentially unfeeling world, but really only intensifies its indifference: 'Ay me! Whilst thee the shores, and sounding seas / Wash far away, where'er thy bones are hurled' (ll. 154–5). 'Sounding' is menacingly vague beside 'wash' and 'hurled', which dramatically alter the idea of nature as a pretty picture by introducing insensitive and impersonal violence. Transitive participial adjectives significantly acknowledge that nature can be uncontrollably active: Lycidas' death is 'as killing as the canker to the rose' (l. 45). Milton changed the non-transitive adjective in 'humming tide' in the Trinity manuscript for the more fearsome 'whelming tide' (l. 157). On one side, the gentleness and quiet joy associated with pastoral are represented by the adjectives in the phrases 'the glad sound', 'joyous leaves', 'soft lays', and 'mild whispers' (ll. 35, 44, 44, 136). On the other, a rough and ominous wildness is acknowledged through 'shaggy top', 'felon winds', 'rugged wings', 'beakèd promontory', and 'stormy Hebrides' (ll. 54, 91, 93, 94, 156). The adjectives in the line describing Neptune's plea crystallize the opposition: 'What hard mishap hath doomed this gentle swain?' (l. 92). It is the awareness that the world is really harsh to life that underlies the austere tone of the opening verse-paragraph: the bitter truth is that nature and man reflect each other's cruelty rather than sympathy. The pastoral and real worlds are found to be equally indifferent, or equally vicious, to human life, and a dark, nihilistic view is opened out in which the muse is 'thankless' (l. 66), nature in the form of the unpredictable, unknown sea is 'remorseless' (l. 50), and man as represented by the dead Lycidas is 'hapless' (l. 164). The 'false surmise' involved in the traditional pastoral rite of strewing flowers on the hearse is replaced by a deeper, more vexing uncertainty:

> Ay me! Whilst thee the shores, and sounding seas
> Wash far away, where'er thy bones are hurled,
> Whether beyond the stormy Hebrides
> Where thou perhaps under the whelming tide
> Visit'st the bottom of the monstrous world;
> Or whether thou to our moist vows denied,
> Sleep'st by the fable of Bellerus old . . .
>
> (ll. 154–60)

The idle speculations of the 'Fair Infant' and the roving of 'The Passion' are checked; attention is cogently redirected to the body in the sea's grip. The speaker's rumination ('where'er . . . whether . . . perhaps . . . or whether . . .') cannot be released into mere escapism, but pathetically dramatizes his own helplessness as he thinks of the helplessness of Lycidas. Sadly, the fact of death seems to make even strong thoughts dally: even though every adjective faces up to what has happened, the speaker at this point can find no acceptable comfort. Rosemond Tuve and John Reesing note the 'intimate communication' and 'softening note of humanity'[69] in the words 'visit'st' and 'sleep'st', and both rightly stress the piteousness of such feeling in such an unaccommodating context. The 'monstrous world' need not be only the world of sea monsters:[70] in 1637 'monstrous' could imply deviation from the natural order and express indignation and contempt for atrocity.[71] As such, the word marks a moment of intense perception of the apparently irrational, careless, and outraging determination of the world. Charles Williams catches something of this when he writes, ' "The bottom of the monstrous world" has already in it a sense of metaphysical prophecy: "bottomless perdition" is to be found there.'[72] Even after the Christian consolation, Milton does not opt for an easy escape from the constant threat represented by the sea: it remains 'that perilous flood' in which men, being fallen, 'wander' (l. 185).

Far from being digressive, the invective of the Pilot of the Galilean Lake is consistent with this world-view.[73] It is important that it should be disturbing, to the poem as well as the corrupt clergy who ignore, and even further, diabolic influence. And the citation of precedents for satire on the clergy in other pastorals in no way lessens the impact of the impassioned speech:

> How well could I have spared for thee, young swain,
> Enow of such as for their bellies' sake,
> Creep and intrude, and climb into the fold?
> Of other care they little reckoning make,   115
> Than how to scramble at the shearers' feast,
> And shove away the worthy bidden guest;
> Blind mouths! that scarce themselves know how to hold
> A sheep-hook, or have learned aught else the least   120
> That to the faithful herdman's art belongs!
> What recks it them? What need they? They are sped;
> And when they list, their lean and flashy songs
> Grate on their scrannel pipes of wretched straw,
> The hungry sheep look up, and are not fed,   125
> But swoll'n with wind, and the rank mist they draw,
> Rot inwardly, and foul contagion spread:
> Besides what the grim wolf with privy paw
> Daily devours apace, and nothing said,
> But that two-handed engine at the door,   130
> Stands ready to smite once, and smite no more.

The only thing left undisturbed is the art with which Milton fits this out-burst into the poem's structure. The speech manifests the pastoral grammar: 'the shearers' feast', 'the worthy bidden guest', 'the faithful herdman's art', 'the hungry sheep', 'the rank mist', and 'the grim wolf' are phrase units familiar from the third verse-paragraph, and they are supported again by generalities – 'blind mouths', 'lean and flashy songs', 'scrannel pipes', 'wretched straw', 'wind', and 'foul contagion'. What is different is the trenchancy with which the Pilot's attitude is expressed. The adjectives 'lean', 'flashy', 'scrannel', 'wretched', 'hungry', 'swoll'n', 'rank', and 'foul' help characterize a 'dread voice' that reflects the harshness of the religious world. Clay Hunt comments on line 122, 'This is stuff to splinter a syrinx', and indicates the predominance of 'harsh' /r/ and /s/ sounds throughout the passage.[74] Through the verbs too the speaker acknowledges that ceremony is abolished, and that reality must be faced: 'creep and intrude . . . scramble . . . shove . . . grate . . . rot . . . . devours'. In religion the cruelty and injustice are human, and therefore controllable, whereas the sea and 'the blind Fury' remain apparently anarchic. The rapid sequence of verbs in the Pilot's speech stresses strong action, just as 'and nothing said' implicitly calls for a remedy before the 'two-handed engine' does its final work. Adjectival severity and an emphasis on verbs are the chief means whereby the motivation expressed so forcefully in the opening verse-paragraph is recalled: the Pilot echoes the tone of the swain's voice in speaking out against pastoral wrongs. The imagery of 'bellies . . . feast . . . mouths . . . not fed . . . swoll'n . . . devours' is the corrupted version of 'nursed upon the self-same hill', 'fed the same flock', 'battening our flocks with the fresh dews of night', and 'weanling herds that graze': conventional idyll has become actual disaster. The most disruptive attack on indifference in 'Lycidas' is thus shaped to the design behind the other disruptions. Dramatic representation blends with structural harmony.

Earthly pastoral and religious pastoral give way to heavenly pastoral:

Weep no more, woeful shepherds weep no more,	165
For Lycidas your sorrow is not dead,	
Sunk though he be beneath the watery floor,	
So sinks the day-star in the ocean bed,	
And yet anon repairs his drooping head,	
And tricks his beams, and with new spangled ore,	170
Flames in the forehead of the morning sky:	
So Lycidas sunk low, but mounted high,	
Through the dear might of him that walked the waves;	
Where other groves, and other streams along,	
With nectar pure his oozy locks he laves,	175
And hears the unexpressive nuptial song,	

In the blest kingdoms meek of joy and love.
There entertain him all the saints above,
In solemn troops, and sweet societies
That sing, and singing in their glory move,   180
And wipe the tears for ever from his eyes.

Christopher Hill thinks that these consolations of immortality play a 'rather perfunctory part' in 'Lycidas' since Milton's this-worldly interests are likely to be committed to curing the diseases of the clergy.[75] But Milton's undoubted wish for religious reform does not result in the marring of his art. Though a Christian consolation may be regarded as perfunctory by Hill, an aesthetic judgement is involved in dismissing the consolation of 'Lycidas'. Milton is committed to a poetic structure, and the care with which the consolation is fitted into the poem makes it far from superficial or disinterested. The familiar phrase units of 'the watery floor', 'the day-star', 'the ocean bed', 'the forehead of the morning sky', and so on, and the generalities of 'woeful shepherds', 'blest kingdoms meek of joy and love', 'all the saints', 'solemn troops', and 'sweet societies', signal that the consolation will, at deeper levels, recall the poem before it. The command 'weep no more . . . weep no more' recalls both 'yet once more' (*l.* 1) and the willows and hazels fanning their leaves 'no more' to Lycidas' song (*ll.* 42–4),[76] suggesting that comfort is precisely made appropriate to the nature of the grief. The act of wiping the tears for ever from Lycidas' eyes reflects back on the 'melodious tear' offered in commemoration (*l.* 14), revealing that all previous mourning has been earthly and impermanent. The 'watery floor' beneath which he is 'sunk' reminds the reader of the bark which 'sunk so low' his 'sacred head', of the deep closing over him, and of the 'level brine' (*ll.* 50–1, 98, 102); while the use of 'floor' makes the water reassuringly more solid for Christ's triumphant walk over it. The 'day-star', suggestive of Christ and fixed with heraldic permanence in the sky, is the antitype of 'the opening eye-lids of the morn', 'the star that rose, at evening', and 'the swart star' (*ll.* 26, 30, 138),[77] and its movement into the ocean and back again to the sky figures forth death and resurrection.[78] Lowry Nelson, Jr notes that the expressions 'the dear might of him that walked the waves' and 'other groves and other streams' avoid explicit naming of Christ and heaven so that their relation to the natural imagery of the poem is preserved.[79] It is not that the phrase 'other groves and other streams' 'unsettlingly returns [Lycidas] to the pattern that groves and streams obey',[80] for 'other' can denote a difference in kind as well as in location. The description throughout the passage identifies the after-life with this life, implying a comprehensive and comprehensible life-view, and establishing some consistency and discernible plan in what has seemed chaotic. Pastoral song (*ll.* 10–11, 36, 44), and indeed the Orphean music which was once drowned out by the 'hideous roar' of his murderers (*ll.* 58–63), are transcendently re-instated, with pastoral companionship, in the 'unexpressive nuptial song' of the saints at the marriage supper of the Lamb. The vicious, impersonal acts of wild nature against Lycidas' body are past: he hears the heavenly music, is entertained, and has his tears wiped away. Whereas the sea has previously washed him in its pitiless tides (*ll.* 154–5), now he, in control, washes his hair, 'oozy' from 'the bottom of the monstrous world', in the paradisal 'nectar pure' of heaven.[81] Milton transforms earthly pastoral; he does not relinquish it.

Nor should he: the return to a rehabilitated earthly pastoral is possible only after the glimpse of the heavenly vision. All through 'Lycidas' Milton has not absorbed *or* revolutionized pastoral; he has done both, evolving from the anxious turbulence of the start the rapturous calm and quiet seriousness of the close. A whole range of feeling is realized without the qualities of damaging self-consciousness, wordiness, or irrelevance, and the pastoral convention is fully exploited. 'Lycidas' is the most dramatic pastoral ever written. If it was significant personally to Milton when he wrote it to be able to 'build the lofty rhyme' in defiance of the apparently annihilating forces in the world, that consideration can only make his achievement in 'Lycidas' the greater.

NOTES

1. *The Enduring Monument: A Study of the Idea of Praise in Renaissance Literary Theory and Practice* (1962), p. 108.
2. 'Literature as Context: Milton's *Lycidas*', *Milton's 'Lycidas': The Tradition and the Poem*, ed. C. A. Patrides (1961), p. 206.
3. *Lives of the English Poets*, ed. G. B. Hill, **1**, 163.
4. ibid., **1**, 292.
5. *The Rambler*, No. 92.
6. On the structural use of movement, especially of rising and falling, throughout the poem see D. C. Allen, *The Harmonious Vision*, pp. 47–8; Hugh N. Maclean, 'Milton's *Fair Infant*', *ELH*, **24** (1957), 302–3; and Jackson I. Cope, 'Fortunate Falls as Form in Milton's "Fair Infant"', *JEGP*, **63** (1964), 660.
7. *John Milton: Samson Agonistes, Sonnets, &c.*, ed. Broadbent and Hodge (1977), p. 30.
8. See also Hugh N. Maclean, 'Milton's *Fair Infant*', *ELH*, **24** (1957), 299; Isabel Gamble MacCaffrey, '*Lycidas*: The Poet in a Landscape', *The Lyric and Dramatic Milton*, ed. Summers, p. 69; and A. S. P. Woodhouse, *The Heavenly Muse: A Preface to Milton*, ed. Hugh R. MacCallum (1972), p. 33.
9. For similar views see Daiches, *Milton*, p. 21, and Parker, *Milton: A Biography*, **1**, 40.

10. 'Literature as Context: Milton's *Lycidas*', *Milton's 'Lycidas': The Tradition and the Poem*, ed. Patrides p. 208.

11. *Milton: A Biography*, **1**, 72.

12. *John Milton: Odes, Pastorals, Masques*, ed. Broadbent *et al.* (1975), p. 47*n*.

13. 'Notes on Milton's Early Development', *UTQ*, **13** (1943), 81.

14. Philip J. Gallagher ('Milton's "The Passion": Inspired Mediocrity', *MQ*, **11** (1977), 44–50) makes a virtue of necessity. He argues that 'The Passion' is successful if regarded as a prologue to a poem about 'The Passion'; that it is 'a deliberate failure' whose purpose is 'to show the futility of attempting to write a divine poem in the absence of divine inspiration'; and that 'Milton's procedure is to turn his speaker's failures into occasions for the construction of a successful poem about those failures.' This is ingenious, but unconvincing. Any poem that fails is in a sense a dramatization of failure, so that Gallagher's judgement is insignificant because it may be applied so widely and so easily; 'deliberate' in 'deliberate failure' is difficult to substantiate, and crucial to Gallagher's argument; and, since we cannot imagine the non-existent poem on the Passion to which Milton's poem 'The Passion' is allegedly a prologue, we can hardly use that non-existent poem as a means of establishing that the existing poem is, in fact, a prologue.

15. *Lives of the English Poets*, ed. G. B. Hill, **1**, 163.

16. *Milton's 'Lycidas'*, ed. Patrides, p. 78.

17. *Milton*, p. 55.

18. ibid., p. 57.

19. See Edward Le Comte, *Milton's Unchanging Mind*, pp. 5–68.

20. See pages 11–15, above.

21. *Milton: A Biography*, **1**, 86–7.

22. Lowry Nelson, Jr, *Baroque Lyric Poetry*, pp. 65–75.

23. I am indebted to Parker's biography here, especially **1**, 7–8, 28, 29, 31–2, 96, 155.

24. A. S. P. Woodhouse, 'Milton the Poet', Sedgewick Memorial Lecture at the University of British Columbia (1955), p. 9. See also Rosemond Tuve, *Images and Themes*, p. 73.

25. 'Milton in *Lycidas*', *CE*, **7** (1945–6), 395. See also Brooks and Hardy in Patrides (p. 139), and G. S. Fraser, 'Approaches to *Lycidas*', in *The Living Milton*, ed. Kermode, p. 40.

26. See John Spencer Hill's account of Milton's developing sense of vocation in *John Milton: Poet, Priest and Prophet* (1979), chs. 1 and 2.

27. *English Poetry and Prose, 1540–1674* (1970), p. 258. Northrop Frye shows that starting with a handful of peripheral facts about the poem rather than with the poem itself eventually causes the fragmentation of the poem (Patrides, p. 205).

28. E. M. W. Tillyard, *Milton*, p. 70; James Holly Hanford, *A Milton Handbook* (5th edn, rev. Taaffe, 1970), p. 137; Ransom (Patrides, p. 78); Richard P. Adams (Patrides, p. 124); Roy Daniells, *Milton, Mannerism and Baroque* (1963), p. 47. Lowry Nelson, Jr provides a necessary curb for this reading by tracing 'the evolution of an attitude' and a 'process of self-objectification' in

the poem (*Baroque Lyric Poetry*, pp. 75, 151, 152). B. Rajan, *The Lofty Rhyme*, p. 55, and C. F. Stone, III, 'Milton's Self-Concerns and Manuscript Revisions in Lycidas', *MLN*, **83** (1968), 873, detect this process in the closing verse-paragraph.

29. 'The Pattern of Milton's "Nativity Ode"' (1941), rpt. in *Milton: Modern Judgements*, ed. Alan Rudrum (1968), p. 47.

30. *John Milton* (1949), p. 56.

31. *Lives of the English Poets*, ed. G. B. Hill, **3**, 456. See also Joseph Wood Krutch, *Samuel Johnson* (1963 edn), pp. 486–7, 594.

32. 'A Definition of the Pastoral Idyll', *PMLA*, **19** (1904), 583.

33. Patrides, p. 67.

34. Introduction to *Collected Plays* (1958), p. 53.

35. *English Pastoral Poetry from the Beginnings to Marvell*, ed. Kermode (1952), p. 11. See also Herbert E. Cory, 'The Golden Age of the Spenserian Pastoral', *PLMA*, **25** (1910), 241.

36. Christopher Ricks, *English Poetry and Prose, 1540–1674*, pp. 257–8.

37. Patrides, p. 76.

38. *The Primary Language of Poetry in the 1640s* (1948), p. 88. Though her comments on 'Lycidas', *ll*. 1–10, are excluded from the revised version of her study in Patrides, she still applies the same analytical principles.

39. Isabel Gamble MacCaffrey, '*Lycidas*: the Poet in a Landscape', *The Lyric and Dramatic Milton*, ed. Summers, p. 66, finds the opening of 'Lycidas' 'brutally direct', and Michael Lieb, ' "Yet Once More": The Formulaic Opening of *Lycidas*', *MQ*, **12** (1978), feels that 'if Milton invokes the pastoral elegiac tradition "Yet once more", he does so in a decidedly destructive manner' (25).

40. See H. V. S. Ogden, 'The Principles of Variety and Contrast in Seventeenth-Century Aesthetics, and Milton's Poetry', *JHI*, **10** (1949), 181; Wylie Sypher, *Four Stages of Renaissance Style: Transformations in Art and Literature 1400–1700* (1956), pp. 22, 105, 183, 192; Roy Daniells, *Milton, Mannerism and Baroque*, pp. 40–7.

41. Charles H. Hinnant, 'Freedom as Form in Milton's "Lycidas"', *Papers of the Michigan Academy of Science, Arts, and Letters*, **53** (1967), ed. Ralph A. Loamis, 322–3. Alastair Fowler, applying numerological criteria, finds that 'the broken stanzas are broken with grief' (*Silent Poetry: Essays in Numerological Analysis*, ed. Fowler (1970), p. 172). Ransom (Patrides, pp. 68, 69, 71) interprets the dramatic agitation of the poem as evidence merely of Milton's insubordinacy, without concluding, of course, that this makes the poem less anonymous.

42. Ants Oras, 'Milton's Early Rhyme-Schemes', *MP*, **52** (1954), 15.

43. Isabel G. MacCaffrey, op. cit., p. 71.

44. Joseph Frank, 'The Unharmonious Vision: Milton as a Baroque Artist', *Comparative Literature Studies*, **3** (1966), 100–1; Michael Lieb, op. cit., 26.

45. *Images and Themes*, p. 79. See also *John Milton: Odes, Pastorals, Masques*, ed. Broadbent *et al.*, p. 189.

46. Josephine Miles in Patrides (p. 97).

47. Roy Daniells, op. cit., p. 46.

48. Lowry Nelson, Jr, op. cit., pp. 65–75; Ransom in Patrides (p. 79). William C. Riggs, 'The Plant of Fame in *Lycidas*', *MS*, **4** (1972), 158–9, regards tense-shifts as the means whereby a recreative process is represented throughout the poem.

49. See Oras, op. cit., 12–22; J. A. Wittreich, Jr, 'Milton's "Destin'd Urn": The Art of *Lycidas*', *PMLA*, **84** (1969), 60–70, and *Visionary Poetics: Milton's Tradition and his Legacy* (1979), pp. 167–78. Alberta Turner, 'The Sound of Grief: A Reconsideration of the Nature and Function of the Unrhymed Lines in *Lycidas*', *MQ*, **10** (1976), 67–72, suggests that if 'slant rhyme' (whereby internal and terminal sounds are linked and extended) is taken into account, then 'Lycidas' contains no wholly unrhymed lines.

50. Alastair Fowler, *Silent Poetry*, p. 180.

51. op. cit., 21. See Arthur E. Barker's idea of the poem's 'three successive and perfectly controlled crescendos' (*Milton: Modern Judgements*, ed. Rudrum, p. 48), and Clay Hunt, *'Lycidas' and the Italian Critics* (1979), ch. 5.

52. B. Rajan, *The Lofty Rhyme*, p. 45.

53. Jon S. Lawry, ' "Eager Thought": Dialectic in *Lycidas*', *PMLA*, **77** (1962), 27; W. J. Grace, *Ideas in Milton* (1968), p. 145; Walter W. Greg, *Pastoral Poetry and Pastoral Drama* (1959), p. 132. Ransom's hypothesis that 'Lycidas' was 'written smooth and rewritten rough' (Patrides, p. 71) is not supported by the manuscript evidence: see Winifred Lynskey, 'A Critic in Action: Mr. Ransom', *CE*, **5** (1944), 243; F. T. Bowers, *Textual and Literary Criticism* (1949), p. 3; and Martin C. Battestin, 'John Crowe Ransom and *Lycidas*: A Reappraisal', *CE*, **17** (1956), 226–7.

54. See the articles by Josephine Miles, Richard P. Adams, Wayne Shumaker, Brooks and Hardy, and M. H. Abrams in Patrides (pp. 95–100, 120–5, 125–35, 136–52, 224–5).

55. *Milton*, p. 56.

56. Patrides, p. 97.

57. See G. S. Fraser's examples in 'Approaches to *Lycidas*', *The Living Milton,* ed. Kermode, p. 43.

58. 'The Poetic Powers of Repetition', *Proceedings of the British Academy,* **55** (1969), 70.

59. Mother M. Christopher Pecheux, 'The Dread Voice in *Lycidas*', *MS*, **9** (1976), 236; Michael Lieb, ' "Yet Once More": The Formulaic Opening of *Lycidas*', *MQ*, **12** (1978), 26.

60. John Carey (*Milton*, p. 58) is unsettled by the fact that 'the sun poised "in the forehead of the morning sky" (171) symbolizes impermanence . . . and makes the point by dropping, with Lycidas, back to the Irish Sea before the poem ends (191).' The sun in line 171 is not permanently positioned: it is seen from the human point of view. And Lycidas' position is expressible only by simile (*ll.* 167–73). The sun at the end of the poem is seen to be timelessly permanent from the heavenly point of view. The change is reflected in the new 'voice' in the last verse-paragraph, where the speaker is able to view the 'uncouth

swain' objectively. The ideal timelessness of pastoral (*ll.* 25–37) is thus made Christian.

61. Ants Oras, 'Milton's Early Rhyme-Schemes', *MP*, **52** (1954), 17, F. T. Prince, *The Italian Element in Milton's Verse* (rev. edn, 1969), pp. 71–88, John Reesing, *Milton's Poetic Art: A Mask, Lycidas, and Paradise Lost* (1968), p. 28, and Balachandra Rajan, *The Lofty Rhyme*, p. 54, make relevant comments on the style of the last paragraph.

62. *John Milton: Odes, Pastorals, Masques*, ed. Broadbent *et al.*, p. 189.

63. Thomas Perrin Harrison, Jr, *The Pastoral Elegy: An Anthology* (1939), p. 17.

64. See J. P. Hardy, *Reinterpretations: Essays on Poems by Milton, Pope and Johnson* (1971), p. 30; and Michael Lieb, ' "Yet Once More": The Formulaic Opening of *Lycidas*', *MQ*, **12** (1978), 25: 'What results is an undermining of convention by means of convention.'

65. Stewart A. Baker, 'Milton's Uncouth Swain', *MS*, **3** (1971), 41.

66. This view is shared by Stewart A. Baker (ibid., 44); by Donald M. Friedman, '*Lycidas:* The Swain's Paideia', *MS*, **3** (1971), 9; and by Clay Hunt, who demonstrates how Milton has modified the conventions of eclogue to incorporate the style of high lyric ('*Lycidas' and the Italian Critics*, ch. 5).

67. 9.8 per cent of the words are definite articles, 5.8 per cent more than George Rostrevor Hamilton's average figure for the period, and 3.8 per cent more than his average figure for Milton (*The Tell-Tale Article*, pp. 5–6).

68. See pages 25–8, above.

69. *Images and Themes*, p. 96; *Milton's Poetic Art*, p. 23.

70. *OED*, 3.b; *Variorum Commentary*, **2**, 720.

71. *OED*, 1, 5, 6.

72. *The English Poetic Mind* (1932), p. 115. The poem does not substantiate David Shelley Berkeley's over-specific view that we are meant to imagine Lycidas in Leviathan's belly. However, Berkeley is right to stress the diabolic significance in the typology of the sea in the poem, and to find it intensified at the 'bottom of the monstrous world' (*Inwrought with Figures Dim: A Reading of Milton's 'Lycidas'* (1974), pp. 60, 62, 114–30).

73. J. M. French, 'The Digressions in Milton's *Lycidas*', *SP*, **50** (1953), 485–90, argues against the digression theory. For him, lines 64–84 and 113–31 are passages of 'increased intensity' (485).

74. '*Lycidas' and the Italian Critics*, pp. 11, 135–6.

75. *Milton and the English Revolution*, pp. 52, 460.

76. Mother M. Christopher Pecheux, 'The Dread Voice in *Lycidas*', *MS*, **9** (1976), 236, and Michael Lieb, ' "Yet Once More": The Formulaic Opening of *Lycidas*', *MQ*, **12** (1978), 26, note the verbal echoes.

77. Berkeley, *Inwrought with Figures Dim*, pp. 45–6.

78. ibid., p. 46; Lowry Nelson, Jr, *Baroque Lyric Poetry*, pp. 148–9; and *Variorum Commentary*, **2**, 725–6.

79. loc. cit.

80. John Carey, *Milton*, p. 58.

81. Berkeley (op. cit., p. 202) thinks that the 'he' of line 175 refers to Christ, not

to Lycidas, because Lycidas is passive – receiving baptism in 'nectar pure', hearing the heavenly song, and having his tears wiped away. But if Christ washes Lycidas' hair, then he must also be the one who hears the heavenly song and has his tears wiped, for the same pronoun is used throughout the passage. Lycidas *avails himself* of a kind of baptism by washing his own hair, and though it is possible that the 'he' of line 175 could be Christ, it is not plausible. Berkeley's regret that his interpretation depends on there being no 'express *object*' – he must surely mean subject – for 'hears' (*l.* 176) reveals a more serious vagueness about syntax than he attributes to Milton.

CHAPTER FOUR
Psalms and Sonnets

Generalizations about an author's style all too often amount to little more than hastily indulged prejudices or crude abstractions, but some provide useful beginnings for investigation of the more specific functions of style in varying contexts. James Holly Hanford offers one of the best of the latter kind for studying Milton:

Milton really has two styles, corresponding to two different kinds of object or two qualities of poetic inspiration. The one is abundant, highly coloured, pictorial, figurative; the other direct, closely woven, and relatively plain. The first is the language of Milton's impassioned visual imagination, the second, of his ethical and intellectual intensity. Many passages, to be sure, show the two modes in combination, and both have the fundamental Miltonic qualities already analysed. The contrast between them in their purity is, nevertheless, strongly marked.[1]

Hanford sensibly distinguishes between the 'purity' of the styles as analytical abstractions and their actual combinations in the poems. It is just this adaptation of style to a variety of functions, such as sensuous evocation, dramatization of characters and symbolic attitudes, and control of structural cohesion, that is ultimately important. The consideration of stylistic *function* raises the crucial issue of the appropriateness of the style; and this, in turn, reveals the limitations of prejudiced judgement or of mere abstraction, and makes precise inquiry necessary. The first general style delineated by Hanford is that found in 'L'Allegro' and 'Il Penseroso', the 'Nativity Ode', 'Comus', the 'Fair Infant', 'The Passion', and 'Lycidas', all early poems with high adjective frequencies. At deeper levels, these poems have, of course, been shown to be significantly different from each other. The second general style, characterized by a relatively low adjective frequency, is found in Milton's versified psalms, his sonnets, *Paradise Regained*, and 'Samson Agonistes'. Again, however, it is the function of the basic style, modified by different individual contexts, that invites critical inspection.

99

No-one has claimed remarkable literary merit for Milton's three groups of versified psalms, written in 1624, 1648, and 1653 respectively. But they serve to illustrate the general, though by no means strictly linear and unvaried, tendency of his style towards a lower adjective frequency. The following table adduces evidence from three other psalters in order to suggest that the change in this aspect of his style does not necessarily represent a translator's response to the style of the Hebrew originals:[2]

Work				*Adjective/Word*
	Sternhold & Hopkins	*Sandys*	*Ford*	*Milton*
Group 1: Psalms cxiv, cxxxvi.	6.6%	10.9%	6.1%	11.5%
Group 2: Psalms lxxx–lxxxviii.	3.2%	10.4%	6.9%	8.1%
Group 3: Psalms i–viii.	4.2%	10.0%	7.6%	5.2%

If the constant refrain from Psalm cxxxvi, 'For his mercies ay endure, / Ever faithful, ever sure', is counted more than once, the figure for Milton's first group rises to 15 per cent. The figure for the third group is the lowest in all of Milton's poetry. And even if the term 'colour adjective' is taken loosely to denote or imply light and shade (as in 'wan', 'cloudy', 'glowing', etc.) as well as the colours of the spectrum, then a similar change is manifest throughout the three groups: in group 1, 18 per cent of the adjectives are colour adjectives; in group 2, 4.6 per cent; and in group 3, 2 per cent.

Milton's style in Psalms cxiv and cxxxvi is unadventurous – understandably so, since he was only fifteen when he wrote them. Compound adjectives such as those in the phrases 'froth-becurlèd head', 'golden-tressèd sun', 'large-limbed Og', and 'thunder-clasping hand' disclose a mode of contrived embellishment familiar from Elizabethan writing. David Daiches has noted an affinity with the style of Joshua Sylvester.[3] The only line in which the young Milton attempts a group of two adjectives before a noun conflates Sylvester with the Bible, with a result that is both clumsy and sexually unfortunate: 'The high, huge-bellied mountains skip like rams' (Psa. cxiv, 11). This line must be the worst that Milton ever wrote. Throughout the two early psalms 'ornate' adjectives are drilled into normal prenominal positions in a way that imposes artifice on nature: 'That glassy floods from rugged rocks can crush, / And make soft rills from fiery flint-stones gush' (Psa. cxiv, 17–18). Only once is there a hint of strong visual credibility in the artifice – in the account of the Israelites passing through the Red Sea: 'The floods stood still like walls of glass, / While the Hebrew bands did pass' (Psa. cxxxvi, 49–50). Ambiguities in such syntax are unsuspected, justifiably for the most part; but the very slight ambiguity in 'stood still | like walls of glass' and 'stood | still like walls of glass' is mimetically arresting. Only once in these two early psalms does Milton alter the prenominal position of the adjective in a phrase, in Psalm cxxxvi, 33–4: 'The hornèd moon to shine by night, / Amongst her spangled sisters bright'. The moon, conventionally 'hornèd',[4] may be 'bright' or shine 'bright(ly)'; and 'bright' may apply to 'moon', or to 'spangled sisters', thus spreading radiance. But, even allowing for such possible subtleties, one must agree with Dr Johnson's judgement, echoed by many critics, that these psalms 'would in any numerous school have obtained praise; but not excited wonder'.[5]

Most literary critics have followed Dr Johnson in politely neglecting to mention the second and third groups of psalms. These belong to the prose years. The Revd Stopford A. Brooke, a man who makes a fairly constant effort to wax eulogistic about Milton, merely records the writing of group three, and comments on group two, 'What [Milton] did in the way of poetry was to translate nine of the Psalms . . . into metre, and badly done they were.'[6] Discussions of these psalms are usually confined knowingly to the safe matters of prosody, or to puzzled speculations about Milton's possible motives for bothering to write them.[7] It seems certain that there is no arguing away their conventionality on grounds of literary merit. When Marian Studley praises them flatly for showing the force and dignity of the originals,[8] she effectually ignores E. C. Baldwin's allegations that the adjectives in particular are conventional.[9] William B. Hunter has shown that when Milton's phraseology is compared with that of other psalters 'it is frequently similar or identical'.[10] Miss Studley's observation that the period 1600-1653 saw 206 metrical versions of the complete psalter and her comment that Milton was 'doing the customary and popular thing'[11] argue against originality. Certainly, the placing of adjectives after their nouns fails to relieve the dullness of the writing: 'wonders great', 'dwellings fair', and 'affliction great' are typical. The phrase 'grace divine' occurs three times in formulaic fashion, and Todd notes that the phrase 'honour due' occurs in Spenser, in biblical translation, and elsewhere in Milton.[12] When Milton uses the apparently ordinary phrase 'rivers wide' in 'L'Allegro', he sets it in a context where the prenominal and postnominal positions of adjectives are alternated to evoke the variety of the landscape described:

> Russet lawns, and fallows grey,
> Where the nibbling flocks do stray,
> Mountains on whose barren breast
> The labouring clouds do often rest:
> Meadows trim with daisies pied,
> Shallow brooks, and rivers wide.

(*ll.* 71–6)

101

In Psalm lxxx, 47, the same phrase achieves nothing:

> Her branches on the western side
> Down to the sea she sent,
> And upward to that river wide
> Her other branches went.

The lines possess all the imaginative thrill of a surveyor's report. The pedestrian regularity of pace and the reliable-sounding, matter-of-fact tone only make the horizontal pull of 'wide' after 'down' and 'upward' more bewildering. William B. Hunter could have extended his observation that Milton avoids feminine endings in these two groups of psalms[13] by adding that twenty-five of the forty-five adjectives placed after their nouns are monosyllables in rhyming positions. This suggests that Milton uses the device as a metrical expedient. Certainly, the 'noun-adjective' phrases create no discernible poetic effects of the kind created by comparable phrases in the 'Nativity Ode' and 'Comus'.[14] Milton's language throughout these two groups of psalms can be praised only for coping with the mechanics of versification.

If writing psalms was almost a communal activity, Milton was virtually alone in cultivating the sonnet in the middle of the seventeenth century.[15] Commentators agree that his originality lies in replacing the 'abundance and vague luxuriance' common among the Elizabethans with 'precision of utterance, careful selection of words, [and] the simple and clear expression of definite ideas',[16] and in writing generally with a 'classical restraint' involving 'less ornament'.[17] In his sonnets Milton rescues the plain style from the banality prevalent in his versified psalms. A chief characteristic of the plain style is a low adjective frequency. The following table gives the figures for each sonnet:

Sonnet	Words	Adjectives	Adj./Wd.
I	120	12	10.0%
VII	116	12	10.4%
VIII	111	9	8.1%
X	101	11	10.9%
IX	114	11	9.7%
XIII	115	11	9.6%
XII	118	8	6.8%
XIV	122	11	9.0%
XI	133	9	6.8%
'Fairfax'	106	15	14.2%
'Cromwell'	109	13	12.0%
'Vane'	114	14	12.3%

XVI	113	10	8.9%
XVII	113	17	15.0%
XV	111	12	10.9%
XVIII	107	10	9.4%
'Cyriack Skinner'	117	8	6.9%
XIX	119	12	10.0%
	2059	205	average 10.0%

On average, 10 per cent of the words in these fourteen-line sonnets are adjectives.[18] This compares with an average for all the early poems, including the psalms and sonnets, of 11.9 per cent, and an average of 11.2 per cent for the whole of Milton's poetry. The average for the psalms, sonnets, *Paradise Regained*, and 'Samson Agonistes' is 9.4 per cent; and the figure for 'Samson' of 10 per cent is exactly that for the sonnets. This is one of the reasons why their styles have been impressionistically described by such terms as 'intense', 'strict', 'austere', and 'bold'. Macaulay, for instance, finds a quality of 'severe dignity' in 'Samson Agonistes', and also finds a certain 'severity of style' in the sonnets.[19]

The adjectives in Milton's sonnets are in general 'severe' in that less than one fifth of them are sensory. Many of the sensory adjectives are not used memorably either ('soft lay', 'sun's bright circle', 'golden rod', etc.). Only four of the 205 adjectives in all the sonnets denote colour, three of them in the heavenly vision of 'Sonnet XIV' ('golden rod', 'purple beams', 'azure wings'), and the other in the phrase 'the broad way and the green' ('Sonnet IX', 2). The suggestion of youthful immaturity in 'green' dulls the colour *per se*. Even if words denoting or implying light and shade are included with colour adjectives, the resulting total constitutes only 5.9 per cent of all adjectives used in the sonnets.

The sonnets in general are not remarkably 'visual' poems. Like Samson, the speaker in 'When I consider how my light is spent' questions providence for leaving him in the restricting 'dark world and wide' of blindness. And though it embodies no aesthetic effect that may influence critical judgement, the knowledge that the writer of the last of the sonnets lacks physical sight intensifies its poignancy:[20]

> Methought I saw my late espoused saint
> Brought to me like Alcestis from the grave,
> Whom Jove's great son to her glad husband gave,
> Rescued from death by force though pale and faint.
> Mine as whom washed from spot of childbed taint,   5
> Purification in the old Law did save,
> And such, as yet once more I trust to have

> Full sight of her in heaven without restraint,
> Came vested all in white, pure as her mind:
> Her face was veiled, yet to my fancied sight,   10
> Love, sweetness, goodness in her person shined
> So clear, as in no face with more delight.
> But O as to embrace me she inclined
> I waked, she fled, and day brought back my night.

The sonnet is concerned with the speaker's necessarily limited perception of the difference between the physical and the spiritual.[21] His dead wife, the 'late espoused saint', inhabits the perfect spiritual world of heaven,[22] but he remains confined by the imperfect physical world in which he can but see 'through a glass, darkly' (I Corinthians 13:12). The opening phrase 'methought I saw', the similes (*ll.* 2, 5, 7, 9), and the knotty syntax of lines 5–9, all testify to tentativeness and difficulty.[23] After the struggle of lines 1–8, the sudden simplicity of line 9 makes the appearance of the 'saint' an almost unanticipated quiet intrusion; while the affectionate accumulation of her virtues, running over into line 12 and endorsed by the elated compliment of 'in no face with more delight', touchingly discloses how much she has been wished for. Only her moral qualities are 'clear': she remains 'pale and faint', 'vested', 'veiled'; and 'full sight', implying the speaker's perfected spiritual perception, will be possible only in heaven. At present she is accessible, but uncertainly so: only the speaker's 'fancied sight', his imagination prompted by devoted wishing, is able to apprehend her presence. 'But O' (*l.* 13) follows 'though pale and faint' (*l.* 4) and 'yet to my fancied sight' (*l.* 10) as the last, and the most frustrating, of the poem's enforced qualifications: the speaker is left with the certainty that the uncertain vision has vanished. As William McCarthy has commented, 'the poet's dream is a promise and a reminder: a promise of bliss to be granted in the next world and a reminder of how inferior this one is. His pain on waking is of having to wait for the dream to fulfill itself.'[24] Just as the 'saint' seems most real, most near to the speaker – Kurt Heinzelman notes the syntactic nearness of 'me' and 'she' in line 13[25] – and most active,[26] she becomes least so. 'Inclined' (*l.* 13) obviously may mean that she leans over to embrace him, but it may also represent the speaker's fond interpretation of something in her appearance that suggests her *disposition* to embrace him: sadly, her apparently independent action emerges partly as his wish. He is left startled, uttering a paradox in monosyllables (*l.* 14). At the start of the poem the speaker thinks he sees his dead wife brought to him; at the end only his 'night' is brought back. 'Day' (*l.* 14), associated with heaven and spiritual perception,[27] is for him no more than a 'night' of emotional bewilderment and spiritual limitation. The lack of well-defined visual images is therefore of particular significance in the sonnet. As Marilyn L.

Williamson has said, 'we are constantly made aware of the fragile nature of the experience.'[28] The vision is also only a glimpse.

Milton's sonnets are in general not characterized by pervasive sense impression. In the opening lines of 'Sonnet I' an adjectival amplitude is symptomatic of the lover's youthful optimism:

> O nightingale, that on yon bloomy spray
> Warblest at eve, when all the woods are still,
> Thou with fresh hope the lover's heart dost fill,
> While the jolly hours lead on propitious May,
> Thy liquid notes that close the eye of day,
> First heard before the shallow cuckoo's bill
> Portend success in love;

But this is immediately questioned by a potentially more serious tone:

> O if Jove's will
> Have linked that amorous power to thy soft lay,
> Now timely sing, ere the rude bird of hate
> Foretell my hopeless doom in some grove nigh:

And the close of the sonnet scorns adjectives altogether in a plain statement of devotion that foreshadows the self-examining sonnets 'How soon hath time' and 'When I consider':[29]

> As thou from year to year hast sung too late
> For my relief; yet hadst no reason why,
> Whether the Muse, or Love call thee his mate,
> Both them I serve, and of their train am I.

Even in 'Sonnet I' the voice that was to become most characteristic of Milton's sonnets can be heard.

The only sonnet notable for sustained sense experience is 'Sonnet XVII', which has the highest adjective frequency of all the sonnets (15 per cent):

> Lawrence of virtuous father virtuous son,
> Now that the fields are dank, and ways are mire,
> Where shall we sometimes meet, and by the fire
> Help waste a sullen day; what may be won
> From the hard season gaining: time will run   5
> On smoother, till Favonius reinspire
> The frozen earth; and clothe in fresh attire
> The lily and the rose, that neither sowed nor spun.
> What neat repast shall feast us, light and choice,
> Of Attic taste, with wine, whence we may rise   10
> To hear the lute well touched, or artful voice
> Warble immortal notes and Tuscan air?

> He who of those delights can judge, and spare
> To interpose them oft, is not unwise.

A remarkable balance of austerity and indulgence is achieved here. The feeling for the 'hard season', the awareness of time passing, the reference in line 8 to Christ's words about the lilies (Matthew 6:28), and the judicious restraint of the close, all suggest an undercurrent of seriousness in the speaker's temperament. And yet the poem wears a smile, in the ready heartiness of its opening compliment, the knowing justification of the passing of time in self-indulgence, the good-natured invitation to dinner, and the mock-serious understatement of the double negative at the end. The succession of 'neat repast . . . light and choice, / Of Attic taste, with wine', and so on, in lines 9–12 freshly presents each ingredient of the meal and each aspect of the entertainment as a pleasant, spontaneous afterthought: the speaker seems to be making up his mind about a possible menu and programme. Thus the poem preserves a relaxed Horatian intimacy of tone[30] and a degree of adjectival specificness amounting in itself to convivial indulgence, and reconciles these qualities with an altogether more controlled sensibility. It is neither hedonistic nor glum.

Characteristically, the adjectives found in Milton's sonnets are of the kind readily found in prose, often staunchly 'moral', and very much in the 'sober, predominantly serious, and factual'[31] vein. The style is not surprising in poems of public affairs; and in such poems as 'When I consider' an ornate, elaborate style involving a high adjective frequency would have threatened to turn solemn, moving meditation towards artful self-display and insincerity. The same applies to the sonnets of eulogy, which Peter Hellings has praised for their unhyperbolical 'restraint and sincerity'.[32] Above all, Milton's cultivation in his sonnets of a 'determined forward movement'[33] and of 'authoritative directness'[34] of tone seems to dictate his strict reduction of adjectives in their prevalent style. Nine of the sonnets have a vocative in their opening line, so that they are supposedly in direct speech. Pronouns are also used to achieve a representation of a speaking voice: six of the sonnets contain first-person pronouns, and two announce their public-spiritedness by using the plural form.[35] In the tenth sonnet, 'To the Lady Margaret Ley', there are no less than three vocatives, thirteen pronouns, and three occurrences of the demonstrative 'that' assuming intimacy between speaker and addressee. Monosyllables are also used to point straight-talking: in 'When I consider', 81 per cent of the words are monosyllables; in the Piedmont sonnet and 'I did but prompt the age to quit their clogs', 87 per cent.[36] Of course, this kind of style has its hazards:

> Avenge O Lord thy slaughtered saints, whose bones
> Lie scattered on the Alpine mountains cold,

Even them who kept thy truth so pure of old
When all our fathers worshipped stocks and stones,
Forget not: in thy book record their groans   5
Who were thy sheep and in their ancient fold
Slain by the bloody Piedmontese that rolled
Mother with infant down the rocks. Their moans
The vales redoubled to the hills, and they
To heaven. Their martyred blood and ashes sow   10
O'er all the Italian fields where still doth sway
The triple Tyrant: that from these may grow
A hundredfold, who having learnt thy way
Early may fly the Babylonian woe.

Taylor Stoehr catches the blatantly partisan allegiance represented in the pronouns ('ev'n them', 'thy truth', 'thy book', 'their groans', 'thy sheep', 'their ancient fold'), which, in his words, establish 'a kind of holy bond . . . violated by "*the* bloody Piedmontese", marked as outsiders by the impersonality of the definite article'.[37] And John Broadbent says, rightly, that 'the power of the poem comes from the simplicity of the basic feeling of outrage, unqualified by any moral complexities. The Waldensians are completely innocent and good, the Piedmontese soldiers wholly evil.'[38] The sonnet's tone is unmistakably Hebraic: Kester Svensden has pointed out that every word except five occurs in some form in the Bible,[39] and Charles E. Goldstein has demonstrated, by accumulating the biblical references, that the sonnet can be read as 'a kind of traditional Hebrew lament or call for revenge'.[40] Nicholas R. Jones has noted that 'the imagery – hard, penetrating, and extreme – also unifies the poem with its implications of a world of bare, uncompromising strife: "bones", "mountains cold", "groans", "woe".' Nevertheless, he feels that the sonnet dramatizes the 'religious self-education' of its speaker:

His wisdom grows from a temporary state of indignation to a more balanced and durable state of charity. The harsh zeal of the opening lines, a prayer for vengeance on the enemies of the church, develops into a more profound feeling of compassion, expressed in a prayer for conversion.[41]

But there is no evidence in the poem of 'a more balanced and durable state of charity' or of 'compassion' towards 'the bloody Piedmontese'. God is asked to do two things: exercise his prerogative and take revenge on the Piedmontese; and prevent the future slaughter of an increased number of Italian Protestants. The two requests are not mutually exclusive: the second one may specify the form that the vengeance will take – of overcoming the 'Babylonian woe' by force of numbers (*ll.* 12–14). On the other hand, it may not. But the prayer for vengeance is not revoked. The sonnet's extreme style matches the uncompromising attitude of its speaker.

The plain style serves bigotry, albeit of a less frighteningly grand sort, in 'Sonnet XII. On the Detraction which followed upon my Writing Certain Treatises':

> I did but prompt the age to quit their clogs
> By the known rules of ancient liberty,
> When straight a barbarous noise environs me
> Of owls and cuckoos, asses, apes and dogs.
> As when those hinds that were transformed to frogs   5
> Railed at Latona's twin-born progeny
> Which after held the sun and moon in fee.
> But this is got by casting pearl to hogs;
> That bawl for freedom in their senseless mood,
> And still revolt when truth would set them free.   10
> Licence they mean when they cry liberty;
> For who loves that, must first be wise and good;
> But from that mark how far they rove we see
> For all this waste of wealth, and loss of blood.

This sonnet contains the lowest adjective frequency of all the sonnets. The steely scorn, deliberately measured and relentlessly vented, descends to moral bullying in 'known rules', 'barbarous noise', 'senseless mood', 'free', 'wise and good'; and to mere name-calling ('owls and cuckoos', 'asses', 'apes and dogs', 'frogs', 'hogs'). The style represents hardened emotion so convincingly and thoroughly that in itself it provokes the reader's aversion. It accommodates none of the 'fine raillery' in which Dryden considered the 'nicest and most delicate touches of satire' lay.[42] Raillery has been reduced to railing.

If, however, there are dangers in a style that cultivates a 'massive simplicity of diction and thought',[43] the sonnets in general are to be valued as 'essays, on a small scale, in the "magnificent" style'.[44] As has been indicated in this chapter, the sonnets display a range of style within general limits. But if 'magnificence' implies not elaborate sensuousness but an 'element of plainness and harshness',[45] Milton's stylistic achievement in his sonnets is greatest when the plain style does not disown, but rather correlates with, a mode of feeling that can be called magnanimous.

NOTES

1. *A Milton Handbook* (5th edn, rev. James G. Taaffe, 1970), pp. 256–7.
2. Editions used are: Sternhold & Hopkins, *The Whole Boke of Psalms* (1566), Bodl. MS. Ps verse 1566e.1; *The Poetical Works of George Sandys*, ed. Hooper

(1872); Simon Ford, *A New Version of the Psalms of David* (1688), *Bodl. MS. 8o P266 Th.*

3. *Milton*, p. 14.

4. Examples from Shakespeare and Spenser are cited in *Variorum Commentary*, 2, 117. Others are to be found in Phineas Fletcher, *Apollyonists*, V.xxiv.5, and in Thomas Campion, *Works*, ed. Vivian, p. 231.

5. *Lives of the English Poets*, ed. G. B. Hill, 1, 87.

6. *Milton* (1881), pp. 56, 49.

7. Carolyn P. Collette, 'Milton's Psalm Translations: Petition and Praise', *English Literary Renaissance*, 2 (1972), 243–59, suggests that Milton versified the psalms in response to civil events and his conscience, and to find comfort through meditation.

8. 'Milton and his Paraphrases of the Psalms', *PQ*, 4 (1925), 364–72.

9. 'Milton and the Psalms', *MP*, 17 (1919), 458.

10. 'Milton Translates the Psalms', *PQ*, 40 (1961), 485.

11. op. cit., 365, 366. See also *Variorum Commentary*, 2, 111.

12. H. J. Todd, ed., *The Poetical Works of John Milton* (3rd edn, 1826), 6, 130–1n.

13. 'The Sources of Milton's Prosody', *PQ*, 28 (1949), 135, 143.

14. See pages 37, 66 above.

15. J. S. Smart, *The Sonnets of Milton* (1921; rpt., 1966), p. 10.

16. ibid., pp. 21, 11.

17. E. A. J. Honigmann, ed., *Milton's Sonnets* (1966), p. 40, and Peter Hellings, 'A Note on the Sonnets of Milton', *Life and Letters*, 64 (1950), 165.

18. . If the sixteen-line poem 'On Shakespeare. 1630' and the twenty-line poem 'On the New Forcers of Conscience under the Long Parliament', are taken into account, the resulting average is 10.3 per cent.

19. *Macaulay's Essay on Milton*, ed. Charles Wallace French (1898), pp. 44, 23.

20. Leo Spitzer, 'Understanding Milton', *Hopkins Review*, 4 (1951), rpt. in *Essays on English and American Literature* (1962), pp. 121, 123.

21. John Spencer Hill, ' "Alcestis from the Grave": Image and Structure in *Sonnet XXIII*', *MS*, 10 (1977), 129, notes the paradox in the poem's structure: 'while the spiritual progression of the imagery records an ascent from flesh to spirit, the narrative progression records a tragic countermovement which emphasizes in purely human terms the irreparable loss of the "late espoused Saint".' 'Irreparable' is not quite accurate, for as Hill himself notes, desolation is 'tempered by the consolatory assurance of an Alcestis-like restoration' (137). John C. Ulreich, 'Typological Symbolism in Milton's *Sonnet XXIII*', *MQ*, 8 (1974), 10, feels that 'the speaker's present helplessness is qualified by his future hope'. But he too is aware of a paradox: 'against the triumphant evolution of types Milton has balanced a sense of overwhelming loss . . . the typological structure of the poem . . . does not correspond in any obvious way with what most readers feel to be its emotional force' (8).

22. John J. Colaccio, ' "A Death Like Sleep": The Christology of Milton's Twenty-Third Sonnet', *MS*, 6 (1974), 181–97, shows how she is made to typify the heavenly condition.

23. John Spencer Hill (*MS*, **10** (1977), 131, 134) notes the uncertainty of 'methought', and Kurt Heinzelman (' "Cold Consolation": The Art of Milton's Last Sonnet', *MS*, **10** (1977), 117) acutely notes that the expression 'methought I saw' also occurs in Adam's account of his sensations during the creation of Eve (*PL*, VIII.460–90). The similes in the sonnet are noted by Ulreich (*MQ*, **8** (1974), 7), and by Heinzelman (111, 114). For Heinzelman, the sonnet 'illustrates both the achievement and limitation of seeing comparatively, through likenesses, as the paradox of the human imagination', and 'the resemblance-making power of the poet *is* the experience of the poem' (114). An interesting parallel to the syntax of lines 1–9 is in lines 1–8 of 'When I consider how my light is spent', of which Gary Stringer has said, 'the sinuous, overstuffed period . . . connotes confusion and an inability to grasp facts surehandedly' ('Milton's "Thorn in the Flesh": Pauline Didacticism in *Sonnet XIX*', *MS*, **10** (1977), 143).

24. 'The Continuity of Milton's Sonnets', *PMLA*, **92** (1977), 107. Dixon Fiske takes a similar view, commenting that the speaker 'must achieve her condition rather than having her impossibly returned to him in his', and that 'the moment of the dreamer's unconsummated embrace dramatizes what the veil symbolizes – the insufficiency of the dreamer himself' ('The Theme of Purification in Milton's *Sonnet XXIII*', *MS*, **8** (1975), 158, 160).

25. ' "Cold Consolation": The Art of Milton's Last Sonnet', *MS*, **10** (1977), 122.

26. John Huntley comments: 'At first, she seemed to be *his* espoused saint, but by the end of the poem, passive in his trance, he is nearly espoused again, possessed and embraced by the inclining figure' ('Milton's 23rd Sonnet', *ELH*, **34** (1967), 477).

27. See Macon Cheek, 'Of Two Sonnets of Milton', *Renaissance Papers* (1956), rpt. in *Milton: Modern Essays in Criticism*, ed. Barker, p. 130.

28. 'A Reading of Milton's Twenty-Third Sonnet', *MS*, **4** (1972), 143.

29. William McCarthy, 'The Continuity of Milton's Sonnets', *PMLA*, **92** (1977), 96–109, views the sonnets as a sequence divided into three stages that correspond to the youth, maturity, and old age of the poet: the first, Italianate in character, deals in youthful poems with love as an inspiration to poetry; the second is devoted to a consideration of public themes; and the third presents the poet in retirement. The three stages are demarcated by two sonnets that represent turning-points in the poet's career: 'How soon hath time', and 'When I consider'.

30. J. H. Finley, Jr points out the Horatian parallels with the sonnet in 'Milton and Horace: A Study of Milton's Sonnets', *Harvard Studies in Classical Philology*, **48** (1937), 64.

31. This phrase is from Thomas Wheeler, 'Milton's Twenty-Third Sonnet', *SP*, **58** (1961), rpt. in *Milton: Modern Essays in Criticism*, ed. Barker, p. 138.

32. 'A Note on the Sonnets of Milton', *Life and Letters*, **64** (1950), 168.

33. The phrase is Taylor Stoehr's, from 'Syntax and Poetic Form in Milton's Sonnets', *ES*, **45** (1964), 300.

34. This phrase is Christopher Ricks's, from *English Poetry and Prose, 1540–1674*, p. 279.

35. 'Sonnet VII', 13, and 'Sonnet XV', 4. See also 'New Forcers', *ll.* 6, 7, 13, 17.

36. Kester Svensden, 'Milton's Sonnet on the Massacre in Piedmont', *The Shakespeare Association Bulletin*, **20** (1945), 148 and *n*; and *John Milton: Samson Agonistes, Sonnets, &c.*, ed. John Broadbent and Robert Hodge (1977), p. 50. Stephen Wigler finds the first-person pronouns in 'When I consider' significant: 'the reader discovers that the octave is dominated by egocentricity and fruitless bitterness. The first person pronouns *I, me*, and *my* occur eight times. In the sestet, the first person does not appear at all, but "God" and pronouns to which he is antecedent occur six times' ('Outrageous Noise and the Sovereign Voice: Satan, Sin, and Syntax in *Sonnet XIX* and Book VI of *Paradise Lost*', *MS*, **10** (1977), 156).

37. 'Syntax and Poetic Form in Milton's Sonnets', *ES*, **45** (1964), 300.

38. *John Milton: Samson Agonistes, Sonnets, &c.*, ed. Broadbent and Hodge, p. 45.

39. 'Milton's Sonnet on the Massacre in Piedmont', *The Shakespeare Association Bulletin*, **20** (1945), 148.

40. 'The Hebrew Element in Milton's *Sonnet XVIII*', *MQ*, **9** (1975), 111–14. However, Goldstein also feels that the reference to blood and ashes (*l.* 10), through its association with Old Testament purificatory rites, 'helps reinforce the ironic reversal at the end of the sonnet where, instead of demanding the bloody retaliation so characteristic of the tradition he is exemplifying, he pleads in a truly Christian vein that Reformation and Truth triumph over barbarism and bloodshed' (113). But purification applies only to the Italian Protestants. And there is no 'ironic reversal' at the end of the poem: the speaker asks for divine vengeance, and then asks that Italian Protestants may increase in number and be delivered from Catholic persecution.

41. 'The Education of the Faithful in Milton's Piedmontese Sonnet', *MS*, **10** (1977), 167–76. The passages quoted are on page 168 of the article.

42. John Dryden, *Of Dramatic Poesy and other Critical Essays*, ed. George Watson (1962), **2**, 136. Dryden exclaims, 'How easy it is to call rogue and villain, and that wittily! But how hard to make a man appear a fool, a blockhead, or a knave, without using any of those opprobrious terms!' (ibid., 136–7).

43. The phrase is taken from *John Milton: Samson Agonistes, Sonnets, &c.*, ed. Broadbent and Hodge, p. 38.

44. F. T. Prince, *The Italian Element in Milton's Verse* (1962 edn), p. 103.

45. ibid., p. 107.

CHAPTER FIVE
Paradise Regained

Macaulay remarks that Milton 'could stoop to a plain style, sometimes even to a bald style, but false brilliancy was his utter aversion'.[1] Many critics are likely to think this grimly true of *Paradise Regained*: between Mark Pattison's choleric overstatement that it is 'probably the most unadorned poem in any language'[2] and W. Menzies's temperate reflections on its 'extreme simplicity and plainness',[3] there exists a fairly unanimous judgement that the poem's language is adequately described as 'bare', 'flat', 'colourless', 'chastened and dimmed', 'muted', 'dry', 'cold', or 'bleak'.[4] But only John Carey and Christopher Ricks,[5] and to a lesser extent a few other critics,[6] have taken a close look at the allegedly bare language and attempted to analyse its functions. This lack of penetration means that the nature of Milton's stylistic range remains largely unexplored, and that comparisons between, say, 'Samson Agonistes', *Paradise Regained*, and the sonnets are not as exact as they could be. More serious is the fact that statements about the poem's language are left sufficiently impressionistic for metaphoric terms like 'bare' or 'colourless' to serve ambiguously as unsupported value judgements. This, in turn, allows the prescription for 'Good Poetry' implicit in the value judgements to remain elusive. Perhaps this is just as well, for though many critics have championed such qualities as 'sensuous vitality', who would be so bold as to demand the qualities, more objectively specified, that constitute 'vitality'? If precise anaylsis causes embarrassment to a literary taste that depends on catch-phrases readily applied, that is only because literary taste *should* depend on precise analysis.

What critics have observed about the style of *Paradise Regained* is that imagery, especially in the form of epic similes,[7] is relatively scarce; though such imagery as the poem does possess has been shown to be as tightly structured as that of 'Comus'.[8] The 'bare' style has also been correlated with 'prosaic', and often uncompromisingly monosyllabic, speech, particularly with that typical of the Son.[9] Rhetoric has been shown to be used to a considerable degree throughout the poem;[10] but if Frank Kermode is mistaken in speaking of its 'cold, unrhetorical diction',[11] he provides one of the most acute insights into the style, albeit unsupported by evidence, when he suspects that Milton has banished epithets from the poem;[12] Milton's style in *Paradise Regained* accords in general with the hero's contempt for 'swelling epithets thick-laid' (IV.343). On average only 9.4 per cent of the words are adjectives. Further, only about 13 per cent of the adjectives convey sense impression: the others, as in the sonnets, are 'moral' or of the kind that could readily be found in prose. However, *Paradise Regained* is by no means written uniformly in this 'bare' style:

Context	Words	Adjectives	Adj./Wd.
II.337–65 (Banquet)	313	32	10.3%
III.251–344 (Worldly glory; Parthians)	676	79	11.7%
IV.25–89 (Rome)	465	62	13.4%
IV.236–84 (Athens)	336	57	17.0%
IV.397–438 (Storm)	324	54	16.7%
	2114	284	average 13.5%

The set-piece temptation passages are all adjectival, and increasingly so; and the presence of three markedly adjectival sections in the fourth book explains the rise of adjective frequency in that book to 10 per cent of the words.[13] The banquet in the second book is, as a temptation to indulge *voluptaria*,[14] overtly sensuous. Two long sentences (II.337–47, 350–65) amass luxury, while the short sentence between them gives a bitter and pointed reminder of the 'crude apple that diverted Eve'. This technique accentuates the exhibition and excess of the whole pageant. Theodore H. Banks comments that the copiousness of the banquet shows that 'it is . . . Nature . . . supposedly tendering the feast, and [she] would therefore bring forth her choicest delicacies out of mere zeal,' so that 'her most profuse and elaborate offering could not be excessive.'[15] But it must be remembered that the banquet is produced not by nature but by Satan (II.393–9), and that it is Satan's claim that nature provides the feast (II.331–6). Banks's parallel with Comus's argument that nature's profuse offerings are not to be rejected[16] is not strictly relevant, because Comus describes a fantastic natural abundance, and not built pastries, wine, a sideboard, and the sounds of musical instruments that suddenly materialize in the desert. Milton undermines the plenitude by suggesting its suspicious artifice. As Charles Lamb comments, 'The mighty artillery of sauces, which the cook-fiend conjures up, is out of proportion to the simple wants and plain hunger of the guest.'[17] The adjectival element in the banquet description, set against the generally less adjectival style of the poem, is one of the means by which Milton alerts the reader to its pretentiousness. In the other set-piece temptation passages, suspicion is aroused not so much by overt sensuousness as by Satan's passion for 'total inclusiveness', 'pelting generality', and dizzying shifts of perspective and direction.[18] The increase in adjectives correlates with the increased specificness and definition noted in the later temptations by John Carey and Jon S. Lawry.[19]

The adjectival temptation passages, as tabulated, together contain 13.5 per cent of the poem's words, but about 30 per cent of the sensory adjectives. As the temptations are not always overtly sensuous, these facts reveal just how little sense impression *Paradise Regained* incorporates. Jackson I. Cope has observed how 'we hear of flight and do not view it', how 'the first two books . . . contain only the most negligible landscape perspectives', and how 'there is no depth to the sensual matter of the temptations or to the physical guises of tempter and tempted'.[20] Perhaps this is so because Milton distrusts a visual emphasis as potential idolatry;[21] or because he wishes to allow the speeches of the protagonists to pass directly to the intellect;[22] or because the poem is concerned with spiritual discernment, with perception that penetrates more deeply than the potentially misleading senses can do.[23] What is certain is that Milton has reduced visual effects in *Paradise Regained*. Only twelve of the 1474 adjectives in the poem denote colour, and even if words such as 'fiery', 'dark', 'glittering', and 'crystal' are included in the reckoning, the resulting total constitutes only 1.5 per cent of all the adjectives. Where flashes of light do pierce the prevailing sombre atmosphere, they come from allusions or temptations: 'crystal doors' (I.82), 'fiery wheels', ' a crown, / Golden in show' (II.16, 458–9), 'amber stream' (III.288), 'gilded battlements', 'dusk faces with white silken turbans wreathed', 'golden spires' (IV.53, 76, 548). The foot of the 'mountain high' is described as 'verdant' (II.252–3), and the three occurrences of the adjective 'green', two of them in the fourth book (*ll.* 435, 587), bear witness to the truth of John Carey's observation that Eden is raised in the wilderness as the poem progresses.[24] For the most part, however, 'the landscape is of twilight',[25] as the adjectives 'grey' (I.498; IV.427), 'brown' (II.293),[26] 'dark' (I.41, 194; IV.456), and 'dusk'

(I.296; IV.76) indicate; and into this darkness Milton, in Tillyard's words, 'projects brilliant visions'.[27]

Barbara K. Lewalski has observed the pervasive contrast in *Paradise Regained* between Satanic darkness and heavenly light.[28] However, the symbolism and wordplay are more subtly managed than she seems to estimate. Satan, who has lost his 'native brightness' (I.378), is first presented with his peers 'within thick clouds and dark tenfold involved' (I.41), and his very speech is 'dark' with deceitful ambiguity (I.434). Shades, clouds, and night are consistently associated with him (I.194, 296, 304, 500; II.242; III.326–7; IV.397–400, 410). Hell is, of course, a place of darkness (I.116, 364; IV.456), and heaven a place of light (I.81–2, 128–9; IV.597–8). Christ, like Job, is at first 'obscure' (I.24–5; III.94), but 'in his face / The glimpses of his father's glory shine' (I.92–3), and his baptism marks the time when he 'no more should live obscure' (I.287). In the world, represented by the wilderness, he is seen as a light shining in darkness. At his birth a 'glorious choir' announces his presence 'by night', and the magi follow his 'star new-graven in heaven' (I.242–5, 253). Milton makes the symbolism explicit by describing him as 'our morning star, then in his rise' (I.294), and by surrounding him with 'a pathless desert, dusk with horrid shades' (I.296). A subsidiary of the light-darkness pattern is the imagery of flame, used with telling irony as the Son resists Satan's temptations. The thought of lost bliss 'inflames' Satan (I.418), whereas the Son scorns the 'blaze of fame' that could follow the time when 'victorious deeds / Flamed in [his] heart, heroic acts' (III.47; I.215–16). When, in a beguiling passage, Satan asks the Son to serve as 'a shelter and a kind of shading cool / Interposition, as a summer's cloud' (III.221–2) to shield him from the heat of divine wrath, there is little possibility of such protection: the cloud image works against Satan, for he, not the Son, is associated with clouds. This is perhaps why the Son denounces worldly wisdom as 'an empty cloud' (IV.321). When the establishment of David's kingdom is said to be 'like a tree / Spreading and overshadowing all the earth' (IV.147–8), kindly shade is contrasted with the 'horrid shades' of the wilderness. Just as the star in the night sky prefigures the Son in the desert darkness, so the sunny morning chasing the clouds (IV.426–42) typifies the end of Satanic rule 'in the clouds' (IV.619).[29] Satan falls from heaven 'like an autumnal star / Or lightning' (IV.619–20), but this envisaged downfall and the Son's ascendancy begin, in effect, with the events of the poem: Satan, Prince of Darkness (IV.441), is 'discovered' (IV.3), and the identity of Jesus as Son of God is triumphantly 'declared' (I.121, 385; II.4; IV.521).

Colour in this image pattern is virtually reduced to black and white, and sense impression is governed by conceptual significance. *Paradise Regained*

115

includes occasional instances of sense perception for their own sake, such as the description of the 'horny beaks' of the raven that fed Elijah (II.267) or of the 'sharp sleet of arrowy showers' shot by the retreating Parthian army (III.324), but in general it avoids mere sensory gratification and adapts images to its overall didactic design. For instance, the adjective in the phrase 'star new-graven in heaven' (I.253) suggests the star's sculpted permanence, but the 'star' symbolizes the Son, and the adjective describes his moral durability. The adjective in the phrase 'withered sticks' (I.316) is similarly specific about physical quality, and there is even a sad appropriateness in an old man gathering such sticks; but the old man is Satan, and 'withered' takes on the suggestion of moral decay.[30] Description serves moral design in the portrayal of the poem's setting as 'a pathless desert, dusk with horrid shades' (I.296): 'horrid', meaning 'rough' or 'bristling', appropriately characterizes the branches or foliage of trees, but becomes sinister and insubstantial when applied to the more abstract 'shades'.[31] In fact, the 'shades' are also 'horrid' in the sense of 'detestable' – the meaning was available to Milton — through their association with Satan.

Milton's descriptive economy and controlling moral purpose are manifested at their best at the much-admired close of Book I:

> He added not; and Satan bowing low
> His grey dissimulation, disappeared
> Into thin air diffused: for now began
> Night with her sullen wing to double-shade
> The desert, fowls in their clay nests were couched;
> And now wild beasts came forth the woods to roam.

W. W. Robson merely says that this passage possesses 'a certain ideal dignity of its own',[32] and F. W. Bateson, while purporting to disagree with Robson over the poem, praises the 'condensed and laconic art' of its 'bare ascetic style'.[33] But neither critic analyses the language of the passage in sufficient detail to engage the reader's agreement. Bateson notes the 'sarcastic polysyllables' that echo each other ('dissimulation', 'disappeared', 'diffused'), says that the verb 'double-shade' is 'bold and sophisticated', and then lapses unhelpfully into name-dropping: the last line is 'Blakean', and the passage 'spans a whole range of English poetic style from Sidney to Keats'.[34]

The art and dignity of the passage inhere in its stylistic brilliance. The adjective 'grey' suitably blends the fading figure of the old man with the dull light that obscures him. The polysyllables in 'dissimulation' and 'disappeared' are deflated into 'thin air'; and 'thin', associated with Satan, suggests moral inadequacy.[35] The very conglomeration of polysyllables noted by Bateson seems to trace the process of evanescence phonologically. And the succession of 'bowing', 'disappeared', and 'diffused' makes it gradual and yet surprisingly sudden: one minute Satan is 'bowing'; the next he is 'diffused'. The adjective 'diffused' is syntactically and semantically ambiguous: it applies to Satan and to 'air', and the merging wonderfully duplicates Satan's; and since the verb 'diffuse' may mean in physics 'to intermingle or interpenetrate by diffusion' or 'to spread out the body or limbs',[36] Milton uses 'diffused' precisely to catch the moment when Satan is mysteriously both a vapour and a body.[37] 'Double-shade' is wittily exact too, since Satan as shade is present in the physical shade; and his lurking participation is further suggested by the attribution of agency to 'Night'. The predominance of monosyllables in the last three lines of the passage itself intimates physical deprivation; the indefinite plural 'fowls' leaves the desert birds opaquely nondescript; and 'clay' threatens to chill the comfort of 'nests' and 'couched'. The collapsed time perspective in the parallel structures 'for now began / Night . . . to double-shade' and 'now wild beasts came forth' furthers the ominous association of wild beasts with darkness,[38] and the succession of 'began . . . to double-shade' and the more sudden 'came forth' makes the emergence of evil progressively more blatant.[39] In addition, the word 'roam' is strongly reminiscent of accounts of Satan and the fallen angels in *Paradise Lost*.[40] Thus six lines at the close of Book I of *Paradise Regained* reinforce, with considerable verbal delicacy, several of the poem's chief associative and moral patterns, while evoking its bare but richly symbolic landscape.

This analysis of the close of Book I serves to illustrate the misleading ambiguity in calling the poem 'bare' or 'colourless'. The desert setting, the concern with physical strain and deprivation, and even the superficial simplicity of the language, all make for a kind of bareness, just as the lack of colour makes the poem, in the most obvious sense, 'colourless'. But the poem *qua* poem is not therefore to be adjudged bare or colourless. The language used to evoke the bareness is often poetically rich, and the colours blend with the sombre atmosphere and promote the significance of the setting.

But what do critics mean by the term 'bare'? And is the judgement defensible? First it is necessary to become more fully acquainted with the language in which the criticism is made. Mark Pattison finds the style of *Paradise Regained* 'as of set purpose divested of the attributes of poetry', and thinks that Milton has carried simplicity 'to the verge of nakedness'.[41] John Bailey agrees: Milton's style is 'stripped of almost all ornament'.[42] However, Bailey modifies Pattison's metaphor to turn it rhetorically against him (thus deftly avoiding analysis of the poem, but not self-contradiction):

There is no poem in English, perhaps none in any language of the world, which exhibits to the same degree the inherent power of style itself, in its naked essence, unassisted by any of its visible accessories. There are in it, of course, some passages of

117

characteristic splendour, the banquet in the wilderness, the vision of Rome, and others; but a large part of the poem is as bare as the mountains and, to the luxurious and conventional, as bleak and forbidding.[43]

Modern critics may find such a blend of metaphoric quibbling and soaring hyperbole amusing, but many are essentially in agreement with Pattison and Bailey. Though David Daiches commendably discerns some purpose in the writing, he notes that the banquet description shows something of 'the richer passages of *Paradise Lost*', and that the accounts of Greece and Rome are also in the 'grandest style'.[44] For John Carey, 'the stylistic oases (the banquet, the panoramas) are Satan's territory.'[45] And in James G. Taaffe's revised version of Hanford's *A Milton Handbook* the banquet and the storm passages are cited as 'patches' of Milton's abundant, figurative style.[46] Kenneth Muir probably also has the set-piece temptation episodes in mind when he speaks of the 'few "poetic" passages' in the poem, and he also emphasizes the lack of 'poetic ornament' in a style he considers generally 'desiccated and prosaic'.[47]

The terminology used by the critics is of interest. In particular, the metaphor, cited by Rosemond Tuve as an 'accepted Renaissance commonplace',[48] of style as the garment of thought recurs with remarkable frequency in the words 'divested', 'naked', 'stripped', 'unadorned', 'ornament', and even 'accessories'. Other metaphors are used – of richness, refreshment, and abundance – but it is useful to focus on the main one. Tuve equates the 'garment' with imagery, and then points out the inadequacy of the whole metaphoric concept:

It would seem to tempt poets to think of imagery as something added onto meaning, and of 'embroidered' prettiness as a desideratum, with one added temptation – to make garments that could stand alone, so stiff with 'external Gorgiousness' that they needed no body within.[49]

Tuve assumes that a large number of modern critics have misunderstood the metaphor, and suggests that it contains 'the notion of style as a garment in the sense that the flesh is the soul's garment, its bodying-forth or manifestation'.[50] This mystical view is calculated to postulate a more organic relation between style and meaning than is implied in the original metaphor, but fails to circumvent the problem inherent in the metaphor; for style and meaning are inseparable in the artefact, and taking off the 'garment' reveals no 'body'. Tuve's expressing one metaphor in terms of another still leaves her committed to metaphor, and so opens her to her own criticisms: if a poem cannot be analysed into garment-words and body-words, it certainly cannot be analysed into body-words and soul-words. Tuve speaks of possible 'irrelevancy of ornament' and of the 'relation between meaning and ornament',[51] overlooking the fact that the concepts of relevance and relation require at least two separable entities *in* some relation, and the fact that her analysis by metaphor is not able to separate them consistently or clearly. Her whole procedure demands faith in a correspondence between vague notions used by poets to facilitate the act of composition and what can be deduced from their poems by using equally vague notions in analysis. And though she implicitly absolves the poets' ideas from criticism, she is not herself exempt: the inadequacies of ill-defined, general techniques of composition may be obscured in the poem, but they can only become more evident when they are used for analysis.[52]

The critics who use the metaphor of style as a garment, or other metaphors, when discussing *Paradise Regained* are difficult to challenge, if only because their meaning is left obscure. It is important to realize that the metaphors describe not the language but impressions of the language; and that instead of describing the language as objectively as possible these critics offer metaphoric formulations of such descriptions.[53] Thus the linguistic evidence, the basis of the metaphoric description and of the reader's judgement, is withheld. If the reader happens to agree with the metaphoric description, he agrees only with what he thinks he understands. If he disagrees and uses an alternative metaphor to describe the poetic language, the critical dispute has reached a stalemate. Only clearer, more testable descriptions of the language can provide a way out of such critical confrontations, provided, of course, that the confrontation arises in the first place from obscurity or inaccuracy in literary-critical terminology. If a conflict of literary tastes is involved, the whole problem is much more complex, more permanent, and perhaps ultimately insoluble.[54]

To return to the problems raised by the descriptions of the language of *Paradise Regained*: what, precisely, do the critics mean? Pattison is too irritated to say just what he means, and Bailey and Muir say unhelpfully that the poem is 'prosaic' or 'unpoetic'. Perhaps the best clue to their meaning lies in their shared delight in the temptation passages: they all pant after these 'stylistic oases', as John Carey calls them.[55] Adjectives, and in particular sensory adjectives, occur more frequently in these passages than in the rest of the poem, and though it would be oversimple and unkind to allege that critics who admire the passages merely demand 'sensuous', 'adjectival' writing, their taste would appear to include such a demand. Those who simply lament that *Paradise Regained* lacks 'the most obvious graces of poetry', that it is 'divested of the attributes of poetry', or that it contains 'few poetic passages', are applying an undefined, limited, and prejudiced definition of 'poetry' to the poem. They stipulate, by implication, that 'poetry' must possess certain qualities, discover that *Paradise Regained* does not include those particular qualities, and condemn it as 'poetry'. And the attempt to be more accurate and discriminating about the poetic language is hardly helped by singling out some passages and awarding them the distinction of being 'poetic'. Matthew Arnold saw the shortcomings of critics who do no more than this:

They will permit the poet to select any action he pleases, and to suffer that action to go as it will, provided he gratifies them with occasional bursts of fine writing, and with a shower of isolated thoughts and images.[56]

Everyone is welcome to his taste, but, as Christopher Ricks has said, 'we have a right to some degree of substantiation – an insight must be plausible.'[57] If a critical term like 'bare', or any other critical term, is evaluative, then it should be supported, or supportable, by analysis of the language to which it applies; if descriptive, it can be re-expressed by a more technical terminology. Life may be too short to refer every critical remark to a detailed supporting analysis (though to do this could only prove illuminating!); but descriptive clarity is essential in critical controversies. Where it does not change taste, penetrating descriptive criticism can help reveal the nature of taste. In the twentieth-century debate over Milton, many of these problems have been highlighted. The debate survived for a long time on 'dogma, built on unexamined premises and unsupported by demonstration'.[58] Is it not the case that Ricks's *Milton's Grand Style* has answered the anti-Miltonists most convincingly because it examines more of the poetry, in greater detail, than they were prepared to examine?

In his discussion of *Paradise Regained,* Christopher Ricks consistently provides detailed support for his allegation that the poem is written in 'a curiously over-emphatic style' in which 'emphasis is called in to do work which should be done by precision'.[59] The case that Ricks makes amounts to the most precise and important criticism of the poem's style, and perhaps also the clearest exposition of the 'bareness' possibly felt, but not sufficiently demonstrated, by other critics. And Ricks has not been answered: the *Variorum Commentary* merely summarizes his views in a footnote, either because the serious implications of his criticisms are not fully realized, or because the criticisms are acceptable.[60]

Ricks's final statement of his views on *Paradise Regained* is preceded by two others.[61] (It is perhaps worthy of a smile that he should allege that Satan's arguments 'may well depend for their power on nothing more than "what I tell you three times is true" '.)[62] One comment which appeared only in the original version applied to the line 'With sound of harpies' wings, and talons heard' (II.403). 'What is that limp *heard* doing there?', Ricks scolded, 'It blurs the swift vanishing, and adds absolutely nothing to the meaning.'[63] But 'heard' emphasizes that the harpies vanished so quickly that only their sound remained behind; and by not saying *who* 'heard' their sound Milton makes the disembodiment already implied by mere 'wings' and 'talons' even more sinister and unsettling. Ricks was right to excise this particular criticism from his final version.

Ricks's main criticisms of the style of *Paradise Regained* concern alleged forms of tautology. When the Son calls Satan a 'poor miserable captive thrall' (I.411), Ricks comments:

> But how can a thrall be anything but captive, since that is what the word means? And though *poor* and *miserable* are not exact synonyms, that is mainly because there are not in the end any exact synonyms. Yet wasteful writing certainly exists, and it can be argued that *poor* and *miserable* – in a context offered as austerely economical – duplicate too much of each other.[64]

It can also be argued that the context is not offered as austerely economical in quite the way Ricks assumes it should be. He concedes that 'poor' and 'miserable' do not mean the same thing. Might not this be true also of 'thrall' and 'captive'? The Son may be saying that Satan is both captive to his own desires and God's thrall; that Satan is a slave in more senses than one. But this rationalization of the meaning is of secondary importance when the whole expression 'poor miserable captive thrall' is seen to represent the breakdown of strict logical distinctions typical of fervent, and especially denunciatory, speech: one is reminded of such expressions as 'stupid fool' and 'silly idiot'. In achieving the tone of such speech, the writing is not 'wasteful'. The same is true of the tone of violent indignation achieved in the Son's allegation that Satan's answers are 'dark / Ambiguous and with double sense deluding' (I.434–5). Ricks says that if Satan's answers were ambiguous 'it is hardly necessary to tell us that they had a "double sense"'.[65] An ambiguous utterance may delude by means other than its ambiguity, and an ambiguous utterance need not delude (as Ricks knows if anyone does). The Son is making valid logical distinctions.

Ricks is least sensitive to the language of *Paradise Regained* when he alleges that the opening of Book III is the 'least satisfying' of certain passages in which Milton writes badly 'in order to see that Satan comes out badly'.[66] It is hard to imagine Milton writing in order to make Satan come out well, but if Satan comes out badly that need not be because the writing is bad. Ricks quotes the first four lines of Book III, but it is helpful to add the two lines that complete the verse-paragraph:

> So spake the Son of God, and Satan stood
> A while as mute confounded what to say,
> What to reply, confuted and convinced
> Of his weak arguing, and fallacious drift;
> At length collecting all his serpent wiles,
> With soothing words renewed, him thus accosts.

Ricks objects:

'Confounded what to say' contains 'mute', and 'what to reply' adds nothing to 'what to say' except the utterly misleading impression that Satan might speak to someone other than Christ. And the 'weak arguing' is the 'fallacious drift'. At least, it is hard to see what distinctions are being made.[67]

Milton writes 'stood / A while *as* mute confounded what to say' to suggest, with ambiguity appropriate to Satanic cunning, that Satan not only pretends to be mute but also to be confounded what to say. Arguably, too, if the Son has just finished speaking, *he* is 'mute', and Satan, for the moment, is 'as mute' as he is, but for the reason that he is confounded what to say. 'Confounded what to say' does not therefore contain 'mute', but rather explains its cause. Nor is 'weak arguing' identical to 'fallacious drift'. A perfectly valid distinction is being made between the argument in itself and the way it ultimately tends. Charles Jerram, in his 1877 annotated edition of *Paradise Regained,* glosses 'drift' as 'intention', and cites other examples in Shakespeare and Chapman.[68] And the *OED* records two meanings of the word that are relevant: one, basically that suggested by Jerram, where 'drift' means 'the conscious direction of action or speech to some end; the end itself; what one is "driving at"; purpose, intention, object, aim' (I.4); the other, where 'drift' simply means 'meaning, purport, tenor, scope' (I.4.b). Satan's drift is 'fallacious' in that it is deceptive or misleading (*OED*, 2): one is reminded of the 'fallacious fruit' in *Paradise Lost* (IX.1046). And if 'weak arguing' is not the same as 'fallacious drift', 'what to reply' is similarly distinct from 'what to say': Satan could 'say' something without actually answering the Son's allegations. Ricks's suggestion that 'what to reply', coming after 'what to say', gives a misleading impression that Satan might address someone other than the Son is puzzling and far-fetched: is such an abrupt switch at all likely at III.2–3? In fact, Satan immediately continues in direct address of the only other protagonist present, saying rather than replying:

> I see thou know'st what is of use to know,
> What best to say canst say, to do canst do;
> Thy actions to thy words accord, thy words
> To thy large heart give utterance due, thy heart . . .   (III.7–10)

Regarded out of context, such rhetoric may well invite Leavis's description 'mechanical as bricklaying';[69] but it is important to see its function. William E. McCarron has pointed out that Satan's lines contain *sorites* – 'an argument based on a chain of enthymemes whereby the last term of one series becomes the first term in the next' – and that Satan's illogicality is manifest in 'the alteration of meaning of a term from one proposition to the next'.[70] The lines do more than display Satanic sophistry, however: the rhetoric represents Satan's protracted embarrassment as he struggles to restart his flow of words. Characteristically, he does not give an answer; he merely 'accosts' his opponent.

The opening of Book III dramatizes Satan's mental processes between his severe reprimand by the Son and the resumption of temptation. The repetition of the empty 'what to' formula (*ll.* 2, 3) and the pause at the line-break ('Satan stood / A while') highlight the lack of development in his thinking; and the alliterated past-participial adjectives 'confounded', 'confuted', and 'convinced', all linked in turn to the main verb 'stood', fix him in his temporary unresourcefulness. The present participle 'collecting' marks the return of facility, though the ambiguity in 'at length' (*l.* 5) implies the very difficulty of the 'collecting' that the grammar of the preceding lines has dramatized. The adjective 'renewed' signals that Satan's mental *impasse* has been surmounted. The whole passage thus progresses with remarkable psychological realism from the past tense of 'stood' to the boldly stressed present of 'him thus accosts'. And 'accosts' pierces through the pretence of 'soothing' in 'soothing words', betraying the sudden return of Satanic guile. The lines contain what seem to be plain, rather ordinary words, and may even be dismissed as constituting no more than a bridge passage; but they are carefully written. Even the simple opening – 'So spake the Son of God, and Satan stood / A while ... ' – uses the line-break to make 'a while' seem a mere addendum, and so to suggest that Satan is killing time rather than standing firm. The effect is accentuated by the appropriately staunch parallels in 'Tempt not the Lord thy God, he said and stood. / But Satan smitten with amazement fell' (IV.561-2),[71] or by the participial buttress in 'ill wast thou shrouded then, / O patient Son of God, yet only stood'st / Unshaken' (IV.419-21). The stylistic contrast is structurally important too, for standing in *Paradise Regained* assumes moral significance. Standing recurs in temptation contexts (II.298, 350-2, 354-5, for example) to help give the displays their strange, mirage-like fixity. And standing is chiefly used to point the attitudes and status of the protagonists. Satan has lost his 'station' in heaven (I.360), is accused by the Son of standing up to David (III.409-10), and gradually loses moral standing (III.145-7; IV.1-2, 571); whereas the Son ultimately triumphs by standing on the pinnacle (IV. 551-5, 561-2, 571),[72] and is received by angels from his 'uneasy station (VI. 584). Ricks criticizes God's praise of Job, 'Whose constant perseverance overcame / Whate'er his [Satan's] cruel malice could invent' (I.148-9), on the grounds that 'perseverance virtually includes constant, just as malice virtually includes cruel.'[73] Ricks is right about malice being by definition cruel. But perseverance is by no means always constant; and in a poem which regards the perseverance of moral standing as a virtue, it is important that the perseverance should be 'con*stant*'.

Ricks's general observation that much of *Paradise Regained* is written in an emphatic style still retains important truth, however; for a marked tendency towards a form of wordiness is so prevalent that it amounts, in W. W. Robson's words, to a 'habit of emphasis'.[74] Does this justify Ricks's allegations of wasteful writing? Is Robson right to regard the habit of emphasis as a bad habit?

It is rather equivocal of Ricks to say that the style of *Paradise Regained* is not altogether to be equated with the kind of repetitiveness he detects, any more than with the showpieces usually selected to illustrate the poem's economy and Gospel simplicity.[75] If passages of repetitive writing occur as frequently as he suggests, then surely the repetitiveness is an important feature of the style, and one that is purposeful on Milton's part? Ricks's focus does not dilate enough to detect any such purpose, though perhaps he ought to have found a hint when finding the same stylistic feature in every passage he cites. In fact, Ricks strangely detaches the words from their context for scrutiny: he extracts four allegedly lax passages from the Son's speech at I.411–35, and then complains that they occur 'in a context offered as austerely economical'.[76] Austere it may be, but economical it patently is not – at least by Ricks's criterion of economy. This ontological approach to the language of the poem, by no means typical of Ricks's criticism, has the effect, in Helen Gardner's words, of 'putting it under a kind of mental bell-jar';[77] and in this case it smothers the dramatic potential of the words that only the poem's larger atmosphere will release.

Certain adjective groups serve to illustrate the emphatic style:

(1) *adjectives in series*: 'obsure, / Unmarked, unknown', 'the slightest, easiest, readiest recompense' (I.24–5; III.128)[78]

(2) *conjoined adjectives*: 'defeated and repulsed', 'disheartened or dismayed' (I.6, 268)[79]

(3) *adjectives in parallel, near-synonymous phrases*: 'victorious deeds / Flamed in my heart, heroic acts', 'placid aspect and meek regard' (I.215–16; III.217)

(4) *adjectives of moral or heroic connotation*: 'great', 'high', 'pure', 'wise', 'just', 'divine', 'false', 'vain', etc.

Similar formations occur that use nouns and verbs, and in the following discussion these will be related to those that use adjectives.

Adjectives in series are mostly characteristic of the speeches of the Son and Satan. An adjective series occurs only once in the narrator's discourse (I.24–5), and once in Mary's (II.80–2). In Satan's speeches the device is used four times (I.679, 486; II.413–16; III.243), and in the Son's speeches, six times (I.411, 413–16, 434–5; III.127–8, 429; IV.301–2). All of the examples reveal a tendency towards extreme, trenchant statement of the kind that intends to leave nothing unsaid. In the stalemate temptation-rejection pattern of the poem's 'action', such a form of counterstatement introduces an element of traditional fliting, and this is promoted by parody.[80] Satan's accusation that the Son is 'irresolute, unhardy, un-adventurous' (III.243) is answered by the Son's reciprocal accusation that Satan is 'unhumbled, unrepentant, unreformed' (III.429). The Son crushes Satan verbally with the allegation that he is

> deposed,
> Ejected, emptied, gazed, unpitied, shunned,
> A spectacle of ruin or of scorn
> To all the host of heaven;   (I.413–16)

And Satan later retaliates in a similar manner:

> Thou art unknown, unfriended, low of birth,
> A carpenter thy father known, thyself
> Bred up in poverty and straits at home;
> Lost in a desert here and hunger-bit: (II.413–16)

Read aloud, these passages are dramatic. The parallel in 'of ruin or of scorn' steadies the tone into measured, deliberate derision, 'carpenter' is slight-ingly weighted, and the conjoinings in the last two lines of Satan's speech, making quick leaps from the time of the Son's birth to his present hardship, reveal a technique of slander based on a high degree of selection. It is impor-tant that the Son should parody Satan's language, and not just for the sake of rhythmic vigour or tone: his imitation signals that he has seen through the techniques of temptation and denunciation; replying in their style impairs their success.[82]

Some groupings in the style of *Paradise Regained* show a tendency to accumulate parts of speech, either by conjoining them or by arranging them in formations of three or more. The evidence for this may be tabulated as follows:[82]

		Narrator	Son	Satan	Others	Totals
Adjectives	conjoined	17	14	23	3	57
	3 or more	1	4	3		8
Nouns	conjoined	49	34	48	6	137
	3 or more	16	19	43		78
Verbs	conjoined	5	15	17	1	38
	3 or more	3	1	4	2	10
		91	87	138	12	328

Patrick Grant notes the frequent use of the word 'or' in the description of the banquet:[83]

> A table richly spread, in regal mode,
> With dishes piled, and meats of noblest sort
> And savour, beasts of chase, or fowl of game,
> In pastry built, or from the spit, or boiled,
> Grisamber-steamed; all fish from sea or shore,
> Freshet, or purling brook, of shell or fin,
> And exquisitest name . . .
> And ladies of the Hesperides, that seemed
> Fairer than feigned of old, or fabled since
> Of faëry damsels met in forest wide
> By knights of Logres, or of Lyonesse,
> Lancelot or Pelleas, or Pellenore,
> And all the while harmonious airs were heard
> Of chiming strings, or charming pipes and winds
> Of gentlest gale Arabian odours fanned
> From their soft wings, and Flora's earliest smells.   (II.340–6, 357–65)

He develops his observation on the curious indefiniteness achieved by the use of the device into a penetrating explanation of its dramatic function: 'How we are to envisage all these alternatives as part of a sensual temptation, actually presented, is not clear unless we assume that this sensuality is deliberately phantasmagoric.'[84] The non-naturalistic, dream-like presentation achieved by the use of 'or' (and of plural and often indefinite nouns) is significant in that it arranges for Satan's temptations to make their appeal to the non-rational side of the Son's (and reader's) mind. Satan works subtly by vague suggestion rather than by bold definition. And, as in 'Il Penseroso',[85] 'or' makes a connection between things in a way that traces the reflective mind's drift through possibilities.

As the tabulated evidence suggests, conjoining and cataloguing are notable characteristics of the style of *Paradise Regained*. They may be correlated with the thoroughness in the temptation process, which several commentators have stressed. Arnold Stein, for instance, emphasizes the poem's statement of its theme: that a single protagonist will be *fully* tried through *all* temptation by a single antagonist; and that the antagonist will be foiled in *all* his wiles, making possible the celebration of recovered paradise to *all* mankind (I.1–7).[86] Satan throughout *Paradise Regained* is relentlessly energetic, expending his every resource in a nervous, hectic, and increasingly desperate attempt to search out the Son's weakness and overpower him. At the beginning Satan announces excitedly to the fallen angels that he has 'found him, viewed him, tasted him', and realizes that there is 'far other labour to be undergone' than there was when he tackled 'Adam first of men' (II.131–3). It is ironic that after his 'vain battery' has met with 'repulse upon repulse' (IV.20–1) the grammar of his temptation technique continues as he admits that temptation has been pointless:

> Since neither wealth, nor honour, arms nor arts,
> Kingdom nor empire pleases thee, nor aught
> By me proposed in life contemplative,
> Or active, tended on by glory, or fame,
> What dost thou in this world?   (IV.368–72)

Satan's subsequent effort to brainwash the Son into submission involves the same oppressive flurry of the temptations. He threatens the Son:

> Sorrows, and labours, opposition, hate,
> Attends thee, scorns, reproaches, injuries,
> Violence and stripes, and lastly cruel death.   (IV.386–8)

Later still, Satan even reveals his tactics towards his opponents to his opponent:

> Good reason then, if I beforehand seek
> To understand my adversary, who
> And what he is; his wisdom, power, intent,
> By parle, or composition, truce, or league
> To win him, or win from him what I can.

This prompts him to consider the degree of success he has enjoyed with his present opponent:

> And opportunity I here have had
> To try thee, sift thee, and confess have found thee
> Proof against all temptation as a rock
> Of adamant, and as a centre, firm
> To the utmost of mere man both wise and good . . .   (IV.526–35)

He immediately bites his tongue – 'not more' – and presses on with 'another method'. The grammar of his confession is highly significant. The series of nouns reveal his typical ferreting, opportunistic restlessness; and they are checked by the plain statement – part realization, part admission – that opportunity has passed. From this moment the grammar works subtly against Satan. The verb triad ending with 'found thee' (*l.* 532) is an ironic echo not merely of such groups in temptations[87] but of Satan's original 'found him, viewed him, tasted him': the parallel is exact; the excitement of the one has become the dazed realization of the other; the style signals precisely that Satan has got nowhere. He stumbles as though in shock on the words 'proof', 'rock', and 'firm', providing a suggestion of the simile which likens his temptations to waves dashing themselves to froth on the Son's rock-like integrity (IV.18–22). The phrase 'of adamant' (*l.* 534), a timely reminder that the resistance of 'Adam first of men' has been surpassed, seems to slip out unconsciously, in mesmerized surprise. Satan must acknowledge that the person he has slandered as 'unknown, unfriended, low of birth' is, in fact, 'firm . . . wise and good': the Satanic language has been taken over morally. The Son has shown that he resembles his Father in being 'holy, wise and pure' (I.486); and Satan is 'foiled / In all his wiles, defeated and repulsed' (I.5–6).[88] Thus Milton exploits the potential of the repetitive style for irony and parody, and uses its resonances to establish the poem's harmonious structure.

Some of the adjective groups ('holy, wise and pure', etc.) manifest a tendency in the style of *Paradise Regained* for 'moral' and 'heroic' terms to conglomerate:

> Turned recreant to God, ingrate and false. . .   (III.138)

> That people victor once, now vile and base,
> Deservedly made vassal, who once just,
> Frugal, and mild, and temperate, conquered well. . .   (IV.132–4)

>   his virtuous man,
> Wise, perfect in himself, and all possessing,
> Equal to God.   (IV.301–3)[89]

This patterning extends to nouns even more noticeably:

>   displaying
> All virtue, grace and wisdom to achieve
> Things highest, greatest . . .   (I.67–9)

> Therefore with manlier objects we must try
> His constancy, with such as have more show
> Of worth, of honour, glory, and popular praise;
> Rocks whereon greatest men have oftest wrecked. . .   (II.225–8)

> Contempt instead, dishonour, obloquy?   (III.131)

>   . . . who of his own
> Hath nothing, and to whom nothing belongs
> But condemnation, ignominy, and shame?   (III.134–6)

The moral approval or disapproval shown by the Son is absolute – it could hardly be otherwise in a conflict with Satan. The grouping of moral terms suggests the unfragmented firmness of his nature. The syntactic catalogues of his speeches exhibit his unshakeable integrity in dramatic contrast to the scurrying catalogues of Satan's temptations.[90] When close groups of moral terms occur in Satan's speeches, they produce an effect of flattery, or of insincerity incurred by trying to gain the Son's confidence and simultaneously paralyse his critical faculties:

> Thy father, who is holy, wise and pure. . .   (I.486)

>> thy heart
> Contains of good, wise, just, the perfect shape.   (III.10–11)

Elsewhere Satan significantly fragments moral qualities:

> What I see excellent in good, or fair,
> Or virtuous . . .   (I.381–2)

and glibly asserts that God conflates distinctions between good and evil:

>> requires
> Glory from men, from all men good or bad,
> Wise or unwise, no difference, no exemption;   (III.113–15)

The stylistic repetition and accumulation of moral terms is therefore one of the chief means by which *Paradise Regained* dramatizes the manifest intention which Christopher Ricks feels it possesses: 'to contrast the restless temptation by Satan with the massive simplicity and singleness (integrity) of Christ.'[91] Ricks does not detect this stylistic function because he adheres to the oversimplifying principle that the Son should say things only once because Satan says things three times.[92] By presupposing that a stylistic feature must always be interpreted in the same way, Ricks rules out the possibility of stylistically-pointed contrast.

The main objections raised by Ricks to the style of *Paradise Regained* concern near-synonymous or closely-associated noun phrases in apposition to each other. Most of these contain adjectives that might be thought to aggravate the alleged stylistic failure:

>> the happy place
> Imparts to thee no happiness, no joy,
> Rather inflames thy torment . . .   (I.416–18)

> For lying is thy sustenance, thy food. . .   (I.429)

> And what the people but a herd confused,
> A miscellaneous rabble . . .   (III.49–50)

> Hard recompense, unsuitable return
> For so much good, so much beneficence.   (III.132–3)

Ricks's objections are that no logical distinctions are being made between happiness and joy, sustenance and food, and so on, with the result that 'far from getting, as we do when Milton's verse is really working, two for the price of one, we are being fobbed off with one for the price of two.'[93]

Ricks has not really got such a bad bargain as he thinks. These aspects of the style may frustrate cravings for ambiguity, but they are used with considerable psychological insight. K. M. Lea delineates the principle behind their function when she says that 'we have it on the authority of the Bellman that "What I tell you three times is true", and while logically this is not true, psychologically it often is.'[94] It is significant that the style which uses near-synonymous or closely-associated noun phrases in apposition to each other is almost exclusively characteristic of the speech of the two protagonists 'locked in cerebral combat'.[95] In the narrator's language the style represents contemplation:

> In fleshly tabernacle, and human form . . .   (IV.599)

> From thy demoniac holds, possession foul. . .   (IV.628)

In the report of Mary's speech to the Son it reveals private mental fixation:

>   High are thy thoughts
> O son, but nourish them and let them soar
> To what highth sacred virtue and true worth
> Can raise them, though above example high;
> By matchless deeds express thy matchless sire.   (I.229–33)

When the Son meditates on his earthly mission, the style traces the disposition of his thought and discloses his singleness of purpose:

>   myself I thought
> Born to that end, born to promote all truth,
> All righteous things . . .   (I.204–6)

>   victorious deeds
> Flamed in my heart, heroic acts . . .   (I.215–16)

Satan, expert in indoctrination and therefore in the knowledge of the mind's habits, uses the same stylistic device in trying to penetrate the Son's defences:

> Not force, but well-couched fraud, well-woven snares . . .   (I.97)

> Perfections absolute, graces divine . . .   (II.138)

> Now at full age, fulness of time, thy season . . .   (IV.380)[96]

When the Son addresses Satan his thoughts are shaped by the style. What John Broadbent sensitively describes as 'the obsessional repetitions of inner thought'[97] constitute not so much a prepared speech as a kind of externalized rumination, simultaneously revealing and implanting ideas as they form in the mind:

> the happy place
> Imparts to thee no happiness, no joy,
> Rather inflames thy torment . . .   (I.416–18)

> The other service was thy chosen task,
> To be a liar in four hundred mouths;
> For lying is thy sustenance, thy food
> Yet thou pretend'st to truth; all oracles
> By thee are given, and what confessed more true
> Among the nations? that hath been thy craft,
> By mixing somewhat true to vent more lies.   (I.427–33)

> . . . since his word all things produced,
> Though chiefly not for glory as prime end,
> But to show forth his goodness, and impart
> His good communicable to every soul
> Freely; of whom what could he less expect
> Than glory and benediction, that is, thanks,
> The slightest, easiest, readiest recompense
> From them who could return him nothing else,
> And not returning that would likeliest render
> Contempt instead, dishonour, obloquy?
> Hard recompense, unsuitable return
> For so much good, so much beneficence.   (III.122–33)[98]

The Son is convicting Satan by insistent probing of the nerves of his conscience, and doing it with the skill of a good hypnotist. The repetitive style does imply a certain 'leisure and expansiveness',[99] as John Carey has said; but this is by no means incompatible with its function in representing a mind 'engaged in an immense effort at self-control . . . poised, tense, alert, watching any tendency towards elaboration, luxury, self-indulgence'.[100] Arnold Stein's acute observation on one of the Son's speeches can be usefully extended to describe the function of the style that is predominant in *Paradise Regained*: 'As logical argument . . . [it] is far less impressive than it is if we read it as a process of thought defining itself in motion, under the pressure of concrete dramatic circumstances.'[101]

NOTES

1. *Macaulay's Essay on Milton*, ed. Charles Wallace French (1898), p. 24.
2. *Milton* (1879), p. 193.
3. 'Milton: The Last Poems', *ESEA*, **24** (1938), 104.
4. See John Bailey, *Milton* (1915; rpt., 1957), pp. 196, 208, 209; E. M. W. Tillyard, *Milton*, pp. 266, 268; Frank Kermode, 'Milton's Hero', *RES*, NS **4** (1953), 329; Kenneth Muir, *John Milton*, p. 166; Louis L. Martz, '*Paradise Regained*: The Meditative Combat', *ELH*, **27** (1960), 228; Barbara K. Lewalski, *Milton's Brief Epic: The Genre, Meaning, and Art of 'Paradise Regained'* (1966), p. 332; Christopher Ricks, *English Poetry and Prose, 1540–1674*, p. 303.
5. Carey and Fowler, pp. 1070–7; Ricks, op. cit., pp. 303–6.
6. W. W. Robson, 'The Better Fortitude', *The Living Milton*, ed. Kermode, pp. 124–37; F. W. Bateson, '*Paradise Regained*: A Dissentient Appendix', ibid., pp. 138–40; Stewart A. Baker, 'Sannazaro and Milton's Brief Epic', *CL*, **20** (1968), 116–32, especially 125, 127, 131–2; Joan Malory Webber, *Milton and His Epic Tradition* (1979), pp. 168–9.
7. Charles S. Jerram, ed., *Paradise Regained: A Poem in Four Books by John Milton* (1877), p. 141; Kenneth Muir, *John Milton*, p. 166; Barbara K. Lewalski, *Milton's Brief Epic*, p. 335; Carey and Fowler, p. 1074; John Carey, *Milton*, p. 122; William E. McCarron, 'The "persuasive Rhetoric" of *Paradise Regained*', *MQ*, **10** (1976), 19.
8. See Lee S. Cox, 'Food-Word Imagery in *Paradise Regained*', *ELH*, **28** (1961), 225–43; Lewalski, pp. 337, 340, on the light-darkness and martial imagery; Mother Mary Christopher Pecheux, 'Sin in *Paradise Regained*: The Biblical Background', *Calm of Mind: Tercentenary Essays on 'Paradise Regained' and 'Samson Agonistes' in Honour of John S. Diekhoff*, ed. J. A. Wittreich, Jr (1971), pp. 60–1, on the imagery of sin as bondage and servitude. Balachandra Rajan (*The Lofty Rhyme*, p. 126) suggests that the two similes relating to the pinnacle episode celebrate contemplation (Oedipus) and valour (Hercules), thus indicating the Son's perfection of Adam's manhood (*PL*, IV.297: 'For contemplation he and valour formed'). René E. Fortin detects a 'dual and paradoxical' function in the same similes: 'while they initially enlarge the meaning of Christ's victory by offering very rich analogies drawn from the classical world, they also, upon reconsideration, underscore the crucial differences between the pagan and Christian worlds. Hercules and Oedipus are conspicuously imperfect types of Christ, embodying within themselves the self-assertiveness of classical ethics: in Hercules' active heroism and Oedipus' aggressive search for knowledge we are given negative examples of the virtues of patience and humility embodied so perfectly in Christ, the true pattern of the Christian hero' ('The Climactic Similes of *Paradise Regained*': "True Wisdom" or "False Resemblance"?', *MQ*, **7** (1973), 43).
9. Bailey, pp. 208, 209; Robson in *The Living Milton*, ed. Kermode, pp. 125–6; Carey and Fowler, p. 1070; John Carey, *Milton*, p. 122.
10. Carey and Fowler, p. 1073.

11. 'Milton's Hero', *RES*, NS **4** (1953), 329.

12. loc. cit.

13. See p. 175.

14. Lewalski, *Milton's Brief Epic*, p. 331. Frank Kermode ('Milton's Hero', *RES*, NS **4** (1953), 324) and A. S. P. Woodhouse ('Theme and Pattern in *Paradise Regained*', *UTQ*, **25** (1955–6), 176) contrast Satan's 'banquet of sense' with the celestial banquet of IV.588–95. Burton Jasper Weber offers the following account of the structuring of the various temptations, based on the neo-Platonic tripartite soul: 'The first day is a trial of sense, and emotional appeals typify it. The second day is a trial of reason, and that faculty is represented not only by the kind of argument, but by the complexity of the offer, its division and subdivision: reason is the analytic faculty. The third day tries the soul's highest faculty, the intellect. The coercion which characterizes Satan's assaults represents the perverted will. The antithesis to this coercion is fortitude' (*Wedges and Wings: The Patterning of 'Paradise Regained'* (1975), p. 56). Weber points out, however, that each temptation contains subsidiary temptations, and that the temptations interlock and are mutually dependent. The banquet, for instance, 'tests whether the just man will abandon justice for appetitive satisfaction', but also contains temptations of a political and religious nature (ibid., pp. 25, 30–2).

15. 'The Banquet Scene in *Paradise Regained*', *PMLA*, **55** (1940), 776.

16. loc. cit., referring to 'Comus', *ll.* 705–35.

17. *Grace Before Meat, Works*, ed. Lucas (1903–5), **2**, 93–4, quoted in *Variorum Commentary*, **4**, 129. Weber (*Wedges and Wings*, p. 20), comments that 'the sensory element in Satan's opening attack is the temptation to eat in excess of need.'

18. These phrases are taken from John Carey's penetrating analysis of the temptations (Carey and Fowler, pp. 1074–6).

19. Carey and Fowler, p. 1076; and *The Shadow of Heaven*, p. 328.

20. 'Time and Space as Miltonic Symbol', *ELH*, **26** (1959), 506–8.

21. This is Northrop Frye's suggestion, made in *The Prison and the Pinnacle: Papers to Commemorate the Tercentenary of 'Paradise Regained' and 'Samson Agonistes', 1671–1971*, ed. B. Rajan (1973), p. 151.

22. William B. Hunter, Jr offers this explanation for the lack of characterization of God speaking to Adam in *PL*, VIII ('Prophetic Dreams and Visions in *Paradise Lost*', *MLQ*, **9** (1948), 279).

23. Joan Malory Webber stresses the importance of spiritual 'discernment' in *PR*, I.348 and IV.497, and connects this with 'the power of insight, especially at crucial times of spiritual decision' described by St Paul as belonging to the early church (I Corinthians 12:10): *Milton and His Epic Tradition*, pp. 184–5.

24. Carey and Fowler, p. 1076.

25. E. M. W. Tillyard, *Milton*, British Council Pamphlet (rev. edn, 1959), p. 38.

26. Cf. III.326 ('The field all iron cast a gleaming brown'). C. L. Wrenn ('The Language of Milton', *Wiener Beiträge zur englischen Philologie*, **65** (1957), 263) tries to connect the word 'brown' in III.326 with the Old English poetical

word *brun* ('gleaming'). But Milton's line would contain a tautology if 'brown' meant 'gleam'. And Wrenn's case is damaged by other considerations: 'brown' already describes 'iron' aptly; Milton nowhere else uses 'brown' to mean 'gleam'; and the *OED* does not record the noun 'brown' with this meaning, and regards the adjectival meaning as obsolete.

27. Tillyard, *Milton*, British Council Pamphlet, p. 38.

28. *Milton's Brief Epic*, pp. 337–9. Theodore H. Banks (*Milton's Imagery* (1950; rpt., 1969), p. 124) suggests on the evidence provided by Milton's images that 'it might perhaps be said that he thought more in terms of light and darkness than of colour'. Banks also notes that Milton seems to become less conscious of colour in his late poems (p. 127).

29. Burton Jasper Weber disagrees with Northrop Frye's view that the Son cannot shield Satan from God's wrath because the cloud image represents 'the direct opposite of Christ's true nature' ('The Typology of *Paradise Regained*', *MP*, **53** (1956), 237). He argues that 'Satan's faulty knowledge would at least cast doubt on the depth of his contrition – it might even suggest his insincerity – but Frye's deprecation is ill-founded. Satan's view of the Son as saviour tallies with Jesus' own belief' (*Wedges and Wings*, p. 98). But surely Satan is far wrong in thinking that the Son can be *his* saviour? The imagery of clouds in the poem is used in such a way that Frye's view seems more plausible than Weber's.

30. See also my note on *Paradise Regained*, I.314–19, in *N & Q*, NS **25** (1978), 509–10.

31. B. A. Wright (' "Shade" for "Tree" in Milton's Poetry', *N & Q*, **203** (1958), 205–8) shows that Milton uses the word 'shade' for 'shadow' and 'darkness', and as a metonymy for 'tree'. Both meanings enhance the description of the 'horrid shades', and the ambiguity contains the good or evil significance that 'shade', according to Wright, held for Milton. Phillip McCaffrey notes that shade in *Paradise Regained* 'is consistently associated with the desert . . . and consequently with Jesus' spiritual obstacles, his uncertainty and Satan's temptations' ('*Paradise Regained*: The Style of Satan's Athens', *MQ*, **5** (1971), 11). Anne D. Ferry illuminates 'shade' in *Paradise Lost* in *Milton's Epic Voice: The Narrator in Paradise Lost* (1963), pp. 168–76.

32. *The Living Milton*, ed. Kermode, p. 129.

33. ibid., p. 140.

34. loc. cit.

35. Jerram provides a cross-reference to the account of the 'middle region of *thick* air' where Satan and the fallen angels hold sway (*PR*, II.117), and comments that Milton founds his idea of the air as the realm of Satan on Ephesians 2:2 (where Satan is called 'prince of the power of the air'): *Paradise Regained: A Poem in Four Books*, ed. Charles S. Jerram (1877) pp. 101*n*, 67*n*, 68*n*. Ira Clark says that when the Son stands on the pinnacle he 'visually prophesies himself to be the new king of the middle air, the true mediator between God and man. He regains the middle air, that medium which literally and figuratively transfers to man the influence of the prophetic stars and God's providence, the kingdom Satan usurped to obstruct first the old then the new

covenant between God and man' ('Christ on the Tower in *Paradise Regained*', *MQ*, **8** (1974), 107).

36. *OED*, I.5.b; 3.

37. Cf. *PL*, VII.265–6, and 'Samson Agonistes', *l.* 118. D. Douglas Waters notes Milton's consistent use of sorcery as a metaphor for false rhetoric in his poems, and comments that 'in *Paradise Regained* Satan's sorcery emphasizes his disguises, appearances from and disappearances into thin air, his serpentine nature, his trickery, his transportation of the Son of God through the air, and many other antics. As sorcerer-rhetorician he produces optical and auditory illusions that aid his verbal illusions of false rhetoric' ('Milton's Use of the Sorcerer-Rhetorician', *MQ*, **8** (1974), 114).

38. Cf. Psalm 104:20 ('Thou makest darkness, and it is night: wherein all the beasts of the forest do creep forth'). This parallel implies that evil, however it may appear, is in fact part of a divinely-ordained and controlled order.

39. Dustin H. Griffin ('Milton's Evening', *MS*, **6** (1974), 259–76) points out that evening in Milton's poetry is typically 'a time of relaxation . . . a time of gradual process and transition' (268); and that, associated with Eden, it 'creates . . . the very essence of Eden – its harmony, its order, its creativeness and self-renewal as sustained by the powers of heavenly beings' (261). By contrast, the post-lapsarian evening found in Virgil is abrupt and sinister: 'it is a time of cold shadows and dangerous mists. It comes rapidly . . . Evening is not so much sadness and tranquility as the sudden end of a Mediterranean day, lasting but a moment before the hostile night takes control' (262). Griffin shows that the evening in *Paradise Regained* is Virgilian, and cites accounts of similar evenings after the Fall in *Paradise Lost*, X.845–8, XII.628–31 (272–3).

40. See, e.g., *PL*, I.382, 521; II.614; III.430–2; IV.538; IX.82, 575. Cf. *PR*, II.179.

41. *Milton*, pp. 192, 193.

42. *Milton*, p. 208.

43. *Milton*, p. 209.

44. *Milton*, pp. 223, 226.

45. *Milton*, p. 122.

46. 5th edn (1970), p. 257.

47. *John Milton*, p. 166.

48. *Elizabethan and Metaphysical Imagery* (1947), p. 61.

49. loc. cit.

50. loc. cit.

51. op. cit., pp. 64, 65.

52. W. K. Wimsatt, Jr, *The Verbal Icon: Studies in the Meaning of Poetry* (1954), p. 173, remarks that the idea of nature to advantage dressed 'would appear to be the Augustan version of a paradox which literary criticism has so far by no means solved'. The problem arises from the inadequacy of the critical apparatus used, and literary criticism might more fruitfully develop better analytical procedures and terms than worry over unhelpful ones. What applies to nature to advantage dressed applies equally to style as the garment of thought. Rosemond Tuve seems, strangely, to assume the 'living integrity of

thought and expression' that M. H. Abrams has found a post-Romantic commonplace (*The Mirror and the Lamp: Romantic Theory and the Critical Tradition* (1953), p. 291), and yet to persist in ignoring the idea's implications.

53. J. P. Thorne, discussing the notion of a grammar as the explicit statement of a native speaker-hearer's knowledge of his language, makes the point that 'difficult as it is to formulate this statement, it is still easier to formulate it than it is to comment upon the formulation. (A point which might explain much of the obscurity of literary criticism)': 'Stylistics and Generative Grammars', *Journal of Linguistics*, **1** (1965), rpt. in *Linguistics and Literary Style*, ed. D. C. Freeman (1970), p. 190. For related statements see Richard M. Ohmann, 'Prologomena to the Analysis of Prose Style', *Style in Prose Fiction*, ed. H. Martin (1959), rpt. in *Essays in Stylistic Analysis*, ed. Howard S. Babb (1972), p. 43 and *n*; and J. P. Thorne, 'Generative Grammar and Stylistic Analysis', *New Horizons in Linguistics*, ed. John Lyons (1970), p. 189.

54. See C. S. Lewis's account of his disagreement with F. R. Leavis over the style of *Paradise Lost*: *A Preface to 'Paradise Lost'* (1942), p. 134.

55. *Milton*, p. 122.

56. *On the Classical Tradition*, ed. R. H. Super (1960), p. 7. John Press has a lively discussion of prejudiced ideas of 'poetry' in *The Chequer'd Shade: Reflections on Obscurity in Poetry* (1963), pp. 83–4.

57. *Milton's Grand Style*, p. 20. See also his *Poems and Critics* (1966), p. 14.

58. Carey and Fowler, p. 430.

59. *English Poetry and Prose, 1540–1674*, pp. 303, 304. See also *Milton's Grand Style*, p. 17.

60. *Variorum Commentary*, **4**, 312*n*.

61. 'Over-Emphasis in *Paradise Regained*', *MLN*, **76** (1961), 701–4, and an edition of *Paradise Lost and Paradise Regained* (1968), p. xxix.

62. *English Poetry and Prose, 1540–1674*, p. 303. All references are to this version, unless otherwise indicated.

63. *MLN*, **76** (1961), 703.

64. *English Poetry and Prose, 1540–1674*, p. 303.

65. ibid., p. 304.

66. ibid., p. 305.

67. loc. cit.

68. p. 122.

69. *Revaluation*, p. 62.

70. 'The "persuasive Rhetoric" of *Paradise Regained*', *MQ*, **10** (1976), 16, 17.

71. James R. McAdams, 'The Pattern of Temptation in *Paradise Regained*', *MS*, **4** (1972), 189, states the opinion held by many critics when he says that Christ's standing on the pinnacle is to be seen as 'signifying his full recognition of his nature'. Ira Clark, 'Christ on the Tower in *Paradise Regained*', *MQ*, **8** (1974), 106, remarks that 'the Son's stand during Satan's fall is the central emblem of *Paradise Regained*.'

72. A. B. Chambers says that 'on the pinnacle, for the first time in the poem, Christ exercises powers exceeding those of man. He becomes *Theanthropos*, and Satan, smitten with amazement, falls': 'The Double Time Scheme in

Paradise Regained', *MS*, **7** (1975), 202. Burton Jasper Weber comments that 'Satan's punishment is his progressive deterioration; he is punished internally, and it is significant that his story ends with a fall which – whatever its further meanings – is a realistically probable consequence of psychological exhaustion' (*Wedges and Wings*, p. 89).

73. *English Poetry and Prose, 1540–1674*, p. 305.
74. *The Living Milton*, ed. Kermode, p. 126.
75. op. cit., pp. 305–6.
76. ibid., p. 303.
77. *The Business of Criticism* (1959), p. 18.
78. Charles S. Jerram, ed., *Paradise Regained* (1877), p. 140*n*, comments that 'Milton is rather fond of this effect', cites other examples in *PL*, II.185, V.899, and notes the parallel in *Hamlet* ('unhouseled, disappointed, unaneled').
79. John Carey notes that conjoining is popular throughout the poem, especially in Satan's speeches; and that triple groupings of adjectives also occur (Carey and Fowler, p. 1072). His observations are extended and corroborated here.
80. D. M. Rosenberg, 'Parody of Style in Milton's Polemics', *MS*, **2** (1970), 116, shows how Milton in his prose often caricatures the style of his opponents. John Broadbent, 'Milton's Rhetoric', *MP*, **56** (1959), 231, notes that in *Paradise Lost* 'Satan's tempting rhetoric is a parody of the Father's'. Stanley E. Fish, 'Inaction and Silence: The Reader in *Paradise Regained'*, *Calm of Mind*, ed. Wittreich, p. 40, detects a parody of Satan's language in the Son's speech at *PR*, IV.113–21. It may be added that the Son's phrase 'swelling epithets thick-laid' (I.343) is scornfully parodic with its thick-laid epithets.
81. Patrick Cullen, *Infernal Triad: The Flesh, the World, and the Devil in Spenser and Milton* (1974), pp. 133–4, 136, 137, 143, 168, makes relevant comments on parody in *Paradise Regained*. He remarks that one of the Son's replies is designed 'to turn on Satan himself the mirror Satan has perversely used' (p. 155).
82. Where a conjoined group forms part of a series of three or more of a part of speech it is counted once, with the series.
83. *Images and Ideas in Literature of the English Renaissance* (1979), p. 147.
84. loc. cit. See also Carey and Fowler, pp. 1074–5.
85. See pp. 20–1, above.
86. *Heroic Knowledge: An Interpretation of 'Paradise Regained' and 'Samson Agonistes'* (1957), pp. 3–4, 6. See also Jon S. Lawry, *The Shadow of Heaven*, pp. 305, 306, and Roger H. Sundell, 'The Narrator as Interpreter in *Paradise Regained'*, *MS*, **2** (1970), 84. John M. Steadman has shown that the Son is required 'to *sustain* the menaces of adversity and *abstain* from the allurements of prosperity' (' "Like Turbulencies": The Tempest of *Paradise Regain'd* as Adversity Symbol', *MP*, **59** (1961), 84); and that, unlike Paris and Hercules, the Son rejects all the offers of the *vita activa*, *contemplativa*, or *voluptuosa* ('*Paradise Regained*: Moral Dialectic and the Pattern of Rejection', *UTQ*, **31** (1962), 418–19).

87. I.474; III.75, 332; IV.227, e.g. See also the opposed verb triads in the storm episode, which counter evil with good (IV.423–4, 427–9).

88. Weber (*Wedges and Wings*, pp. 40–1) comments: 'Satan ended the first temptation by asking Jesus to imitate the Father, "holy, wise and pure" (I.468). Now, calling Jesus "good, wise, just" (the words are different, but the qualities are the same), Satan attributes divine sinlessness to Jesus.' Edward Le Comte describes Satan as 'confusing and confused, a would-be Christologist who grapples with some real problems – and loses' ('Satan's Heresies in *Paradise Regained*', *MS*, **12** (1978), 263).

89. See also II.468; IV.143, 535, e.g.

90. See II.422, 427, 429–31, and the Son's reply in II.446, 460, 464, 467. John Broadbent notes that the Son 'piles up *exempla* to oppose Satan's *exempla*, knock-for-knock' ('The Private Mythology of *Paradise Regained*', *Calm of Mind*, ed. Wittreich, p. 85).

91. *English Poetry and Prose, 1540–1674*, p. 303.

92. loc. cit.

93. op. cit., pp. 304–5.

94. 'The Poetic Powers of Repetition', *Proceedings of the British Academy*, **55** (1969), 65.

95. The phrase is John Carey's (Carey and Fowler, p. 1071). Jackson I. Cope, '*Paradise Regained*: Inner Ritual', *MS*, **1** (1969), 51–65, views the poem as 'a religious ritual', and argues that it cannot adequately be described as a 'drama of the mind' because of differences between drama and ritual. Richard Douglas Jordan, '*Paradise Regained* and the Second Adam', *MS*, **9** (1976), 273, admits that 'it is not a realistic drama of psychologically complex characters engaged in an intellectual struggle for uncertain victory', and describes it as 'a biblical drama, a ritual drama, which is also . . . something more than simply a ritual'. The stylistic evidence corroborates Jordan's view: the patterning suggests ritual, but is also the means of dramatizing the battle of minds between the Son and Satan.

96. See also I.69; II.410–11; III.217, 248–9; IV.266.

97. 'The Private Mythology of *Paradise Regained*', *Calm of Mind*, ed. Wittreich, p. 85. Broadbent makes many acute observations on the poem's psychology, though he is least convincing when trying to read it as a covert documentary on Milton's sexual hang-ups. As this approach is followed the mythology becomes very private indeed. Stewart A. Baker, 'Sannazaro and Milton's Brief Epic', *CL*, **20** (1968), 131–2, considers that the stress on meditation in *Paradise Regained* is responsible for the poem's 'repetitive and formally symmetrical structure'. Baker seems to mean only the narrative repetition of key episodes such as Jesus' baptism by this phrase, though he could well have extended his observation to include stylistic details.

98. See also IV.124–5, 173.

99. Carey and Fowler, p. 1072.

100. Louis L. Martz, '*Paradise Regained*: The Meditative Combat', *ELH*, **27** (1960), 233. Martz's own style shows how contagious Milton's is.

101. *Heroic Knowledge*, p. 80.

CHAPTER SIX

'Samson Agonistes'

'Samson Agonistes' resembles *Paradise Regained* in style. The similarity is reflected in impressionistic descriptions of the two poems: 'Samson' has also been said to be 'plain', 'bare', 'dry', and 'austere'.[1] Again, the style tends to be taken as evidence of a lack of inspiration in the ageing Milton. Richard Cumberland in 1785 puts it as kindly as he can, saying that Milton 'curbed his fancy'.[2] Mark Pattison is more aggressive: 'his power over language was failing.'[3] Of course, such statements presuppose a post-Restoration date for the poem's composition, which is by no means certain. And, more crucially, they show the critics who make them to be unwilling either to see that their ideas of 'poetry' are ill-defined, inflexible, and prejudiced, or to inspect the poem in order to ascertain how its language functions. When, on the other hand, Alan Rudrum examines the language of the poem, he concludes that it accords with Milton's subject and manifests the qualities of 'strength and honesty – and lack of superficial "attractiveness"' that are appropriate to a mind 'purged of self-deception and compromise'.[4] Mary Ann Radzinowicz finds the style suitable both to the biblical fable and to 'thought, speech, and expression of passion', and notes that at one point 'the effort to order thought is expressed by a perpetual disturbance of normal word order'.[5] Only when the language of the poem is subjected to this kind of investigation can literary criticism really begin.

Few commentators reveal which features of the language of 'Samson' make it 'austere'. Dr Johnson, however, expands his description of the style usefully when he speaks of 'the language, which, in imitation of the ancients, is through the whole dialogue remarkably simple and unadorned, seldom heightened by epithets, or varied by figures'.[6] He has been shown to be wrong about the imagery, which is plentiful;[7] but he is right about the epithets. His statement is an impressionistic one, and is not supported by evidence, but the intuition behind it is exact. Adjectives constitute only 10 per cent of the words in 'Samson Agonistes', and the figure in itself provides support for Hanford's claim that 'Samson' is 'the exact counterpart of *Paradise Regained,* the work to which it is most closely related in style and art'.[8]

It must be stressed that this figure does not constitute reliable evidence for a late composition date for 'Samson', even if one takes into account the gradual fall in adjective frequency throughout *Paradise Lost* to the low level of *Paradise Regained.* The figure represents only adjectives, and at an abstract numerical level. Milton's poems on the University Carrier, for instance, contain a low adjective frequency, but they are much earlier than 'Samson' and very different in style. William Riley Parker and Chauncey B. Tinker note a stylistic and spiritual affinity between 'Samson' and the penitential psalms versified by Milton in 1648,[9] and Mary Ann Radzinowicz lists a sufficient number of parallels between the whole book of Psalms and 'Samson' to suggest pervasive influence.[10] And E. M. W. Tillyard and John T. Onuska, Jr detect in 'Samson' something of the mood of the blindness sonnet 'When I consider how my light is spent',[11] dated by Carey and Fowler and by the *Variorum Commentary* as 1652. Both Milton's versified psalms and his sonnets are, like 'Samson', characterized by a low adjective frequency.

Several problems arise from the application of stylistic criteria to chronology. These usually derive from the assumptions that lie behind the whole procedure. William Riley Parker has pointed out that Ants Oras, simply by assuming in the first place that 'Samson' is a late work, overlooks the fact that much of the evidence he collects from Milton's prosody would make 'Samson' nearer, in fact, to 'Comus' than to *Paradise Regained.*[12] However, the initial thesis for which evidence may be collected is not the only thing to be considered. The main assumption behind the use of style in deciding chronology is that an author's style must manifest the most obvious – usually linear – trend throughout his works, irrespective of the claims of decorum on each one.[13] Mary Ann Radzinowicz states the problem involved: 'it would only be possible to date from stylistic features if all relevant stylistic traits were accurately computed, while all stylistic traits linked to genre or decorum were omitted.'[14] (Even so, she shows a readiness to infer the composition date of 'Samson' from style.[15]) The stylistic evidence presented in this chapter, then, is not *per se* evidence for a late date for 'Samson'. To interpret it as such would be altogether premature: more knowledge about style and its determinants is needed before reliable assumptions based on stylistic evidence can be made about chronology. At the moment, anyway, John Spencer Hill's scepticism seems healthy: he says outright, 'I am not convinced that Milton's imagery and poetic style provide any real help in determining the date of *Samson Agonistes*.'[16]

Hill also states that 'nothing whatever is known for certain about the composition of *Samson Agonistes*,' and that 'any attempt . . . to establish when the poem was written is necessarily grounded on inference and speculation.'[17] This is true. Whatever scholars may *believe*, Milton's nephew Edward Phillips still states the *known* truth about the date of 'Samson':

It cannot certainly be concluded when he [Milton] wrote his excellent Tragedy entitled *Samson Agonistes*, but sure enough it is that it came forth after the publication of *Paradice lost*, together with his other Poem called *Paradice regain'd* . . .[18]

Paradise Regained and 'Samson Agonistes' were published together in 1671, and the two poems share certain stylistic features. Their adjective usage is similar in several respects, and the similarity extends beyond mere frequency of occurrence. Even if words like 'dark', 'fiery', and 'crystalline' are grouped with colour adjectives, the category so defined contains only 2.1 per cent of the adjectives in 'Samson'. If the category is strictly defined – if only adjectives that denote colours of the spectrum are taken to be 'colour adjectives' – then only 11, or 0.8 per cent, of the adjectives denote colour. This is exactly the same percentage as that in *Paradise Regained*. And, as in *Paradise Regained*, colour is reduced virtually to black and white: the comment by Geoffrey and Margaret Bullough that 'there is little precise form and colour . . . merely light and dark, translucency and opaqueness'[19] could be applied generally to both poems. Samson is tortured by an obsession with an impenetrable 'dark' – he uses the word seven times in lines 1–86 – and this is taken up by the Chorus's phrase 'inseparably dark' (*l.* 154), which provides a sympathetic echo of Samson's 'irrecoverably dark' (*l.* 81) but chides him implicitly for no longer being 'separate' to God (*l.* 31). The prevailing gloomy atmosphere of the poem is offset by suggestions of pure, cool relief that is remote from Samson: 'the cool crystalline stream', 'the clear milky juice', 'snowy alp' (*ll.* 546, 550, 628). This is a healing coolness, John Carey observes, pathetically felt in the 'lavers pure, and cleansing herbs' and 'shade / Of laurel ever green, and branching palm' (*ll.* 1727, 1734–5) of Manoa's funeral preparations.[20] The emphasis is on coolness rather than light, just as the adjective 'fiery' (*ll.* 27, 549, 1690), associated with heavenly omens and with a fervent sense of divine mission,[21] stresses heat rather than light. Samson's tomb will be shaded by 'laurel ever green', the symbol of his perpetual fame; but during the main part of the poem, as long as Samson is alive, a stark, cold, chiaroscuro setting evokes no more than the outlines of a blind man's imagination and reflects constantly on the hardship of his plight.

Much of the sense impression in the poem creates an awareness of Samson's dominant presence, and particularly of his blindness. It is appropriate that it should not be a very 'visual' poem.[22] It is when Samson is dead that the Messenger's long account of the 'spectacle' (*l.* 1604) at the temple of Dagon (*ll.* 1596–1659) and Manoa's description of Samson's body 'soaked in his enemies' blood' and encrusted with 'clotted gore' (*ll.* 1725–8) engage the visual imagination. When Samson is alive, even the Chorus's description of Dalila's approach is allowed no more than an indirect visual impact:

> But who is this, what thing of sea or land?
> Female of sex it seems,
> That so bedecked, ornate, and gay,
> Comes this way sailing
> Like a stately ship
> Of Tarsus, bound for th'isles
> Of Javan or Gadire
> With all her bravery on, and tackle trim,
> Sails filled, and streamers waving,
> Courted by all the winds that hold them play,
> An amber scent of odorous perfume
> Her harbinger, a damsel train behind;
> Some rich Philistian matron she may seem,
> And now at nearer view, no other certain
> Than Dalila thy wife.   (*ll.* 710–24)

An adjective frequency of 17.4 per cent of the words, and such phrases as 'of sea or land', 'of Tarsus', 'of Javan or Gadire', and 'with all her bravery on', are clearly characteristic of a thoroughgoing descriptive style. But there is no definite colour in Dalila's elaborate dress, and when Anne D. Ferry thinks this the 'most nearly pictorial "view"'[23] in the poem she overlooks not merely the eventual visual climax of the action as reported by the Messenger but the stylistic subtlety of this particular passage. The opening question, internal semantic conflicts ('who . . . what thing . . . female of sex it . . .'), equivocatory conjoinings ('sea or land', 'Javan or Gadire'), and 'seems' and 'may seem', all cloud over the possibility of sharp visualization until, with a shock arranged by the dramatic suspense of the Chorus's teasing syntax, Dalila emerges clearly to an understandably astounded Samson. The comparison of a woman to a ship is traditional,[24] but Milton's art transcends the commonplace. First, and most obviously, he uses words that apply with clever ambiguity to Dalila and to a ship: 'bedecked' is a fine pun, and though the *OED* cites only nineteenth-century examples for 'sailing' implying the sweeping, dignified movement of a woman or of a ship

under sail,[25] the comparison's traditionalness and the constraints of the immediate context argue for the applicability of this meaning to 'comes this
way sailing'. The *OED* also records that 'stately' is frequently used to refer
to a ship's motion, that 'trim' may imply neatness of dress or readiness to
sail, and that 'streamers' may be either flags or long, flowing ribbons.[26]
Milton makes Dalila even more suspicious than these ambiguities imply:
'gay' may be a conventional epithet of praise for women in poetry, or it
may describe Dalila's brightly-coloured dress; but it may also suggest her
addiction to pleasure, with overtones of her immorality.[27] 'Sailing' may imply a deliberate, bold movement,[28] and beneath the 'bravery' of fine clothes
may lurk bravado.[29] Does 'waving' not suggest deliberate action calculated
to attract attention? Is 'stately' perhaps loaded with threatening memories
of Dalila's association with the Philistine state? Does the description of
Dalila not remind the reader of accounts of Satan likened to a sea-voyager or
to a fleet on the horizon in *Paradise Lost*, as Helen Damico has suggested?[30]
How evil Dalila is may be uncertain, but the word 'rich' in line 722 certainly tilts the balance in favour of Samson's allegation that she accepted
bribes (*ll.* 389, 831, 958, 1114), which she has denied (*l.* 849).[31] And the
'scent' that heralds her approach should be soured by memories of the
'scent' of gold that provoked her to treachery (*ll.* 388–91). The high adjective frequency of the passage, in a poem that contains few adjectives, itself
suggests Dalila's overdone artifice. If the poem's prevalent style represents
Samson's plight, the style of lines 710–24 suggests Dalila's irrelevance to,
or complete lack of understanding of, his spiritual struggle. Semantic repetition serves to mock her elaborateness: 'bedecked', 'ornate', and 'gay'
partly duplicate each other, and the 'amber scent' *is* the 'odorous perfume'.
The symmetrical balancing of phrase units within lines – 'With all her
bravery on, and tackle trim, / Sails filled, and streamers waving' – matches
the contrivance of her appearance between harbinger and train. Even in the
rhythms of the passage – irregular, half-syncopated – one may detect the
bobbing motion of a ship on the tide, but also a quality of fitful unpre-
dictability that invites suspicion. William Empson's view of Dalila as a
'deeply-wronged wife'[32] does not take into account Milton's highly
ambiguous presentation of Dalila in these and other lines.

The complexity of lines 710–24 suggests that Dalila is not, as one or two
critics have thought, simply a comic figure.[33] She is ridiculous and vain;[34]
but latently, potentially, she is deceitful. Mary Ann Radzinowicz has
rightly emphasized that 'Samson treats her with utmost seriousness and argues with her, if hotly also gravely.'[35] The stylistic subtlety of the description of her arrival accords with the subtlety of Milton's general portrayal of
her character. As Anthony Low has said:

One is never quite sure just how much she is telling the truth, or where she is lying; how much she is the conscious temptress and how much the victim of her own passions . . . Dalila quite properly remains inscrutable. It is precisely this ambiguity that gives her so much force as a character in the play . . . she remains a woman, with a human subtlety that still draws our sympathy and baffles certainty – not about her crime, but about the nature of her character and motivations.[36]

The consistency of the ship simile with Dalila's character largely answers Balachandra Rajan's complaint about its 'digressiveness':[37] if it moulds essential traits of character it can hardly be digressive. And if the simile, as he notes, fits into the sea imagery in the poem, then it is even less digressive. Rajan also feels that the simile is 'an ironic culmination of Samson's earlier comparison of himself to a vessel "gloriously rigg'd" ',[38] and John Carey thinks that the two ship images draw Samson and Dalila into 'an implied, and disturbing, parallelism'.[39] But Milton makes the two images quite different from each other. Samson's 'vessel' is his body (as in I Thessalonians 4:4), and he speaks humbly and with self-reproach for misusing his God-given strength:

> How could I once look up, or heave the head,
> Who like a foolish pilot have shipwrecked,
> My vessel trusted to me from above,
> Gloriously rigged . . . ?

(*ll.* 197–200)

Dalila, by contrast, is over-elaborately dressed, partly alluring, partly ridiculous, and possibly deceitful, and the flamboyant style of lines 710–24 is very different from the sober style of Samson's speech. Thomas Kranidas is right to say that Dalila's 'ship' is 'a humanly adorned creation, different from Samson's'.[40]

Samson cannot see, and the 'scent' of Dalila's bribe brings out his scorn for the 'scent' of her perfume. As a Nazarite he has largely scorned the delights of taste, as well as of other senses:

> *Chorus*: Desire of wine and all delicious drinks,
> Which many a famous warrior overturns,
> Thou couldst repress, nor did the dancing ruby
> Sparkling, out-poured, the flavour, or the smell,
> Or taste that cheers the heart of gods and men,
> Allure thee from the cool crystalline stream.
> *Samson*: Wherever fountain or fresh current flowed
> Against the eastern ray, translucent, pure
> With touch ethereal of heaven's fiery rod
> I drank, from the clear milky juice allaying
> Thirst, and refreshed; nor envied them the grape
> Whose heads that turbulent liquor fills with fumes.

(*ll.* 541–52)

With an adjective frequency of 18.2 per cent of the words, this passage about temptation is certainly descriptive; but it is not indulgent or uncontrolled. In fact, it is very much about the government of sensuousness. The wine is represented as attractive, categorized with 'delicious drinks', and regarded as 'wine that maketh glad the heart of man' (Psalm 104:15). Two of the adjectives in the series 'dancing . . . sparkling, out-poured', and the three nouns 'flavour', 'smell', and 'taste', linger behind the 'ruby', like an aftertaste inviting acknowledgement. (One recalls that Comus's drink is an 'orient' [i.e. shining] liquor in a 'crystal glass' that 'flames and dances'; whereas Sabrina sits 'under the glassy, cool, translucent wave'.[41]) 'Taste' partly duplicates 'flavour', but Milton seems to be representing the Chorus's momentary intoxication, while preserving the distinction between the wine's permanent 'flavour' and an instance, an act, of 'taste'. The noun triad 'flavour', 'smell', 'taste', follows the experience of taking the wine, recalling its flavour, smelling its bouquet, and tasting it. But such psychological enticements are checked by 'thou couldst repress', which restores stability after the precariously-poised 'overturns'; and the verb 'allure' is negated in advance. Samson, as a Nazarite, prefers cool, pure water to wine:[42] the adjectives 'translucent, pure' balance 'sparkling, out-poured', and the negative force of 'thou couldst repress' gives way to the simple 'I drank'. The latter verb is also effectively delayed: the water's sensuous qualities are displayed, with the postponed adjective 'ethereal' making the 'touch' of the 'fiery' rod magically hot and cold; and *then* Samson says 'I drank'. The positive act, like the act of repression, is a deliberate and controlled one. 'Refreshed' wittily represents the effect of the 'fresh' water on the partaker. Samson seems more puritanical than the Chorus, which can hardly conceal delight in wine. But the style allows full realization of the effects of the wine while rejecting it: it may be clear from 'the grape / Whose heads that turbulent liquor fills with fumes' that the 'heads' belong to the antecedent 'them', but the succession of 'grape / Whose heads' is appropriately befuddling. The style arranges for will to control sense. As so often in 'Samson Agonistes', the writing admits of a lyrical mimeticism, but also represents the austerity of Samson's moral code.

The treatment of the senses of hearing and touch in 'Samson Agonistes' is designed to make the reader aware of the hero's sightless, intent presence. The moon is 'silent' to Samson (*l.* 87), not merely in the technical sense of 'not shining' or in the Latinate sense of 'inactive',[43] but because it is awesomely quiet. He is sadly dependent on the Chorus's reports of what is happening around him. When for instance, Dalila is finally announced, Samson's panic-stricken yell, 'My wife, my traitress, let her not come near me', leads immediately to an ironic reflection on his tragic passivity: 'Yet on she moves, now stands and eyes thee fixed' (*ll.* 725–6). The flat-adverb form 'fixed' is tellingly ambiguous: Dalila looks at him 'fixed(ly)', but he is so 'fixed' that he can do nothing about it. (When he finally recovers *constantia* between the pillars, his role is reversed: 'with head a while inclined, / And eyes fast fixed he stood', *ll.* 1636–7).⁴⁴ Samson's only defence of his dignity is to forbid Dalila to touch his hand, and to remain 'deaf' to her words (*ll.* 951–3, 960–1). He is, of course, painfully aware of 'words' throughout the poem.⁴⁵ He blames himself relentlessly for displaying the 'shameful garrulity' of a 'blab' (*ll.* 490–6) in disclosing his secret to Dalila, herself full of deceitful words (*ll.* 235, 729, 905–6, 947, 1066). It is remorse for having sacrificed everything for a mere 'word' (*l.* 200) that prevents him from accepting the 'apt words' and 'healing words' of the Chorus (*ll.* 184, 605); and yet, being blind, he finds himself vexingly dependent on words:

> I hear the sound of words, their sense the air
> Dissolves unjointed ere it reach my ear.   (*ll.* 176–7)

The phrase 'dissolves unjointed' obtrudes from stark monosyllables. The half-rhyme of 'air' and 'ear' corresponds to the difficulty of bringing 'air' to 'ear'. Does the 'air' dissolve the 'sense', or vice versa? Is it the 'sound' that is 'unjointed', or the 'sense'? The syntax feelingly dissolves and disjoints. At the end of the poem, it is dramatically important that the catastrophe should take place offstage, and not merely in accordance with the conventions of Greek drama: it is then that, Samson's recovery of active heroism makes of Manoa and of the Chorus the kind of passive, questioning, nervous hearers that he himself has been.

Samson depends as much on touch as on hearing, and the whole poem develops a similar sympathetic dependence in the reader. Samson *feels* thoughts as 'a deadly swarm / Of hornets armed' that attack him and 'mangle [his] apprehensive tenderest parts', raising 'dire inflammation' (*ll.* 19–20, 623–6);⁴⁶ and he thinks of a cure for his torment in terms of touch, whether 'sedentary numbness craze [his] limbs' or 'death's benumbing opium' (*ll.* 571, 630). The Chorus describes Dalila as 'a manifest serpent by her sting', but suggests also that Samson is suffering from 'the secret sting of amorous remorse' (*ll.* 997, 1007). The violence with which Samson expresses his mental torment is evident also in his refusal to allow Dalila even to touch his hand (*ll.* 951–2). Dalila's wish to touch him perhaps represents no more than an offer of affectionate guidance, but since he, presuming to be led by God (*l.* 638), has been led captive by enemies (*ll.* 365, 1623, 1629, 1635), he refuses her offer. After divine guidance has been invoked by the Chorus (*l.* 1428), Samson is led by God, rather than by the 'unsuspicious' Philistine (*l.* 1635), to pull down the pillars. Guidance, an important theme in 'Samson Agonistes', is announced at the beginning of the poem:

> A little onward lend thy guiding hand
> To these dark steps, a little further on. (*ll.* 1–2)

The quality in these lines memorably described by Dr Johnson as 'graceful abruptness'[47] results from the repetition of 'a little onward . . . a little further on', which suggests the intense concentration and the hesitant, groping movements of a blind man. It is a strangely disembodied 'hand', somehow constantly 'guiding', that leads Samson to the stark silhouette of the steps; and though it may be, most obviously, the hand of the Philistine guide, its mysteriousness has led several commentators to suggest that it is possibly the hand of God.[48]

In the earlier part of the poem, it is not a sense of divine guidance but the impression of Samson's confinement in the Philistine prison that creates the strongest awareness of touch. Samson's role as deliverer is reversed as he speaks of

> my task of servile toil,
> Daily in the common prison else enjoined me,
> Where I a prisoner chained, scarce freely draw
> The air imprisoned also, close and damp,
> Unwholesome draught . . . (*ll.* 5–9)

The adjectives 'servile', 'common', and 'unwholesome' express his indignation and depression, but his thoughts cannot break free from the obsessive linkage of 'prison', 'prisoner', and 'imprisoned'. His passive servility is ruthlessly enforced by 'confined', 'chained', and 'imprisoned', and the placing of these adjectives, and of 'close and damp', after their nouns, adds weight to an already cramping degree of qualification. The style sensitively follows Samson's sensations as he feels them.[49] The position of the half-echoing adverbs 'daily' and 'scarce freely' tugs the lines further into the irregular rhythms of anguished speech.[50] Just how much energy is pent up in the words is realized with the contrast that follows:

> but here I feel amends,
> The breath of heaven fresh blowing, pure and sweet,
> With day-spring born . . . (*ll.* 9–11)

Rhythmically, grammatically, and symbolically, these lines relax tension and bring a glimmer of optimism.[51] 'Blowing' breaks the fetters of the past-participial adjectives, and 'pure and sweet' makes compensation for 'close and damp'. The flat-adverb form 'fresh' is ambivalent: the 'breath of heaven' blows freshly or afresh, its nature unaltered by time or by the perceiver. (One recalls Hopkins exclaiming at the beauties of nature, 'These

147

things, these things were here and but the beholder / Wanting.'[52]) The double meaning alerts the reader to the enchantment of the spiritually refreshing breeze that Samson feels.

The dramatic conformity of grammar to the nuances of thought and sensation represents one of Milton's major stylistic achievements in 'Samson Agonistes'.[53] A passage in which the Chorus contrasts Samson's past with his present will serve to illustrate it further:

> See how he lies at random, carelessly diffused,
> With languished head unpropped,
> As one past hope, abandoned,   120
> And by himself given over;
> In slavish habit, ill-fitted weeds
> O'er-worn and soiled;
> Or do my eyes misrepresent? Can this be he,
> That heroic, that renowned,   125
> Irresistible Samson? whom unarmed
> No strength of man, or fiercest wild beast could withstand;
> Who tore the lion, as the lion tears the kid,
> Ran on embattled armies clad in iron,
> And weaponless himself,   130
> Made arms ridiculous, useless the forgery
> Of brazen shield and spear, the hammered cuirass,
> Chalybean-tempered steel, and frock of mail,
> Adamantean proof . . .

Adjectives constitute 25.5 per cent of these words – more than double the poem's average of 10 per cent – and they have a significant function in the style of the passage. In the first part, before the question in line 124, nine participial adjectives fix Samson in still-life, sketching his posture and gradually evoking sadness.[54] A meditative stillness is further induced by the partial semantic duplications in 'slavish habit' and 'ill-fitted weeds', and in 'at random' and 'carelessly diffused'. What Una Ellis-Fermor calls 'the rhythms of flat, inert despair'[55] are symptomatic of a more basic syntactic sluggishness. It is possible to stop the first sentence at points which mark complete sense units: See how he lies | at random | carelessly diffused | with languished head | unpropped | as one past hope | abandoned | and by himself given over | in slavish habit | ill-fitted weeds | o'er-worn and soiled. The syntactic junctures come with the force of dramatically placed rests in music, so that the sentence moves fitfully, as though indifferent to its progression, and each pause seems about to submit finally to awesome silence. Dr Johnson's comment on lines 594–8 –

> So much I feel my genial spirits droop,
> My hopes all flat, nature within me seems

> In all her functions weary of herself;
> My race of glory run, and race of shame,
> And I shall shortly be with them that rest –

is that 'it is not easy to give a stronger representation of the weariness of despondency.'[56] His comment could apply equally to lines 118–23. Samson is in the Slough of Despond.[57] The placing of the past-participial adjectives after their nouns or pronouns ('diffused', 'unpropped', 'abandoned', 'given over', 'o'er-worn', 'soiled') imposes a burden that sinks him deeper in the mire. His very clothes reflect his state of mind: the syntax allows the suggestion that both are 'o'er-worn and soiled'. When Raymond B. Waddington relates the whole description to the traditional iconography of melancholy[58] he confirms what the style has successfully intimated. As so often in 'Samson Agonistes', and in *Paradise Regained*, the language constitutes a 'mimesis of thought',[59] its movement shaped to 'thought following thought, and step by step led on' (*PR*, I.192).

The style of the passage alters with the question, ironic in the presence of a blind man, 'Or do my eyes misrepresent?' The question that follows is less matter-of-fact than the first:

> Can this be he,
> That heroic, that renowned,
> Irresistible Samson?

The tone of surprise that starts with the rising intonation of 'this' is extended through the breathless repetition of 'that' and through the adjective triad 'heroic', 'renowned', and 'irresistible'. The stress built up before 'irresistible' and the sudden absence of 'that' force the word's vocalic beginning out like a grunt of intense effort. The prominent placing of 'fiercest' and 'weaponless' adds to the celebration of heroic action implicit in the negatives ('irresistible', 'unarmed', 'no strength of man', 'weaponless'). The rhythms accelerate in response to Samson's headlong rush, and the verbs 'tore . . . tears . . . ran . . . made' seem to hew their way through the adjectivally-encumbered noun phrases – 'embattled armies clad in iron', 'brazen shield and spear', 'hammered cuirass, / Chalybean-tempered steel', 'frock of mail, / Adamantean proof'. The stress-patterning, especially noticeable on the compound adjectives, amasses unwieldy weight, but Samson brushes it aside. The exhilaration in the chiastic juxtaposition of 'ridiculous' and 'useless' is nearly playful as blows struck to right and left are simulated. The whole passage is dramatically sensitive to Samson's passivity and to his carving out his passage through the enemy. The writing is animated with physical delight.

Such analysis of the style of 'Samson' indicates that the word 'dramatic' need not be applied narrowly to the work's stageability, but fittingly to its language.[60] It also suggests that F. R. Leavis's allegations of 'rhythmic deadness' and 'pervasive stiff, pedantic aridity',[61] already answered in part by Una Ellis-Fermor's fine study of the work's rhythmic variety,[62] are unsound. In fact, Leavis is not as insensitive to the verse as he is to the muddle in his criteria of excellence. On the justly famous lines 'The sun to me is dark . . . Among inhuman foes' (*ll.* 86–109) he comments:

> It might, of course, be said that the jerky, ejaculatory stiffness is dramatically appropriate, expressing an arid, exhausted, uneloquent desperation of agony. Yes, it is true that the general unsatisfactoriness of the verse has a peculiar expressive facility.[63]

If what is (infelicitously) termed 'ejaculatory stiffness' *is* 'dramatically appropriate' and *does* possess 'expressive felicity', by which criteria is the verse judged to be unsatisfactory? Prejudice has blurred Leavis's logic. And it is prejudice that he wishes to create:

> One can grant that it ['Samson Agonistes'] might possibly help to form taste: it certainly could not instil or foster a love of poetry. How many cultivated adults could honestly swear that they had ever read it through with enjoyment?[64]

Readers who have good reasons for enjoying the poetry, and who wish in no way to compromise their adulthood, culture, or honesty, may choose to agree in principle with a slightly less bullying comment by George Steiner: 'Only an ear deaf to drama could fail to experience, sharp as a whiplash, the hurt and tension of the successive assaults on Samson's bruised integrity.'[65] At least Steiner is in touch with the function of the style in its context.

The contrast of participial adjectives and main verbs in lines 118–34 compactly represents an alternation between passivity and action that is basic to Samson's experience and to the concept of his heroism. The pattern is established in Samson's opening monologue, where he sees himself as the object of action rather than the agent: 'relieves me', 'enjoined me', 'yields me', 'rush upon me', 'afflict me' (*ll.* 5, 6, 14–15, 19–21, 114). He is fettered to his affliction: 'chained', 'imprisoned', 'o'ercome', 'exposed', 'bereaved', 'exiled' (*ll.* 7–8, 51, 75, 85, 98). When he suffers a spiritual relapse, the grammar reverts to that of the opening speech:

> My griefs not only pain me
> As a lingering disease,
> But finding no redress, ferment and rage,
> Nor less than wounds immedicable
> Rankle, and fester, and gangrene,
> To black mortification.
> Thoughts my tormentors armed with deadly stings
> Mangle my apprehensive tenderest parts,
> Exasperate, exulcerate, and raise

> Dire inflammation which no cooling herb
> Or med'cinal liquor can assuage,
> Nor breath of vernal air from snowy alp.
> Sleep hath forsook and given me o'er
> To death's benumbing opium as my only cure.
> Thence faintings, swoonings of despair,
> And sense of heaven's desertion. (*ll.* 617–32)

The active hero is acted upon, but his torment is mental and self-inflicted. Abstractions usurp his active role: 'griefs . . . pain me . . . rankle, and fester, and gangrene'; 'thoughts . . . mangle . . . exasperate, exulcerate, and raise dire inflammation'; 'sleep hath forsook and given me o'er'.[66] The intense frustration packed into the series of verbs paralyses Samson; he is his own worst enemy.[67] Only when this disturbance of mind gives way to composure can Samson hope to recover his active heroism. As long as he thinks of himself as unalterably fixed, he is persecuted by an apparent inconsistency in his experience:

> Why was my breeding ordered and prescribed
> As of a person separate to God,
> Designed for great exploits; if I must die
> Betrayed, captived, and both my eyes put out,
> Made of my enemies the scorn and gaze;
> To grind in brazen fetters under task
> With this heaven-gifted strength? O glorious strength
> Put to the labour of a beast, debased
> Lower than bond-slave! Promise was that I
> Should Israel from Philistian yoke deliver;
> Ask for this great deliverer now, and find him
> Eyeless in Gaza at the mill with slaves,
> Himself in bonds under Philistian yoke. (*ll.* 30–42)

'A less promising beginning for any hero would at first be difficult to conceive', comments A. B. Chambers.[68] Samson is struggling with the incompatibility between his role as doer of 'worthiest deeds' and his role as drudge for the Philistines. He cannot reconcile divine appointment with Philistine mockery. On the one hand, he is a person whose life is 'ordered', 'prescribed', 'separate', 'designed', 'heaven-gifted'; but on the other, he is 'betrayed, captived', with his eyes 'put out', 'made . . . the scorn and gaze' of enemies, 'put to the labour of a beast, debased', and 'eyeless'. Duty and circumstance,[69] prophecy and fact,[70] do not seem to coincide. Samson is unable to discern God's purpose from his present state. The tension created between the adjective groups representing his past and present is released in angry, perplexed verbs – 'die', 'grind', 'deliver' – and both the hustled syntax at the phrase 'and both my eyes put out' and the loose connection of

151

the infinitive 'to grind' reveal his impatience. The polysyndeton in 'betrayed, captived, and both my eyes put out' and the accumulation of such phrases as 'in brazen fetters', 'under task', 'in bonds', and 'under Philistian yoke' combine to contain Samson's frustration and inflict torment stroke by stroke. Again it is possible to stop the outburst at several points (after 'prescribed', 'God', 'exploits', 'die', 'betrayed', 'captived', 'out', 'gaze', 'grind', 'fetters', 'task', 'strength', 'beast', 'debased', 'bond-slave', 'deliver', 'eyeless', 'Gaza', 'mill', and 'slaves'): the reader is kept hanging on to Samson's words, and made to feel each pang of anguish freshly. Landor's advocacy of commas after the words 'eyeless', 'Gaza', and 'mill', though textually groundless, derives from an important critical insight: the memorable line he refers to, disjointed and verbless, allows Samson's grief to be 'aggravated at every member of the sentence'.[71]

The language in which Samson gives an account of his past provides the means of understanding his present frustration:

> Meanwhile the men of Judah to prevent
> The harass of their land, beset me round;
> I willingly on some conditions came
> Into their hands, and they as gladly yield me
> To the uncircumcised a welcome prey,
> Bound with two cords; but cords to me were threads
> Touched with the flame: on their whole host I flew
> Unarmed, and with a trivial weapon felled
> Their choicest youth; they only lived who fled.   (*ll.* 256–64)

The significance of 'beset me round', 'yield me', and 'bound' is familiar from Samson's despondent outbursts, but here he decisively counters enemy action with his own vicious and deadly action: the straight verb sequence 'came . . . flew . . . felled' is calculated and trenchment. Samson's frustrated desire to act in this way is, in human terms anyway, the cause of his fury. When he describes how he fell to Dalila, the grammar is again revealing:

> Fearless of danger, like a petty god
> I walked about admired of all and dreaded   530
> On hostile ground, none daring my affront.
> Then swoll'n with pride into the snare I fell
> Of fair fallacious looks, venereal trains,
> Softened with pleasure and voluptuous life;
> At length to lay my head and hallowed pledge   535
> Of all my strength in the lascivious lap
> Of a deceitful concubine who shore me
> Like a tame wether, all my precious fleece,

Then turned me out ridiculous, despoiled,
Shaven, and disarmed among my enemies.   540

The frequency of adjectives in lines 533–4, partial semantic duplication (the 'snare' and 'trains' are the same thing, the 'looks' are the 'trains' referred to, and the 'pleasure' *is* the 'voluptuous life') and alliteration ('fell', 'fair', 'fallacious', 'venereal', 'voluptuous') call attention to the surfeit of Samson's indulgence. Luckily for him, the enemy is unthreatening, even flattering: he is 'admired' and 'dreaded'. But since, being 'softened', he does not act upon the enemy, Dalila usurps his role as active hero – 'shore me', 'turned me out' – and this precipitates the outraged past-participial adjectives in lines 539–40, which gradually, excruciatingly, expose him. Most humiliating of all is the word 'disarmed', for Samson is usually 'unarmed' among foes (*ll.* 126, 263, 1111). His fear on meeting Dalila again is that she will repeat her positive actions, and the significant ritualized style of participial adjectives and verbs recurs:

If in my flower of youth and strength, when all men
Loved, honoured, feared me, thou alone could hate me,
Thy husband, slight me, sell me, and forgo me;
How wouldst thou use me now, blind, and thereby
Deceivable, in most things as a child
Helpless, thence easily contemned, and scorned,
And last neglected?   (*ll.* 938–44)

Act or be acted upon: this is the simple and prevailing ethic of Samson's life.[72] The theme of the poem, Samson's recovery of active heroism, involves his seeing faults in his past actions as the cause of his present inaction, so that he can proceed to further action. He must reject the possibility of rest at all costs.[73] In lines 529–40 the verbs ('I fell . . . to lay') are therefore crucial to recovery, since they acknowledge personal responsibility for actions that have shown irresponsibility towards the values implied by 'precious' and 'hallowed'. Samson must confess, using verbs that will make sense of the participial adjectives that characterize his present condition: 'I . . . have shipwrecked, / My vessel . . . have divulged the secret gift of God'; 'I . . . vanquished . . . Gave up my fort of silence' (*ll.* 197–202, 234–6). By doing this, he realizes that evils have not befallen him unluckily or without reason: 'I myself have brought them on, / Sole author I, sole cause' (*ll.* 375–6).

In the later stages of his spiritual struggle, Samson threatens to tear Dalila apart, and issues commands to her (*ll.* 952–9). Mary Ann Radzinowicz has observed that in the exchange of speech between Dalila and Samson:

Her lines are spoken in a curious falling cadence, six lines ending in unaccented syllables; his reply is couched in strong verbs, not falling nouns, twenty hammer strokes: *break, deceive, betray, submit, beseech, move, confess, promise, try, urg'd, bears, assail, transgresses, submits, reject, forgive, drawn, wear out, entangl'd, cut off.*[74]

Samson is concerned with action. He gives orders to Harapha, urging him to act (*ll.* 1116–17, 1119, 1121, 1146, 1147, 1220, 1237), and offering to meet him and fight (*ll.* 1123, 1151–2, 1237–41). He also gives commands to the Philistine officer (*ll.* 1319–20, 1345). In control of his own actions – 'I will not come ... I will not come' (*ll.* 1332, 1342) – he feels free will operating even when he is apparently ordered about by others: 'Commands are no constraints. If I obey them, / I do it freely' (*ll.* 1373–3). Like the phoenix he is 'vigorous most / When most unactive deemed' (*ll.* 1704–5), and with the 'rousing motions' of conviction in his mind he goes to the temple of Dagon 'nothing to *do*, be sure, that may dishonour / Our Law, or stain my vow of Nazarite' (*ll.* 1385–6, my italics). Ironically for the Philistines, he is led along as though still the object of action (*ll.* 1601, 1615, 1623, 1629, 1635), and for a time he even complies with their commands:

> what was set before him
> Which without help of eye might be assayed,
> To heave, pull, draw, or break, he still performed
> All with incredible, stupendious force.   (*ll.* 1624–7)

But these actions constitute no more than a muscle-man's circus act. The verbs are undramatic, 'performed' carries theatrical overtones,[75] speculation colours 'what might be assayed', and the connective 'or' reduces the infinitive verbs to a list of possible feats that illustrate Samson's versatility. The feats require 'incredible, stupendious force', but the style announces that Samson's heart is not in them. His deep convictions are involved in another action:

> those two massy pillars
> With horrible convulsion to and fro
> He tugged, he shook, till down they came and drew
> The whole roof after them ...   (*ll.* 1648–51)

Advancing the grammatical object 'pillars' gives Samson a firm grip before he pulls; and the polysyllables in 'horrible convulsion' vibrate with the tremor.[76] Even the simple phrase 'to and fro' balances its stress in a rocking movement. The stressed verbs 'tugged' and 'shook' reflect back on all the verb sequences in the poem and transcend the confines of every past-participial adjective. There is a dramatic tumble of stress and enjambment in 'down they came and drew / The whole roof after them'. This final act reverses the role of the Philistines: now it is they who are 'fall'n ... overwhelmed and fall'n' (*ll.* 1558–9).[77] Tragically, it also reverses Samson's

role: he becomes active, but '[pulls] down the same destruction on himself'
(*l.* 1658). His code of life becomes not merely to act or be acted upon, but,
in death, 'at once both to destroy and be destroyed' (*l.* 1587). As Anthony
Low has said, 'Samson's final act is both active *and* passive: he conquers in
defeat, suffers and inflicts, slays and is slain, is reborn and dies.'[78]

G. A. Wilkes's statement that the poem's action is one of 'provocation,
instinctive response, counter-assertion, and defiance'[79] is supported by the
structuring of past-participial adjectives and main verbs. Indeed, so pervasive, narrow, and rigid is the code of behaviour contained by the structure,
and so dedicated is Samson to it, that it completely takes over and simplifies
his character. Perhaps this is why William Riley Parker speaks for many
critics in finding Samson 'anything but lovable ... cold, forbidding,
grand ... unsympathetic to an extreme',[80] and why John Carey feels that it
is difficult to imagine Samson as Dalila's husband.[81] His fall to Dalila is represented as ritual: we are not told what came over Samson's mind, only
that 'thrice she assayed' and 'thrice I deluded her'. Stanley E. Fish has commented that 'he is not taken unaware; his experience with the woman of
Timna has left him suspicious of all Philistines, and Dalila's approach is
hardly subtle'; and that the mode of presentation of the fall 'serves to fix
the combatants in their respective poses'.[82] Frank Kermode even draws a
diagram of Samson's career, paralleling his motivations to action or 'intimate impulse', his two bad marriages, and the ultimate result – in each case
death to the Philistines.[83] The destruction of the temple of Dagon becomes,
for Albert L. Cirillo, 'a kind of liturgical, religious act'.[84] One may not
agree, however, with Thomas B. Stroup, who views the last day of Samson's life as 'a rite generally analogous to a Christian liturgy':[85] it is hard to
forget that Samson is by no means motivated by the pacifist Christian
principle of turning the other cheek and loving his enemies; he kills Philistines. Familiarity with the Judges story only increases the reader's unease at
what Tillyard calls 'a settled ferocity, not very lovely'[86] in the course of the
action, and makes the catastrophe all the more devastatingly inevitable.

Neither Samson, nor the poem which focuses on him, invites the reader
to regard the Philistines with anything approaching equanimity.[87] But are
they merely to be done away with? A third of their lords are, as Manoa testifies, 'generous and civil', and they are prepared to accept a ransom for
Samson (*ll.* 1466–71). In spite of Samson's surliness, the Philistine officer is
courteous to him. And Manoa's description of the Philistines as 'wondrous
harsh, / Contemptuous, proud, set on revenge and spite' (*ll.* 1461–2) fits
Samson too. Samson feels victimized by the Philistines; but has he not persecuted them? Franklin R. Baruch comments on the image of the slain Philistines as chickens and geese (*ll.* 1692–6) that it 'heaps scorn ... but, alas,
makes them innocent as well, and it certainly does no service to Samson's

valour – which, if it was a sign of divine grace, was also a fact on the physical level.'[88] The 'unsuspicious' guide who leads Samson to the pillars, a boy in the Judges account, is also to be presumed dead after the temple roof has come down. Of course the Philistines are far from behaving faultlessly; but does not Samson, living or dying, devote himself to protracted harassment that will do anything but foster peace? Is he not the instigator of violence which they reciprocate? His moving repentance for his past faults, or his developing feeling that he has been justly treated by God, hardly makes his final bloody act less horrible. If, as E. L. Marilla says, 'Samson Agonistes' is intended 'to demonstrate the basic forces of evil that persistently menace man's efforts toward establishing a society compatible with his spiritual needs',[89] then it must also be said that Samson's programme of annihilation, judged by such criteria, is evil. It is barely acceptable, on any account, that people who happen to get in the way of 'spiritual needs' should be wiped out. Given Samson's career and its eventual outcome, it is hard to agree with Mary Ann Radzinowicz when she says that 'the protagonist enlightens us because he stands for us and undergoes experiences typical of his and our humanity', and that '*Samson Agonistes* is a fully Christian and fully theological poem.'[90] She states that the classical hero is traditionally conceived as 'patient in adversity and magnanimous in heroic action';[91] but, if so, it must be hard to reconcile Samson's behaviour with the idea that magnanimity is 'a public virtue, a manifestation of one's general duty to all men, and involves humanity, kindness, and pity'.[92] It must be borne in mind that while the structure of participial adjective and verb may be admired aesthetically, it is a structure centred on killing.

What Tillyard calls 'Samson's tedious butcheries'[93] make any equation of Samson with Christ difficult, if not absurd. The rules of typological exegesis require that type (Samson) and antitype (Christ) be unlike each other in some respects; but if Samson, in spite of Milton's efforts to ennoble the Judges character,[94] remains unlike Christ in the most important respects, then the comparison is invalid. The simplest solution to all the problems incurred by persevering with the comparison – and it has eluded many – is not to persevere with it at all.

'Samson Agonistes' contains no explicit reference to Christ.[95] The phoenix image, traditionally associated with Christ's resurrection and ascension, is used merely as an emblem of Samson's fame.[96] F. M. Krouse in *Milton's Samson and the Christian Tradition* (1949) makes a determined attempt to convert Samson to Christianity, but fails to solve the problems met by the church fathers on account of the diverging Hebraic and Christian conceptions of the poem's awkward hero. Chrysostom was forced to discount the less savoury events of Samson's life, and Augustine both dismissed Samson's visit to the harlot as a prophetic 'dark conceit' and concluded, mystified, that his death and that of the Philistines must have been specially sanctioned by God.[97] Modern allegorists who try to play down the literal atrocities of the Samson story are still faced with the kinds of inconsistency that Hugo of St Victor (d. 1173) tried to remedy: formulations such as 'Samson overcame the lion, and Christ triumphed over Satan; Samson took honey from the lion's mouth, and Christ saved Man from the Devil; Samson married a Philistine, and Christ founded his Church among the Gentiles'[98] display the ingenuity and arbitrary patterns of association of the emblem tradition.[99] But if Satan is the lion and Christ takes man from its carcass, is Satan not therefore dead? And does the happiness of Samson's marriage to Dalila not omen rather badly for Christ and the Church? Krouse concludes that 'Samson Agonistes' neither makes the Samson-Christ parallel nor manifests the allegorical tradition;[100] and lest he should be his work's best critic, he loses himself in the mystery that the poem does not manifest allegory in 'the poetic sense' but in the 'technical exegetical sense'.[101] Those who, like T. S. K. Scott-Craig,[102] follow Krouse in trying to Christianize Samson, trip themselves up with their own ironies: Scott-Craig considers that 'the celebration of the agony of Samson is a surrogate for the unbloody sacrifice of the Mass', but we are only reminded that Samson's end, like that of the Philistines, was decidedly bloody.[103]

Related to the theory that Samson prefigures Christ is the view that the poem is about his 'regeneration'. This has been severely criticized on the grounds that Samson's ultimate redemption would destroy, or seriously impair, the tragedy.[104] A. S. P. Woodhouse, a leading exponent of the Christian regeneration view, tries to solve the paradox of Christian tragedy by saying that 'death, though it be the price of ... victory, and even though it came as a release from suffering, is still death.'[105] But death *is* victory to a Christian (I Corinthians 15:22, 54–7), and if it is 'still death' it may be sorrowful but certainly not tragic.[106] Samson's spiritual condition in the course of the poem turbulently refuses to follow any linear development towards regeneration[107] – he keeps longing for death, and he confesses his past faults in his opening monologue (*ll.* 46–57) and at various points during the poem (*ll.* 197–202, 234–6, 373–80). Above all it is his behaviour that fails to bear the fruits of the spirit. His threat to tear Dalila apart shows, in Balachandra Rajan's words, 'a scarcely Christian ferocity',[108] and he is hardly humble towards Harapha when he might have turned the other cheek. His 'patience', apart from being the suffering he experiences, is little more than endurance to the grim end; his final act, the culmination of his past slaughters (*ll.* 1667–8). The regimented existence represented by the structure of participial adjective and verb throughout the poem in itself reveals a disturbing degree of sameness in all of Samson's 'exploits'. And there are deeper similarities: just as he has in the past killed 'their choicest

157

youth' (*l.* 264) – note the depraved specificness of 'choicest' – so at the temple of Dagon he kills 'their choice nobility and flower' (*l.* 1654). The Messenger escapes the catastrophe by standing 'aloof' (*l.* 1611), reminding us that 'safest he who stood aloof' (*l.* 135) when Samson previously went to war. The acts are frighteningly identical, and that the final one is motivated by religious or nationalistic principle rather than by personal pride hardly makes it more acceptable. Samson is no saint, but a downtrodden national hero who contritely acknowledges his faults before his God, and who sees his way to hit back at his enemies. The story, of course, presents many of the details of his life as 'given', and patriotic allegiance and Samson's role as a judge of Israel who must execute vengeance on tyrannical enemies may also be 'given'.[109] What is not 'given' – and never is – is the reader's moral judgement.[110] If one recalls that Milton invoked vengeance on 'the bloody Piedmontese' and felt that Cromwell's victories were justified, and also that such words as 'anger', 'appease', 'fury', 'ire', 'rage', 'revenge', and 'wrath' are tellingly present throughout *Paradise Lost*,[111] perhaps the representation of the actual slaughter at the temple of Dagon seems less surprising. The Messenger who reports on the carnage shows a human response in running away in horror from it; and the reader may well feel a similar impulse. No poem divides the reader's strictly literary values from moral values more widely than 'Samson Agonistes' does. To trace the pattern of adjective and verb through its style is to uncover a truly fearful symmetry.

NOTES

1. See the accounts of the style in the following: Sir Walter Raleigh, *Milton* (1900), p. 159; Sir Richard C. Jebb, 'Samson Agonistes and the Hellenic Drama', *Proceedings of the British Academy*, **3** (1908), 341; Elbert N. S. Thompson, *Essays on Milton* (1914; rpt., 1968), pp. 204, 212; John Bailey, *Milton*, p. 227; Chauncey B. Tinker, '*Samson Agonistes*', *Tragic Themes in Western Literature*, ed. Cleanth Brooks (1955), p. 61; Geoffrey and Margaret Bullough, eds., *Milton's Dramatic Poems* (1958), p. 58; Michael Hamburger, 'The Sublime Art: Notes on Milton and Hölderlin', *The Living Milton*, ed. Kermode, p. 160; Douglas Bush, *English Literature in the Earlier Seventeenth Century, 1600–1660* (2nd edn, 1962), p. 418; C. V. Wedgwood, *Seventeenth-Century English Literature* (2nd edn, 1970), p. 89.

2. *Observer*, **76** (1785), rpt. in *Milton, 1732–1801: The Critical Heritage*, ed. John T. Shawcross (1972), p. 333.

3. *Milton*, p. 197. P. F. Baum, '*Samson Agonistes* Again', *PMLA*, **36** (1921), 371, agrees. Like Pattison, he presents no evidence.

4. *A Critical Commentary on Milton's 'Samson Agonistes'* (1969), p. 21.

5. *Toward Samson Agonistes: The Growth of Milton's Mind* (1978), pp. 23, 25.

6. *The Rambler*, No. 140 (20 July, 1751).

7. See Barbara K. Lewalski, 'The Ship-Tempest Imagery in "Samson Agonistes"', *N & Q*, NS **6** (1959), 372–3; John Broadbent, *Milton: 'Comus' and 'Samson Agonistes'*, pp. 42, 47, 52, 57, 59, 61; John Carey, 'Sea, Snake, Flower, and Flame in "Samson Agonistes"', *MLR*, **62** (1967), rpt. in Carey and Fowler, pp. 339–43; Lynn Veach Sadler, 'Typological Imagery in *Samson Agonistes*', *ELH*, **37** (1970), 195–210; Albert L. Cirillo, 'Time, Light, and the Phoenix: The Design of *Samson Agonistes*', *Calm of Mind*, ed. Wittreich, pp. 209–33; and William Kerrigan, *The Prophetic Milton* (1974), pp. 232–9, on bird imagery in the poem. The most illuminating and comprehensive study remains Lee Sheridan Cox's 'Natural Science and Figurative Design in *Samson Agonistes*', *ELH*, **35** (1968), rpt. in *Critical Essays on Milton from ELH*, pp. 253–76.

8. 'The Temptation Motive in Milton', *SP*, **15** (1918), 193. See also W. Menzies, 'Milton: The Last Poems', *ESEA*, **24** (1938), 111.

9. 'The Date of *Samson Agonistes*', *PQ*, **28** (1949), 158–61; *Tragic Themes in Western Literature*, ed. Brooks, p. 70. John N. Wall, Jr has indicated similarities between 'Samson' and the Hebraic lament often found in the Psalms: 'The Contrarious Hand of God: *Samson Agonistes* and the Biblical Lament', *MS*, **12** (1978), 117–39, especially 126–9.

10. *Toward Samson Agonistes*, pp. 368–82.

11. *Milton*, p. 162; 'The Equation of Action and Passion in *Samson Agonistes*', *PQ*, **52** (1973), 83–4.

12. 'The Date of *Samson Agonistes* Again', *Calm of Mind*, ed. Wittreich, p. 172. See Oras, 'Milton's Blank Verse and the Chronology of his Major Poems', *SAMLA Studies in Milton*, ed. J. Max Patrick (1953), 128–97, and *Blank Verse and Chronology in Milton* (1966). John Carey criticizes Oras's work in Carey and Fowler, p. 332. Oras admits that the figures for the distribution of polysyllables over the verse-line in Milton's poetry show greater differences between individual books of *Paradise Lost* than between 'Samson Agonistes' and 'Comus', and his figures for pyrrhic verse-endings show a similar variation in parts of *Paradise Lost* and *Paradise Regained*: *SAMLA Studies in Milton* (1953), pp. 154–5, 181.

13. Parker previously found prosodic tests 'inconclusive' because they overlooked the claims of decorum: 'The Date of *Samson Agonistes*', *PQ*, **28** (1949), 155.

14. *Toward Samson Agonistes*, p. 397.

15. ibid., pp. 392–401.

16. *John Milton: Poet, Priest and Prophet* (1979), p. 196.

17. loc. cit.

18. *The Early Lives of Milton*, ed. Helen Darbishire (1932), p. 75.

19. *Milton's Dramatic Poems*, p. 59. The only colour noun in the poem is 'ruby' (*l.* 543).

20. Carey and Fowler, pp. 341–2.

21. See Roger B. Wilkenfeld, 'Act and Emblem: The Conclusion of *Samson*

Agonistes', ELH, **32** (1965), 160–8; Martin Mueller, 'Pathos and Katharsis in *Samson Agonistes'*, *ELH*, **31** (1964), rpt. in *Critical Essays on Milton from ELH*, pp. 245–6; and Lee Sheridan Cox, 'Natural Science and Figurative Design in *Samson Agonistes'*, ibid., p. 253. John Carey misinterprets contrasting parallels as ironic equivalents when he discusses the imagery of fire as it is applied to Samson and to the Philistines. He says that Samson is warned not to add fuel to the 'flame' (*l.* 1351) of the Philistine lords (Carey and Fowler, p. 343). But the Chorus says to Samson that *Harapha* may add fuel to the flame, and the 'flame' is arguably the fervent challenge issued by Samson. The fire with which the Philistines are associated is merely the heat of drunken indulgence (*ll.* 1418–22; cf. 443, 1612–13). Accordingly, John Carey is not strictly accurate in saying that through the fire imagery an 'equivalence' between the religious fervour of the Philistines and that of Samson is revealed (Carey and Fowler, p. 343). Lee S. Cox shows that each element in 'Samson' may be good or bad, and illustrates this principle from the fire images (op. cit., p. 256).

22. Mary Ann Radzinowicz notes that 'the tragedy is stripped of spectacle', and suggests that this is so because of its emphasis on inward experience, on the mind's eye (*Toward Samson Agonistes*, pp. 15–16). T. H. Banks has suggested, on the basis of the evidence of Milton's imagery, that 'his visual sense, judging from his use of colour, weakened, but his other senses – smell, hearing, and touch – became more quick and sharp' (*Milton's Imagery*, p. 137).

23. *Milton and the Miltonic Dryden* (1968), p. 142.

24. See James G. McManaway, 'Women and Ships', *TLS*, 20 February 1937, 131; Peter Ure, 'A Simile in *Samson Agonistes'*, *N & Q*, **195** (1950), 298; and Christopher Hill, *Milton and the English Revolution,* p. 435*n*.

25. 'Sail', 5.b.

26. Again, only nineteenth-century examples are given for 'streamers' meaning 'ribbons'.

27. 'Gay', A.1.d, 3, 4, 2.

28. 'Sail', 5.b. Only nineteenth-century examples are given.

29. 'Bravery', 3.b, 4, 1.

30. 'Duality in Dramatic Vision: A Structural Analysis of *Samson Agonistes'*, *MS*, **12** (1978), 99.

31. John Carey makes this point (*Milton*, p. 142). Lee Sheridan Cox indicates that money in 'Samson Agonistes' is associated with falsehood and corruption (*Critical Essays on Milton from ELH*, pp. 272–3).

32. *Milton's God* (rev. edn, 1965), pp. 211–28.

33. Allan H. Gilbert, 'Is *Samson Agonistes* Unfinished?', *PQ*, **28** (1949), 100, and 'Milton's Defence of Bawdry', *SAMLA Studies in Milton*, ed. J. Max Patrick (1953), pp. 68–9; Chauncey B. Tinker in *Tragic Themes in Western Literature*, ed. Brooks, p. 67; Arnold Stein, *Heroic Knowledge*, p. 167.

34. See David Daiches, *Milton*, p. 241, and Patrick Cullen, *Infernal Triad*, pp. 216, 218. There is a traditional association between the image of the fully-rigged

ship and worldly vanity. See, for example, *Spenser's Minor Poems*, ed. de
Sélincourt (1910; rpt., 1970), pp. 272, 485.

35. *Toward Samson Agonistes*, p. 393.

36. *The Blaze of Noon: A Reading of 'Samson Agonistes'* (1974), pp. 157–8. This is
the view taken by P. F. Baum, 'Samson Agonistes Again', *PMLA*, **36** (1921),
360, A. S. P. Woodhouse, 'Tragic Effect in *Samson Agonistes*', *UTQ*, **28**
(1959), 211, Stanley E. Fish, 'Question and Answer in *Samson Agonistes*',
CQ, **11** (1969), 244, and Patrick Cullen, *Infernal Triad*, pp. 226–7. Virginia
R. Mollenkott, 'Relativism in *Samson Agonistes*', *SP*, **67** (1970), argues that
'only when the conflict is carried onto the ultimate level of God versus Dagon
does Milton's customary absolutism assert itself' (89–90), so that, on the
human level, Dalila, the Philistines, and even Harapha, have much in their
favour. She finds Samson's conduct 'at least as reprehensible as Dalila's' (98),
views 'Samson Agonistes' as Milton's 'sympathetic recognition of the complexity of being fallible' (102), and makes several valid points about the
characterization of Dalila, which she regards as 'an unusually fair portrayal'
(100). John B. Mason, 'Multiple Perspectives in *Samson Agonistes*: Critical
Attitudes Towards Dalila', *MS*, **10** (1977), makes the point that 'critics of
Dalila too often misread the character and the entire play because they insist
upon isolating *the* Dalila. There are three Dalilas . . . how readers view
Dalila's motives depends upon whose viewpoint they choose to adopt: that of
Samson, the Chorus, or Dalila herself' (24).

37. *The Lofty Rhyme*, p. 138.

38. loc. cit.

39. Carey and Fowler, p. 340.

40. 'Dalila's Role in *Samson Agonistes*', *SEL*, **6** (1966), 127.

41. Cf. p. 46.

42. Duncan Robertson, 'Metaphor in *Samson Agonistes*', *UTQ*, **38** (1969),
323–4, makes some good points about the wine-water imagery in general.

43. Anne D. Ferry, *Milton and the Miltonic Dryden*, p. 140. The chilling silence of
the moon in 'Samson' may be contrasted with the 'frendly silence of the quiet
moone' in Surrey's *Aeneid*, II.324 (*Poems*, ed. Emrys Jones (1964), pp. 43 and
143*n*).

44. Nicholas R. Jones, ' "Stand" and "Fall" as Images of Posture in *Paradise
Lost*', *MS*, **8** (1975), 221–46, shows that Milton attaches moral significance
to physical posture in the epic. See also pp. 123, 124, above.

45. The morality of language in 'Samson Agonistes' is studied by Anne D. Ferry
(op. cit., pp. 127–77) and by Marcia Landy ('Language and the Seal of Silence
in *Samson Agonistes*', *MS*, **2** (1970), 175–94).

46. The image pattern is extended by John Carey in Carey and Fowler, p. 341.
Balachandra Rajan observes the contrasting parallel with the swarm of
thoughts in the Son's mind (*PR*, I.196–7) in *The Prison and the Pinnacle*,
pp. 104–5.

47. *The Rambler*, No. 139.

48. See, for example, Anne D. Ferry, *Milton and the Miltonic Dryden*, p. 134, and

Louis L. Martz, 'Chorus and Character in *Samson Agonistes*', MS, **1** (1969), 118.

49. Something of this is noted in 'Samson' by John Bailey, *Milton*, pp. 225–6, John Broadbent, 'Milton's Rhetoric', *MP*, **56** (1959), 227–8, and Leonard Moss, 'The Rhetorical Style of *Samson Agonistes*', *MP*, **62** (1965), 296–301.

50. Bailey (op. cit., p. 225) discerns 'the spasmodic disorder of violent grief' in the inverted stress of 'irrecoverably dark' (*l.* 81), and Robert Bridges, *Milton's Prosody, with a chapter on Accentual Verse and Notes* (1921), pp. 57, 63, 64, makes useful comments on 'descriptive rhythm' in the poem. Edward Weismiller, 'The "Dry" and "Rugged" Verse', *The Lyric and Dramatic Milton*, ed. Summers, pp. 115–52, misses many poetic effects by dissociating stress from other aspects of meaning.

51. William Kerrigan, *The Prophetic Milton* (1974), pp. 210–11, 252, notes that 'almost every line of the opening monologue contains an image or idea redefined or "fulfilled" at the end of the play', and that, in particular, ' "the breath of Heav'n fresh blowing" in which Samson wished to "respire" does in fact return as "Secret refreshings" – he pulls down the temple with the terrible "force of winds" (*l.* 1647).'

52. 'Hurrahing in Harvest', *ll.* 11–12.

53. Mary Ann Radzinowicz, *Toward Samson Agonistes*, p. 25, notes that Samson's speech in his opening monologue '*imitates the mind at work*'.

54. Seymour Chatman, 'Milton's Participial Style', *PMLA*, **83** (1968), 1393, notes that '*Samson Agonistes* . . . uses participles heavily, particularly past participles.' He finds one past participle in five lines on average in the first 800 lines of the poem. See Carey and Fowler, pp. 1071–2, on participles in *Paradise Regained*.

55. *The Frontiers of Drama* (2nd edn, 1964), p. 31. See also her appendix, pp. 148–53.

56. *The Rambler*, No. 140. Mark Pattison thinks 'Samson' 'languid, nerveless, occasionally halting, never brilliant', and cites lines 594–8 as evidence (*Milton*, p. 197). He is ably corrected by W. P. Ker, who distinguishes between Milton's alleged, and Samson's actual, depression, and who notes that 'the representation of weakness . . . is particularly strong' in the lines (*The Art of Poetry: Seven Lectures, 1920–22* (1923), pp. 58–9).

57. John S. Hill, 'Vocation and Spiritual Renovation in *Samson Agonistes*', *MS*, **2** (1970), 161.

58. 'Melancholy Against Melancholy: *Samson Agonistes* as Renaissance Tragedy', *Calm of Mind*, ed. Wittreich, p. 262.

59. This is John Steadman's phrase, from *Milton and the Renaissance Hero* (1967), p. 68. All language may be considered to be a mimesis of thought, though Steadman's phrase is particularly relevant to Milton's style in *Paradise Regained* and 'Samson Agonistes'. Steadman has shown that Italian Renaissance critics expanded Aristotle's idea of catharsis purging the mind into a theory of psychological drama: ' "Passions Well Imitated": Rhetoric and Poetics in the Preface to *Samson Agonistes*', *Calm of Mind*, ed. Wittreich, pp. 175–207. A remark from Piccolomini which he quotes is particularly applicable to

Milton's style in 'Samson': 'as the actor imitates by adapting voice and gesture to the words . . . the poet imitates by making his words conform to the passions of the mind' (p. 196).

60. Max Beerbohm, reviewing a stage performance, ignores the work's style when he says that 'Samson' possesses 'no dramatic quality whatsoever' (*Around Theatres* (1924; rpt., 1953), p. 527). Tillyard takes a similar view (*Milton*, p. 65).

61. *Revaluation*, pp. 65, 66.

62. *The Frontiers of Drama*, pp. 26–31, 148–53. In the rhymed passages spoken by the Chorus, which Leavis considered to be the verse 'at its shocking worst' (op. cit., p. 67), Anthony Low has found a representation of 'rebellion, exasperation, and near insolence in addressing the God whom they feel is responsible for Samson's plight' (*The Blaze of Noon*, pp. 210–17). Michael Cohen has detected several functions of rhyme in the poem: the pointing of irony, the stressing of Samson's situation, imitation of classical choric melody, the achievement of epigrammatic conciseness, and the creation of dissonance and of mournful effects ('Rhyme in *Samson Agonistes*', *MQ*, **8** (1974), 4–6).

63. loc. cit.

64. op. cit., p. 67.

65. *The Death of Tragedy* (1961), p. 32.

66. John Carey notes the use of abstract nouns as grammatical subjects, particularly in the opening speech (Carey and Fowler, p. 338). See also Mary Ann Radzinowicz, *Toward Samson Agonistes*, p. 23.

67. David Daiches speaks of Samson's 'masochistic fury' and 'self-torturing savagery' (*Milton*, pp. 239, 240); and in lines 411–19, which are similar to lines 30–41, Louis Martz feels in Samson's words 'a surge of immense vitality, though turned against himself' ('Chorus and Character in *Samson Agonistes*', *MS*, **1** (1969), 123).

68. 'Wisdom and Fortitude in *Samson Agonistes*', *PMLA*, **78** (1963), 317.

69. See Camille W. Slights, 'A Hero of Conscience: *Samson Agonistes* and Casuistry', *PMLA*, **90** (1975), 395–6.

70. See John Spencer Hill, *John Milton: Poet, Priest and Prophet*, p. 154.

71. 'Southey and Landor', *Imaginary Conversations*, *Works*, ed. Welby, **5**, 295. For similar comments, see Sir Walter Raleigh, *Milton*, p. 204, and Frank Kermode, *English Renaissance Literature: Introductory Lectures* (1974), p. 138. On rhetorical devices in the style which depend upon accumulation, see *Milton 1732–1801: The Critical Heritage*, ed. Shawcross, p. 114; Carey and Fowler, p. 338; and Leonard Moss, 'The Rhetorical Style of *Samson Agonistes*', *MP*, **62** (1965), 296–301.

72. See John T. Onuska, Jr, 'The Equation of Action and Passion in *Samson Agonistes*', *PQ*, **52** (1973), 69–84.

73. The epic hero is usually tempted by the possibility that he can rest, take life easy, and stay where he is: see C. S. Lewis, *Spenser's Images of Life*, ed. Alastair Fowler (1967), p. 95, and Joan Malory Webber, *Milton and His Epic Tradition*, pp. 50–1, 92. John T. Onuska, Jr points out that Samson must reject Dalila's offer of ease (op. cit., 77). And Jeanne K. Welcher, 'The

Meaning of Manoa', *MQ*, **8** (1974), 48–50, points out that Samson's father's name means a resting-place, and derives from a verb meaning to dwell, stay, withdraw, or let alone: hence Samson's rejection of domestic rest as offered by his father – he must be *agonistes*.

74. *Toward Samson Agonistes*, p. 37.

75. Paul R. Sellin shows that *agonistes* may mean simulating, playing a part, acting, and finds words such as 'given', 'deemed', and 'seemed' in the description of the phoenix (*ll.* 1695–1707) significant: 'Milton's Epithet *Agonistes*', *SEL*, **4** (1964), 145, 157, 159.

76. John Broadbent has said that 'all the lines in the poem tend to the word-by-word vibration of Samson's final act': *Milton: Comus and Samson Agonistes*, p. 60.

77. Cf. Isaiah 21:9 ('Babylon is fallen, is fallen; and the graven images of her gods he hath broken unto the ground').

78. 'Action and Suffering: *Samson Agonistes* and the Irony of Alternatives', *PMLA*, **84** (1969), 518.

79. 'The Interpretation of *Samson Agonistes*', *HLQ*, **26** (1962), 374–5.

80. *Milton's Debt to Greek Tragedy in 'Samson Agonistes'* (1937), p. 117.

81. *Milton*, p. 146.

82. 'Question and Answer in *Samson Agonistes*', *CQ*, **11** (1969), 240.

83. *English Renaissance Literature: Introductory Lectures*, p. 135.

84. 'Time, Light, and The Phoenix: The Design of *Samson Agonistes*', *Calm of Mind*, ed. Wittreich, p. 227.

85. *Religious Rite and Ceremony in Milton's Poetry*, p. 55.

86. *Milton*, p. 283.

87. Donald F. Bouchard, *Milton: A Structural Reading* (1974), p. 141.

88. 'Time, Body, and Spirit at the Close of *Samson Agonistes*', *ELH*, **36** (1969), 333.

89. *Milton and Modern Man* (1968), p. 68.

90. *Toward Samson Agonistes*, pp. 111, 312.

91. ibid., p. 97.

92. ibid., p. 241.

93. *Milton*, p. 283.

94. See Parker, *Milton's Debt to Greek Tragedy in 'Samson Agonistes'*, pp. 4–9, and Chauncey B. Tinker, '*Samson Agonistes*', *Tragic Themes in Western Literature*, ed. Brooks, pp. 59–62, for comparisons of the stories in Judges and in Milton.

95. Balachandra Rajan, *The Prison and the Pinnacle*, p. 97.

96. See Christopher Grose, ' "His Uncontrollable Intent": Discovery as Action in *Samson Agonistes*', *MS*, **7** (1975), 69.

97. Cited in Krouse (pp. 36, 37, 41–2). William G. Madsen applies the usual typological rules in 'From Shadowy Types to Truth', *The Lyric and Dramatic Milton*, ed. Summers, pp. 95–114; but Irene Samuel has well said that 'his argument hardly accounts for the extent of Samson's failings', and pointed out that those who prefigure Christ in the last two books of *Paradise Lost* 'are presented with emphasis not on their shortcomings but on their resemblance

to the ultimate Saviour' ('*Samson Agonistes* as Tragedy', *Calm of Mind*, ed. Wittreich, p. 243).

98. Krouse, p. 54.
99. See Rosemary Freeman, *English Emblem Books* (1948), pp. 9, 21–2, 26, 29.
100. op. cit., pp. 120, 122.
101. ibid., p. 123.
102. 'Concerning Milton's Samson', *Renaissance News*, **5** (1952), 47.
103. William Kerrigan proves completely muddled over the Samson-Christ parallel. He assures us that it 'certainly exists' – because 'history is typological' – but then feels that resistance of the typological interpretation 'is not without virtue'. He argues that 'if "Samson" equals "Christ", [his] deep searching doubt is insignificant and insubstantial. The tragic suffering is reduced to ignorance', but sees no contradiction in then saying that 'the final glorious deed of Samson typifies both the Sacrifice of Christ, primarily an act of love, and the Last Judgment, primarily an act of vengeance.' It is scarcely credible that he notes subsequently that 'no sense of universal love either warms or sentimentalizes this nationalistic play', that 'the drama is fulfilled in hatred', and that Samson 'excludes himself from humanity' (*The Prophetic Milton*, pp. 244–8).
104. P. F. Baum, '*Samson Agonistes* Again', *PMLA*, **36** (1921), 365, 369, and George Steiner, *The Death of Tragedy*, pp. 4, 331, are among those who argue along these lines.
105. 'Tragic Effect in *Samson Agonistes*', *UTQ*, **28** (1959), 220.
106. George Steiner makes this useful distinction (op. cit., p. 332).
107. See John Dale Ebbs, 'Milton's Treatment of Poetic Justice in *Samson Agonistes*', *MLQ*, **22** (1961), 383; Stanley E. Fish, 'Question and Answer in *Samson Agonistes*', *CQ*, **11** (1969), 252–5, 260; and Helen Damico, 'Duality in Dramatic Vision: A Structural Analysis of *Samson Agonistes*', *MS*, **12** (1978), 93.
108. *The Lofty Rhyme*, p. 133. Cf. John Arthos, who argues that Samson orders his passions in the course of the action ('Milton and the Passions: A Study of *Samson Agonistes*', *MP*, **69** (1971–2), 209–21), and Michael Atkinson, who states the generalized view that 'beginning in spiritual fragmentation, Samson arrives at spiritual integrity' ('The Structure of the Temptations in Milton's *Samson Agonistes*', *MP*, **69** (1971–2), 286).
109. Anthony Low, '"No Power but of God": Vengeance and Justice in *Samson Agonistes*', *HLQ*, **34** (1970–1), 219–32. Camille W. Slights, 'A Hero of Conscience: *Samson Agonistes* and Casuistry', *PMLA*, **90** (1975) 410, argues that 'the conclusion of *Samson Agonistes* does not recommend Samson's vengeance or Samson's way of death to others, but it does ask us to accept the ethical rightness of Samson's action for him in his particular time and place.' This seems to say that anything, viewed in its context, is morally acceptable.
110. See Christopher Ricks, *English Poetry and Prose, 1540–1674*, p. 315.
111. John Reesing, *Milton's Poetic Art*, pp. 64–5.

Appendix

The purpose of this appendix is to consider some problems of definition and procedure in the use of quantification as evidence in stylistic analysis. As this book is not the first work to draw on statistical data in its investigation of Milton's poetic style, it may prove helpful to clarify some basic principles of analysis by considering the previous studies.

Josephine Miles and Ronald David Emma have conducted notable surveys of the adjectives in Milton's poetry. The former writer finds that 'Milton used more adjectives and fewer verbs ... than any poet of the decade' in his 1645 poems, that his poetry is woven into 'a steady sensory adjectival texture', and that he is the virtually unchallenged 'major master' of what is termed 'the poetry of qualification'.[1] She allows herself the generalization that 'predicates are accessories' for Milton (while 'qualities are accessories, even accidents, for Donne'), and is led to conclude that Milton's writing manifests an 'extreme of style'.[2] Finally, she places Milton high in her charts of those 'phrasal poets' who use many adjectives and few verbs.[3] Emma follows this with the remark that 'Milton's extensive use of descriptive adjectives may be said to mark him as a poet of qualification more than of predication: one who prefers words that qualify and describe to those that express action.'[4]

Both of these studies are tidily executed, plausibly based on an objective consideration of the poetic language, and supported by seemingly immutable tables of figures. As such, they present literary critics with the kind of information they may like to have (but rarely bother to collect) before forming a judgement. The *TLS* review of Emma's book praised it for thoroughness, and shelved it as 'a reference book to which the student can resort for precise information';[5] and A. C. Partridge[6] and John Broadbent[7] represent the general academic response of uncritical acceptance. Though Alastair Fowler is right to welcome the 'objective and descriptive' emphasis of Emma's study as a corrective to 'dogmatic and polemical' statements about Milton's style,[8] the neutrally factual information which Emma provides can be used to confirm prejudice. Indeed, before 'poet of qualification' becomes the shibboleth muttered by all conforming members of the Milton Stylisticians Association, the treatment of the evidence by Miles and Emma, and the evidence itself, should be scrutinized.

Both studies take samples of Milton's poetry, and this is obviously crucial to their general conclusions. Miles takes 1,000 lines of Milton's early poems and compares them with other 1,000-line samples from poets of the sixteenth and seventeenth centuries. After reducing her vast material to manageable fixity in this way, she readily admits that her interpretations relate only to the poems she uses as evidence.[9] But it is clear that she also wishes to suggest that 'the validity of extension is, for most of them, probable.'[10] In Milton's case, this validity is deeply questionable: she claims to select 'lines of early maturity, *usually accepted as characteristic*: not juvenilia, or late work, or special experiments';[11] but her time restriction necessitates the omission of Milton's late work, which constitutes the bulk of his poetry. It is at least counter-intuitive to suggest that, say, 'L'Allegro' and *Paradise Regained* are similar poems. By statistical criteria Miles's sample, set beside the whole of Milton's poetry, is far from ideal: as G. Udny Yule has pointed out, 'if the sample is to be of service, it must be typical, representative, unbiased.'[12] If, in her own words, 'the texts are neither clear random samples for statistical analysis . . . nor demonstrably representative' for Milton's early poems,[13] they are much less so for his entire corpus.

Emma criticizes Miles for presenting her figures 'not in percentages but as absolute numbers determined within lines of unequal length and of an uncounted number of words';[14] but this is a minor point of descriptive accuracy compared to the fact that his sample of Milton amounts to about half of hers. It is true that he spreads it over the poetry more than she does (124 lines of 'Comus', 129 of 'Samson Agonistes', 138 of *Paradise Lost*, and 131 of *Paradise Regained*), but he gives no reasons, intuitive or otherwise, why this particular sample should be representative of Milton's poetry. As his openly-stated purpose is to describe Milton's '*characteristic* grammatical practice',[15] he is more seriously open to criticism than Miles is. Alastair Fowler has shown that Emma's samples are 'too small to support those of his conclusions which concern rare phenomena', and produces results that differ from Emma's for Subject-Object-Verb, Object-Subject-Verb, and Verb-Subject inversion in *Paradise Lost* by increasing Emma's sample of 138 lines to 1,400.[16] There is always some inadequacy in sampling an author, but regarding 522 lines as representative of an author who wrote 17,934 lines approaches 2.9 per cent representation, 97.1 per cent make-believe!

It would be unfair to blame Emma for not being a literary critic, especially since his interest in Milton appears to be primarily philological. But his small sample precludes critical sensitivity to the stylistic nuances of varied contexts, and cannot begin to reveal characteristic poetic uses of grammar. Miles's remarks imply a similar homogeneous style in Milton, simply because her approach requires her sample to be tidily fixed for comparison with other writers. Neither study explores Milton's poetry in great depth, and the figures supplied by each quantify grammatical features without explaining their poetic function.

The methodology of statistical investigation is of the highest importance to any ends it may define for itself, and both studies are inadequate in means and ends. G. W. Turner rightly emphasizes that 'an adequate grammatical description is necessary to identify the forms to be described and counted',[17] and it is at this fundamental level that both studies are flawed. Josephine Miles gathers together 'the normal categories of number and limitation (*some, many, all, several, one, twelfth*, etc.), the participial modifier (*embroidered, moved, shining*), when used adjectivally and not as part of the verb, and the descriptive in its general sense (*good, common, obscure, green*, etc.)'.[18] She excludes 'demonstrative and pronominal adjectives (*that, those, mine*)'.[19] In her view the category thus delineated is sufficiently analytical, and for her purposes 'the adjective's function and position of modification are relatively stable'.[20]

Such explicitness is commendable in quantitative work, for different categories produce different figures and conclusions. But Miles uses her definition of adjective to support her general thesis that Milton emphasizes qualification over predication, description over action, and in this connection her categories need careful examination. First, although she recognizes the distinction between 'the normal categories of number and limitation' and 'the descriptive in its general sense' when drawing up her categories, she effectually ignores it when concluding that Milton prefers description to action. If it is unrevealing to lump together words like 'many' and 'some' with 'green' and 'obscure', it is at least equally so to use them as evidence for 'description' in the poetry. Most grammarians regard these numerical, limiting words as 'quantifiers' and not as adjectives proper; and this separation of quantification from qualification is essential to the description *v.* action thesis.

Josephine Miles's categorization of participles is even more gravely inconsistent with her conclusions about Milton. She says that 'the predicating poet seems to be the limiting, the epithetical, the participial poet', and notes that in comparison with other poets Milton uses many participles.[21] But she includes participial adjectives in her final count of adjectives in order to suggest that Milton is a 'poet of qualification' – in spite of noting also that in the early poems 'the present participles are active and vivid, in sliding, turning, bending, burning, thrilling, brooding, slumbering, whispering'.[22] If her distinction between 'participial' and 'descriptive' adjectives is intended to correlate with action and description respectively, and if Milton uses many participial adjectives, how can he be distinguished on such evidence as a poet who emphasizes description over action?

Miles states that she is counting as 'participial modifier (*embroidered, moved, shining*)' words that are used 'adjectivally and not as part of the verb'.[23] Presumably, this distinction is meant to separate qualification from predication. But a participial adjective can express action: the constructions 'choirboys sing', 'choirboys are singing', 'choirboys singing', and 'singing choirboys' all express it. The truth is that the semantic content of adjectives is not constant, and that 'adjective' is by no means as stable a category as Miles believes it to be.[24]

John Lyons points out that 'adjectives were regarded as a subclass of "verbs" by Plato and Aristotle',[25] and that the participle is so called because of its '"participation" in both nominal and verbal characteristics'.[26] He speaks for many modern grammarians when he says that '"adjectives" and "verbs" have much in common, and . . . in many languages (including English) they are correctly brought together as members of the same deep-structure category.'[27] Adjectives and verbs are not to be entirely dissociated.

Ronald David Emma's grammatical theory is open to criticisms similar to those levelled at Josephine Miles. He does not give an explicit description of his categories, and such indication as he does provide reveals that his categories fail to support his conclusions about Milton. His classification of the parts of speech is based, he says, on the function of 'individual words rather than of the phrases in which they appear: genitives are discussed in the chapter on nouns and pronouns although they are most often used as adjectives.'[28] In effect, then, his classification is not based on the function of the parts of speech, a fact which must affect the validity of his statements about Milton. He follows Jespersen in saying that 'all participles are basically verbs',[29] but he does not recognize the implications of this fact for his categories and conclusions. Jespersen's advice on classification is relevant here:

in order to find out what class a word belongs to it is not enough to consider the form in itself; what is decisive is the way in which other words behave towards it. If we find that one and the same form is used now as a substantive, now as an adjective or verb, this does not mean that the distinction between word-classes is obliterated in English, for in each particular combination the form belongs decidedly to one class only.[30]

The same grammarian indicates elsewhere the freedom in Old and Middle English 'in the use of adjectives (with their adjectival inflexion) as principals',[31] and H. Poutsma's grammar of English contains sixty-one pages on the conversion of adjectives into nouns in the history of English.[32] In fact when Emma talks about 'Adjectives as Nouns' he is talking about nouns, and not about adjectives.[33] The fact that at some stage in the history of a language an adjective form is used as a noun is primarily of etymological interest. Barbara Strang cites the example of the sentence 'There were two firsts in that year' and comments that 'in descriptive study we do not say that the noun *first* is converted from an adjective; it behaves like any other noun, and it is not our business to reflect on its origins.'[34] Emma's attention to the derivation of words therefore conflicts with his descriptive purpose, and presents a misleading account of how many adjectives Milton actually uses. His categories fail to confirm his conclusions about Milton's poetry in other respects, too. One of his subsections on adjectives is headed 'Adjectives Other Than Articles',[35] which implies that he is classing articles as adjectives. This is counter-intuitive, and contributes no evidence which can possibly bear on the description *v.* action thesis. The same applies to 'demonstrative adjectives'.[36] If Emma's grammatical framework is so flimsy, it is hardly able to support the conclusions he constructs around it.

Explicit, soundly-based categorization is necessary in quantitative analysis. In this book the term 'adjective' does *not* include any of the following: (i) articles ('a', 'the') (ii) numerals ('one', 'third') (iii) demonstratives ('this', 'that') (iv) quantifiers ('some', 'many', 'enough', 'all', 'no', 'each', etc.) (v) possessives of nouns or pronouns (vi) participles which are merely part of compound tenses, as in 'he was singing' or 'he had been killed' (vii) 'long passives', i.e. those with an optional expressed agent, as in 'he was shot yesterday [by an enemy]'.[37] Included are all those adjectives categorized by Randolph Quirk, Sidney Greenbaum, Geoffrey Leech, and Jan Svartvik in *A Grammar of Contemporary English* (1972), pages 231–67: attributive, predicative, supplementive, emphasizers, amplifiers, downtoners, and so on;[38] but not those categorized as heads of noun phrases,[39] since in these cases the adjectives function as nouns. Present participles indicating permanent characteristics are included (e.g. 'Typhon huge *ending* in snaky twine'), and 'short passives', that is those in which a participle describes a state, as in the sentence 'He was *wounded* and lying on the ground'.

Emma's assertion that Milton is a 'poet of qualification' contains an ambiguity which must be pointed out. In *Milton's Grammar* he uses the term 'qualification' to denote the use of adjectives; but in his paper 'Grammar and Milton's English Style' he uses it in a more general sense to mean the attributing of qualities to, the characterizing of, an object, and also to mean the modifying of a statement to make it less strong or positive.[40] He describes Milton's listing of the qualities of the 'forbidden fruit' at the start of *Paradise Lost* as 'qualification', and it is clear from his commentary that he is using the term to mean more than the use of adjectives.[41] Perhaps this extension of meaning is motivated by embarrassment at his simplistic correlation of predication-verbs-action and qualification-adjectives-description. Emma's repetition of these magical formulae, with apologies for their crudity, virtually constitutes a wish to exorcise them from his mind; but his implied self-criticism neither breaks the spell of the incantation nor amounts to an alternative interpretation of the evidence.

The term 'action' as used by Miles and Emma is also dangerously ambiguous. It conflates the notion of the class-meaning of verbs, their technical categorization in grammars, with their function in denoting or expressing action. Verbs often do express action, but it is a mistake to think that a grammatical categorization is identical with their lexical meaning.[42] Verbs such as 'to lie', 'to reflect', and 'to sleep' have a grammatical 'action', but their function in expressing what is ordinarily understood as action is not certain.[43]

The ways in which both studies phrase their conclusions about Milton's poetry also require scrutiny. Miles places Milton high in her table on 'Adjectival *Emphasis*', and Emma styles him a poet who '*prefers* words that qualify and describe to those that express action'.[44] But preference and emphasis in poetry are not merely numerical concepts: they relate to every level of structure – metrical, semantic, syntactic, and so on – and they must be defined with close attention to the specific nuances of each poem. Unless this is done, poets who are not similar will appear to be so. Miles, for instance, states that 'no two poets of the 1640s wrote alike',[45] but her tables for adjectives suggest that Sylvester, Phineas Fletcher, Quarles, Henry More, Crashaw, Waller, and Dryden did write alike. While it may be intrinsically interesting that a poet should use a high frequency of adjectives, this fact alone is often of limited significance. Miles's figures for the proportions of 'limiting', 'participial', and 'descriptive' adjectives in Milton are 10 per cent, 30 per cent, and 60 per cent respectively – the same figures as those given for Wallace Stevens![46] If, as she says, 'language is not the sum of words, for their relationship is part of its character',[47] then the relationship between words and phrases, clauses, sentences, paragraphs, and whole poems must be carefully observed before the significant details of any style can be revealed. The fact that a poet uses certain grammatical features must be supplemented by a study of how he uses them.[48]

What 'emphasis' can usefully mean within a poet's work may be illustrated from Marvell. An average adjective frequency may be calculated for a ten-poem sample:

Poem	Lines	Wds.	Adjs.	Adjs./ 10 lines	Adj./Wd.
'To His Coy Mistress'	46	300	28	6.0	9.3%
'An Horatian Ode upon Cromwell's Return from Ireland'	120	657	71	5.9	10.8%
'Upon the Hill and Grove at Bilbrough'	80	498	55	6.9	11.0%
'Upon Appleton House'	776	4827	463	6.0	9.6%
'The Garden'	72	455	47	6.6	10.4%
'On a Drop of Dew'	40	243	38	9.5	15.7%
'The Mower Against Gardens'	40	281	28	7.0	10.0%
'Bermudas'	40	261	22	5.5	8.5%
	1214	7522	752	(average) 6.2	(average) 10.0%

The average adjective frequency of 6.2 adjectives in 10 lines, or 10 per cent of the words,[49] may be used to trace stylistic variation within the poetry. 'On a Drop of Dew' contains a high frequency, and 'Bermudas' a low one. In a sense, then, Marvell emphasizes adjectives in one poem more than he does in the other. However, this is still to use a numerical concept of 'emphasis': the two poems must be inspected more closely before the true significance of the variation can be ascertained. 'On a Drop of Dew' is an elaborate metaphysical comparison of the soul to a dewdrop, precisely visual in its first nineteen lines ('See how ... how ... '), and understandably descriptive throughout in specifying those characteristics of the soul and the dewdrop that make them comparable. 'Bermudas', on the other hand, is written in a style that correlates with Puritan feeling. Its predominantly monosyllabic sentences conform in their couplets to the regular beat of the 'falling oars' (*l.* 40); sensuousness is firmly governed. A long section of supposed speech is placed between two short descriptive sections, and there are lines without adjectives in the speech section (5, 10, 21–4, 29–34). Only one third of the adjectives in the poem are sensory ('watery', 'grassy', 'bright', 'golden', etc.). But this does not preclude memorable adjectival emphasis:

He hangs in shades the orange bright,
Like golden lamps in a green night.   (*ll.* 17–18)

The three adjectives 'bright', 'golden', and 'green' are all strongly stressed
with their nouns, and they shine out from the surrounding 'shades' and
'night' to highlight the vivid 'orange'. 'Bright', though a fairly conventional adjective, is made doubly effective: it is the only adjective in the
poem which follows its noun, and it is cleverly placed at the line-end to
rhyme with the contrasting 'night'. Similarly, 'green' may not be a particularly striking adjective in some contexts, but here it is boldly luminous
when applied to 'night', especially beside 'orange'. The indefinite article
before 'green night' increases the exoticness of the experience: 'the green
night' would have been assumed to have been realistic, recognizable; but 'a
green night' is more specific and unusual, half-metaphorical, cause for
wonder. 'Green', as William Empson has pointed out,[50] is one of Marvell's
favourite words, and carries special weight through association with natural
and contemplative fertility: here one is reminded of the 'green thought in a
green shade' of 'The Garden' (*l.* 48). In several ways, then, the adjectives in
a soberly sensuous couplet receive brilliant 'emphasis' in a poem which does
not use many adjectives.

It emerges that a poet may be seen to emphasize some point of style at
different levels: by comparison with other poets, or with other poems of his
own, or within the structure of a single poem. If purely quantitative comparisons at the first of these levels are to acquire significance, they require
supplementary comparisons at the other two, and especially at the level of
individual poems. For figures alone to give some insight, there has to be a
very marked difference between the poets or poems under consideration;
and, even so, the insight inevitably depends on a reading act that is able to
reveal more of poetic structure than figures alone can indicate. Only the
reader's response can determine what is to be counted in the first place, and
at what level of analysis; and statistics can only begin to be interpreted
when they are related to poetic contexts.[51] Josephine Miles and Ronald
David Emma do not delve deeply enough into Milton's poetic language for
their statistics to be very convincing or significant. P. M. Wetherall has
temperately and rightly insisted that statistical findings about authors
'point not to a particular fact at any particular moment in a text or to a
fixed rigid habit, but rather to a tendency'.[52] The tendencies outlined by
statistics must be related to specific poetic contexts if they are to be ex-
plained. One may accept Josephine Miles's statement that Milton uses a
distinctively high frequency of adjectives, even allowing for the flaws in her
work, if only because her method is applied consistently to a very large
body of evidence. But her statement may perhaps be accepted also because it
is not by itself very illuminating! Milton's adjective frequency varies from

poem to poem, and within poems. The following table gives more detailed information concerning this tendency, as a point of general reference for more particular, and more significant, moments within the structures of the poems under consideration in this book:

Adjective Frequency in Milton's poetry

Works	Lines	Wds.	Adjs.	Adjs./ 10 Lines	Adj./Wd.
Psalm cxiv	16	141	16	10.0	11.4%
Psalm cxxxvi	50	294	34	6.8	11.6%
'Fair Infant'	77	655	83	10.8	12.7%
'Vac. Ex.'	100	786	87	8.7	11.0%
'May Morning'	10	73	9	9.0	12.4%
Horace, *Odes*, I.5	16	100	24	15.0	24.0%
'Nativity Ode'	244	1535	222	9.0	14.5%
'The Passion'	56	456	63	11.3	13.9%
'On Shakespeare'	16	121	13	8.2	10.8%
'Univ. Carrier'	18	154	9	5.0	5.9%
'Another'	34	277	18	5.3	6.5%
'Winchester'	74	439	50	6.8	11.4%
'L'Allegro'	152	902	120	7.9	13.3%
'Il Penseroso'	176	1071	162	9.2	15.2%
'Arcades'	109	827	97	8.9	11.8%
'Solemn Music'	28	205	37	13.3	18.0%
'On Time'	22	151	17	7.8	11.3%
'Circumcision'	28	183	29	10.4	15.9%
'Comus'	1022	7393	1031	10.0	14.0%
'Lycidas'	193	1473	204	10.6	13.9%
Sonnets	252	2059	205	8.2	10.0%
'New Forcers'	20	149	21	10.5	14.0%
Translations	54	430	42	7.8	9.8%
Psas. lxxx–lxxxviii	512	2990	241	4.7	8.0%
Psas. i–viii	262	1785	92	3.6	5.2%
PL, I	798	5990	728	9.2	12.2%
II	1055	7961	989	9.4	12.5%
III	742	5580	687	9.3	12.4%
IV	1015	7779	942	9.3	12.1%
V	907	6839	787	8.7	11.5%
VI	912	6801	818	9.0	12.0%
VII	640	4797	567	8.9	11.9%
VIII	653	4932	500	7.7	10.2%
IX	1189	9049	1114	9.4	12.4%
X	1104	8353	871	7.9	10.5%

XI	901	6905	711	7.9	10.3%
XII	649	4931	447	6.9	9.0%
PR, I	502	3858	368	7.4	9.6%
II	486	3668	317	6.6	8.7%
III	443	3292	303	6.9	9.2%
IV	639	4855	486	7.6	10.0%
'Samson Agonistes'	1758	12918	1290	7.4	10.0%
	17934	133157	14851	(average) 8.3	(average) 11.2%

NOTES

1. *The Continuity of Poetic Language: Studies in English Poetry from the 1540s to the 1940s, University of California Publications in English*, **19** (1948–51), 87, 86, 85. See also her tables on pp. 28–9, and on p. 321 of vol. **12** (1942–6) in the same series, *The Vocabulary of Poetry: Three Studies*, by the same author.
2. *The Continuity of Poetic Language*, pp. 92, 87.
3. *Renaissance, Eighteenth-Century, and Modern Language in English Poetry: A Tabular View* (1960), pp. 42–3. Angus McIntosh finds her analysis of sentence types 'ill defined and puzzling' in McIntosh and M. A. K. Halliday, *Patterns of Language: Papers in General, Descriptive, and Applied Linguistics* (1966), pp. 46–7.
4. *Milton's Grammar* (1964), p. 67.
5. 31 December, 1964, 1182.
6. *The Language of Renaissance Poetry: Spenser, Shakespeare, Donne, Milton* (1971), p. 286.
7. *Paradise Lost: Introduction* (1972), p. 132.
8. Carey and Fowler, p. 430.
9. *The Continuity of Poetic Language*, p. 98.
10. *The Continuity of Poetic Language*, p. 98. Cf. *The Vocabulary of Poetry*, pp. 311, 312.
11. *The Vocabulary of Poetry*, pp. 311–12. The italics are mine.
12. *The Statistical Study of Literary Vocabulary* (1944), p. 35.
13. *The Vocabulary of Poetry*, p. 311.
14. *Milton's Grammar*, p. 68n.
15. ibid., p. 17. The italics are mine.
16. Carey and Fowler, pp. 429, 432.
17. *Stylistics* (1973), p. 25.
18. *The Vocabulary of Poetry*, p. 309.
19. loc. cit.
20. *The Vocabulary of Poetry*, p. 310.
21. *The Continuity of Poetic Language*, p. 42n, and *The Vocabulary of Poetry*, p. 321.

Seymour Chatman endorses this view, with extensive evidence, in 'Milton's Participial Style', *PMLA*, **83** (1968), 1386–99.

22. *The Vocabulary of Poetry*, p. 367.

23. ibid., p. 309.

24. ibid., p. 310.

25. *Introduction to Theoretical Linguistics* (1968), p. 323.

26. ibid., p. 12.

27. ibid., p. 326. Jespersen, in *A Modern English Grammar on Historical Principles* (1909–49; rpt., 1961), **2**, 6–7, and *The Philosophy of Grammar* (1924), p. 87, presents the notion in traditional terms. Dwight Bolinger has suggested by many examples that 'some adjectives are entitled to be classed with the particles that are used in phrasal verbs': *The Phrasal Verb in English* (1971), pp. 71, 67–82. And John Robert Ross, following Paul Postal and George Lakoff, groups adjectives under the major lexical category 'predicate': 'Adjectives as Noun Phrases', *Modern Studies in English: Readings in Transformational Grammar*, ed. David A. Reibel and Sanford A. Schane (1969), pp. 352, 353.

28. *Milton's Grammar*, p. 21.

29. ibid., p. 108*n*.

30. *Essentials of English Grammar* (1933; rpt., 1969), p. 71.

31. *A Modern English Grammar on Historical Principles*, **2**, 272–3.

32. *A Grammar of Late Modern English* (1914), Part 2, *The Parts of Speech*, iA, 365–426.

33. *Milton's Grammar*, pp. 79–80.

34. *Modern English Structure* (1962), p. 97.

35. *Milton's Grammar*, p. 68. He speaks of 'descriptive adjectives (as distinguished from articles)' in *Language and Style in Milton: A Symposium in Honour of the Tercentenary of Paradise Lost*, ed. R. D. Emma and John T. Shawcross (1967), p. 239.

36. *Milton's Grammar*, pp. 78–9.

37. Colloquial English commonly distinguishes this type by using a part of the verb 'get', as in 'he got shot'.

38. As this monumental grammar offers adequate definitions of each type of adjective, it would be superfluous to discuss them here.

39. *A Grammar of Contemporary English*, pp. 251–3.

40. See the distinctions of meaning in the *OED* ('qualify', I.1.a, II.7, and I.1.b). The grammatical correlative of the more general sense of 'qualification' would be subordinate clauses. A. C. Partridge misunderstands Emma's use of the term 'qualification', and cites six *where*-clauses in 'Lycidas' as evidence of Milton's being a 'poet of qualification' (*The Language of Renaissance Poetry*, p. 286).

41. *Language and Style in Milton*, pp. 238–9.

42. See Barbara Strang, *Modern English Structure*, p. 125.

43. John Broadbent falls into the same trap as Emma when he considers that recurring epithets (which he mistakes for kennings) leave less room for 'verbs – that is, for action' (*Paradise Lost: Introduction*, p. 132).

44. *The Continuity of Poetic Language*, p. 30; *Milton's Grammar*, p. 67. The italics are mine.
45. *The Continuity of Poetic Language*, p. 46.
46. *The Vocabulary of Poetry*, p. 321.
47. *The Continuity of Poetic Language*, p. 45n.
48. Emma agrees with this (*Language and Style in Milton*, pp. 239, 241), but does not adequately support the principle by his practice.
49. A 'word' is taken to be a word-length thoughout this study, and compounds are counted as single word-lengths.
50. *Some Versions of Pastoral* (1965 edn), pp. 105–6.
51. See David Lodge, *Language of Fiction: Essays in Criticism and Verbal Analysis of the English Novel* (1966), p. 85, and Roger Fowler, ed., *The Languages of Literature: Some Linguistic Contributions to Criticism* (1971), p. 18.
52. *The Literary Text: An Examination of Critical Methods* (1974), pp. 160–1.

Index